For Margaret – with warm greetings,

[signature]

SURPRISED BY
THE FATHER'S PLAN

A REMARKABLE STORY OF FAITH, RISK, AND ADVENTURE

By Charles David Kelley
with Kristen Zetzsche

Forewords by Luis Palau
and Thomas Kinkade

BRIDGE MEDIA GROUP

Philomath, Oregon
2005

SURPRISED BY THE FATHER'S PLAN

Cover painting, "Sunset Over Riga, Latvia" by Thomas Kinkade
© 2004 Thomas Kinkade Company, Morgan Hill, CA

Book design and layout by Gints Veilands

Unless otherwise indicated,
all photos are from the family archives of Charles Kelley

Bible versions used in the text are identified as follows:
NIV (New International Version)
NKJV (New King James Version)
KJV (King James Version)
NASB (New American Standard Bible)

Published by
Bridge Media Group
Philomath, Oregon

ISBN 0-9767091-0-4
Library of Congress Control Number: 2005903580
1. Latvia 2. Biography 3. Christian missions

Printed in China

What Others
Are Saying

From the prologue to the epilogue, Chuck Kelley's book, *Surprised by the Father's Plan*, will grip you with its amazing story of drama, history, and God's protection and provision. As you read this adventure, I am sure you will be able to relate to many different ways in your own life of how you have been surprised by the wonderful leading of our Heavenly Father.

DR. CLYDE COOK, *President, Biola University, La Mirada, California*

Chuck Kelley is a man of extraordinary faith. The story of his pilgrimage home to Latvia is a story of Kingdom advance. Our God knows how to bring together his instruments to accomplish his purpose. Bridge Builders and the story of Chuck Kelley is a prime example of our Father's active participation in our lives.

DR. KENNETH L. HALL, *President, Buckner Benevolences, Dallas, Texas*

This is an exciting story with evidence of the hand of God on every page. From Nazi occupation to Soviet repression, the fall of the Iron Curtain and the rise of the European Union, it's the story of our times. But it's more that that. It's the story of how God has been faithful in powerful and surprising ways. You won't be able to put this book down!

BILL ZIPP, *President, Extra Mile Media, Albany, Oregon*

What I love about this book is the evidence that God delights in accomplishing his purposes in his time and in his way with his children. Chuck Kelley has experienced this delight of the Father. With authentic integrity he tells the story so the rest of us might enter in wholeheartedly and share the wonder.

ROBIN JONES GUNN, *Author, Vancouver, Washington*

We read so many books these days about great men walking with a small God. This is a book about a small man walking with a great God. That is why I highly recommend it!

THE VERY REVEREND JOHAN CANDELIN, *Goodwill Ambassador, World Evangelical Alliance, Finland*

Chuck Kelley is a bridge builder par excellence: person to person, Russian to Latvian, Latvian to European and beyond; beginning first with Americans to Latvians, churches to churches, schools to schools, musicians and artists to musicians and artists, generations to generations. Time has told and is telling that in the Father's plan, friend Chuck's gospel ministry is proving as significant for Latvia as any we've seen.

DR. HERBERT E. ANDERSON, *Pastor, Mission Executive, Educator, Salem, Oregon*

Charles Kelley tells an amazing story of God's faithfulness in Latvia. It is a story that begins with his grandfather, Charles Singer, and extends to his own ministry and the founding of Bridge Builders International. With a commitment to international missions, a family heritage rooted in a country that had witnessed so much suffering in the twentieth century, and a realization that with the fall of the Iron Curtain Latvia was for the first time in several generations open to the unfettered preaching of the gospel, Kelley pioneered the creation of partnerships between churches in the West and East. It was an approach that was destined to have an impact both on the national life of Latvia and on the wider world of eastern Europe. This book describes this amazing story of BBI and its roots in the lives of two generations (grandfather and grandson) to whom God gave a vision of how the gospel might transform the life of a small Baltic nation.

DR. GARY B. FERNGREN, *Professor of History, Oregon State University, Corvallis, Oregon*

Chuck Kelley has believed God could use him to impact the entire nation of post-Soviet Latvia for Christ—and God has. *Surprised by the Father's Plan* is the personal and moving story of one man's passion for a nation reeling from the oppression of Communist domination, and his experience of "building bridges" between believers in Latvia and the United States. Reading Chuck's book will give you a greater understanding of what a strategic time this is in the history of this Baltic state, and motivate you to pray for all believers who are emerging from behind the Iron Curtain.

REV. HERB REESE, *President, New Commandment Men's Ministries, Broomfield, Colorado*

I love stories about people . . . I love stories about history . . . and I especially love it when the two come together in such a clear way that you cannot deny God's involvement in both. *Surprised by the Father's Plan* is modern-day evidence that God still creates, directs, inspires, and uses people to accomplish his purposes. God's purpose for Chuck Kelley is to build bridges. Bridges that link the heart of God with the hearts of the Latvian people in Chuck's homeland. Bridges that link God's people in America with his people and purposes in Latvia. Through skillfully written stories, through Chuck's witty humor, and through heart-stopping suspense, you will also find yourself inspired to ask God to use you . . . and accomplish the purposes he created you for.

ERIC WEBER, *Vice President, Multnomah Publishers, Sisters, Oregon*

In this account, Chuck Kelley has given us three precious stories of history. The first story is of the church triumphant behind the walls of Communism that has now blossomed in the years following its freedom. The second story is of God's untiring faithfulness to his people under persecution. And the third story is of one man who has yielded his life to God and God's plan for the country of his heritage. *Surprised by the Father's Plan* is an engaging read that will leave the reader thinking, laughing, reflecting, and thankful for servants like Chuck.

ERIC SWANSON, *Leadership Community Director, Leadership Network, Boulder, Colorado*

I have watched Chuck's ministry unfold from starting something with nothing, through the uphill battle to gain credibility, and now the thrill of experiencing God's blessing in ten short years. This is a story of a pastor who became a ministry entrepreneur and did it by faith and fortitude. It is a fresh example for all of us of the balance between God's calling and man's will power.

JOHN D. BRADLEY, *President, IDAK Group, Inc., Portland, Oregon*

Chuck Kelley shows that a seed, watered with faith, can grow to embrace the world. His journey begins in Los Angeles and spans the world to Eastern Europe. Along the way, we see how God uses a few available people to touch a life with hope, and we're reminded that a local church can make a big difference if they are willing to think outside the box.

Rev. Bob Rasmussen, *U.S. Field Director, OC International, Blaine, Washington*

Chuck Kelley tells a great story but gives an even better blueprint. He took his grandfather's "old-school" mission organization and successfully transformed it into a "new-school" template. One church can change a country for Christ by building a bridge. Chuck's church did and this book tells you how. If you have a heart for missions, drop everything and start turning these pages.

Jay Carty, *Speaker, Author, and Church Consultant, Santa Barbara, California*

❖

What would connect a man named Kelley with the country of Latvia? Why would this Oregon pastor leave his cushy American life to take on the daunting task of linking churches and Christ-followers in his country with churches and people in a beautiful spot in the former bureaucratic Soviet bloc? There's only one answer to both questions, and the answer is Jesus. You will be blessed by letting my friend and brother Chuck share his life with you, because in reading his story you too will find that it's all about Jesus.

Rev. Charles Morris, *President and Speaker, Haven Ministries, Costa Mesa, California*

❖

By God's intervention we met in Latvia at the time of its liberation, and since than I have been privileged to participate in a number of Hope conferences in Riga with Chuck and his constantly new and broadening team of co-workers from U.S. churches. The importance of Bridge Builders' Latvian ministry cannot be overestimated. The sister church program that we initiated in Sweden in the late 1970s has developed under Chuck's leadership into a ministry of tremendous importance, both for U.S. churches and especially for the Latvian churches. This development brings a special joy to my heart.

REV. INGEMAR MARTINSON, *Director Emeritus, Solasen, Sweden*

Spreading the Glad News to the people of Latvia and Eastern Europe—that's what this book is about. Exciting. Glorious. No one can stop God's work, as long as we carry on courageously.

BROTHER ANDREW, *President, Open Doors, Author of* <u>God's Smuggler</u>, *The Netherlands*

DEDICATED

To my grandfather, Charles Singer,
whose strength and vision shaped my world view.

To my grandmother, Mary Singer,
whose service and selflessness revealed true Christlikeness.

To my mother, Elizabeth Feldmanis,
who encouraged me to think outside the box.

And most especially to my beloved wife, Nancy,
whose love, insight, and example have always been
a source of encouragement, energy, and joy.

TABLE OF CONTENTS

FOREWORD
BY LUIS PALAU
EVANGELIST, BROADCASTER, AUTHOR

Imagine reaching a nation with the life-changing gospel of Jesus Christ!

When Chuck Kelley came to me in 1998 with the idea for a nationwide evangelistic effort in Latvia, I heartily agreed with his plans. Hope '99 came at a time when Latvia greatly needed the gospel and a message of hope. And in September of 1999, I joined with several evangelists and dozens of churches and ministries from fourteen nations to proclaim the good news of Jesus Christ to the country of Latvia.

Not only did many Latvians and Russians commit their lives to Jesus, but churches of differing backgrounds, cultures, and languages committed to working together. Hope '99 united the nation's diverse denominations and ethnic Christians; for the first time in many years, the Russian Christians and Latvian Christians were a team. A strong testimony of the Lord's work was seen in these men and women who laid aside their personal comfort and familiar boundaries to further God's Kingdom.

Chuck and his ministry, Bridge Builders International, have worked in Latvia for years. While a handful of evangelists and I had the incredible opportunity to present the gospel at Hope '99 and see several thousand make commitments to Christ, Chuck has had a continuous, lasting impact on this country that so desperately needs the Lord. As one woman with the evangelistic team said, "How amazing that a country under Soviet oppression less than a decade ago was more open to the gospel than any public school in the United States."

Latvia needed hope for the future, and Chuck helped to open the doors for Hope '99. As you enjoy the stories of the history of Bridge Builders International's ministry in Latvia over the years, I trust that you will catch a sense of Chuck's love for the good news of Jesus Christ. Chuck's wholehearted commitment to bringing the gospel to Latvians has made a difference for all of eternity.

FOREWORD

BY THOMAS KINKADE
PAINTER OF LIGHT

As an artist, I have a connection with those who painted before me. Their ways of interpreting the world on their canvases lead me to my own expression of light, mood, and color. The stories in this book, and my own experiences with Chuck Kelley and Bridge Builders International, are also about connections—how God uses relationship bridges to bring individuals and groups together to do his work in the Baltic nation of Latvia and beyond.

My own surprising connection to BBI began because of my church's relationship with a church in Riga, Latvia. This deeply enriching relationship of over seven years is a result of Chuck's vision to pair U.S. churches with churches in Latvia. These partnerships are helping to rebuild Latvian congregations after fifty years of Soviet occupation and persecution of believers.

Even before I joined the church, I was aware of the work of Bridge Builders International. The former president of Latvia, Guntis Ulmanis, toured my company during his BBI-arranged U.S tour in 2000, and we'd presented him with a canvas of *Sunrise*. However, it was a Sunday school class presentation that built the bridge for my personal ministry in Latvia.

As Chuck told stories of how God remarkably used the unique talents of hundreds of people to serve him in Latvia, I thought of my own long-held desire to find a way to merge my passion for art with international ministry. And in less than nine months, I stepped off a plane at the Riga, Latvia, airport. . . .

My art was my bridge to talk about my faith to the children at the art camp where I taught; to the national leaders who attended the unveiling of my Latvia paintings; and to fellow artists who shared the love of painting even when we did not share the same language. Having the experience of building these connections has inspired me to expand my vision of merging art and ministry, to build further bridges for Christ as an "Artist Ambassador" to other nations.

I am grateful to Chuck Kelley and BBI for my experience in Latvia, and am pleased that *Sunset Over Riga, Latvia* graces the cover of this book.

Like Chuck, I have been surprised over the years to see how God can weave seemingly unrelated elements of a life into a marvelous master plan of blessing. This book chronicles God's hand of guidance in the life and ministry of Chuck Kelley; but in a larger sense, these stories will be an inspiring challenge for each of us to consider how we might be a part of the Father's surprising plan. I highly recommend this book.

INTRODUCTION

Situated between its Baltic neighbors of Estonia and Lithuania, Latvia has long been the bridge and battleground for Europe's wars. Invading armies have burned fields and fouled wells, burying the dead and dying in the silent forests and leaving the survivors to bear and pass on the scars for generations.

From the beginning, Christianity lodged uneasily in Latvia. When the first German missionaries were rebuffed in their attempts to peaceably spread the gospel, the pope authorized a Crusade to the Baltic region in the early thirteenth century, unleashing

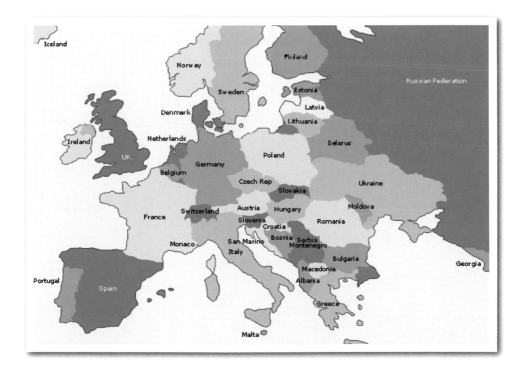

the Teutonic knights to convert and conquer. With the Crusaders came the German overlords, beginning what would become more than 700 years of foreign rule in Latvia.

Not until after World War I, after centuries of alternating German, Swedish, Polish, and Russian rule, did Latvia declare its short-lived independence. But it would take many more decades of warring Soviet and German control, of forced deportations to Siberia and muffled mass executions in the country's deep forests, before Latvians could experience true political freedom. And this time, the opportunity for true spiritual freedom as well.

LENINGRAD 1985

I picked up my suitcase with clammy hands and moved another step forward. The cold gray concrete slabs of the Leningrad airport sent a chill through my bones. Another step forward. I was surrounded by other Latvian-Americans and their assorted luggage, but as one mass we were concentrated on the narrow lanes before us that each converged into a one-on-one stare-down with a hard-eyed Soviet customs officer.

I was part of a group guided by *Intourist*, the tourist arm of the KGB. We were all Americans with Latvian roots, and I had the unmistakable impression that the Soviet guards would do anything to show their power.

I am an American, I recited internally. *I am an American . . . surely they won't harm me.* But we were all Americans here, including the elderly woman trembling in front of me. Suddenly she was whisked away, strip-searched, and interrogated. I waited. When she returned to the line, she was in a state of shock. The guards continued overturning each suitcase, meticulously searching for contraband.

My grandfather's stories flashed before my mind as I took another step closer to the inquisitors. *Men, women, and children herded into cattle cars and left to die in the heat of a Latvian summer. Mass graves in the deep forests. Imprisonment and exile. Interrogation at the Communist headquarters. The flames of his city as he fled with his family on a German cargo ship, a smoked ham strapped on his back.* He had paid such a price for his escape. Was I now to throw it all away?

When I had entered the Soviet Union two weeks earlier, I had been forced by a KGB customs officer to sign a statement that I would take all of the Christian literature I was carrying with me out of the country again when I left. But I had been deeply touched by the commitment, oppression, and deprivation of the Christians I had met with in Latvia, and I had left the Bibles and other theological materials with several pastors in Riga. And now I was leaving with empty hands. Ahead of us a guard ripped the film out of a woman's camera and threw the exposed roll on the floor. My grandfather's warning back in California echoed in my mind: *Chuck, be careful. They will seize any opportunity to take Charles Singer's grandson and arrest him. They can no longer touch me, but you are walking into their hands.* The line lurched forward again.

As I gripped my suitcase and moved another step closer, I repeatedly prayed the prayer made famous by Brother Andrew in his Bible-smuggling adventures into Eastern Europe and the Soviet Union*:* "Lord, in the New Testament it says that you made blind eyes see. Today, Lord, I ask you to make seeing eyes blind."

Too soon I was at the head of the line. The hardened customs official in the dark gray uniform looked at my rumpled suit and my suitcase at my side. I reached out my passport and travel documents, but she ignored them. "Next!" she called, already reaching for the documents of my mother behind me. I looked around dumbly. "Next, next!" she said impatiently, clearly motioning me on.

With a start, I realized I was free to leave now, free to board the plane that would carry me home from this first introduction to the country of my mother and grandparents and my youthful imaginings. I had walked the bridge of my grandfather's sufferings back to the land of his birth, and now God was providing the bridge back to my own home. It was a story that had begun long before my birth, and, after what I had just experienced in these last two weeks, I was certain that it was far from over.

Adventures with Papa

I am a Latvian-American, the product of a short-lived union between my striking Latvian immigrant mother and my outgoing but unstable American father. Though I grew up in a Mexican neighborhood in downtown Los Angeles, my childhood imagination was filled with images of Latvians dodging Russian bullets in the orchards of Jelgava, huddling in underground bunkers like animals in a trap as the Soviet soldiers moved between the trees, guns cocked.

My grandfather, a tall, austere Latvian Baptist pastor we called "Papa," took my mother and sister and me into his home when I was three, and there we lived until I left home for college. Papa loved to tell stories and I loved to hear them, and these stories dominated my childhood fantasies. When I closed my eyes I saw the wooden farmstead where Papa spent his boyhood, nestled into the green fields of the tiny village of Piltene. In my imagination, small groups of muffled Latvian believers gathered there, risking their lives to meet in secret as they prayed and listened to Scripture read from a single, worn copy of the Bible. And the Nazi and Communist armies marched on and on, terrible and threatening, through my dreams both day and night.

When I was eleven, Papa took me with him on a ministry trip to Texas, and on those hot roads, with my sweaty back and legs sticking to the vinyl seat of the '59 Chevy Impala on the long cross-desert trip, he fed me stories of Latvia to my heart's content.

Papa was born as Karlis Wilhelm Zingers into the Latvia of the Russian czar in 1904, just one year before the Baltic Revolution, the bloody uprising that heralded the end of the Russian empire and the beginning of a century of upheaval. The revolution was a protest against the serfdom of Latvians within their own country, and it was aimed

My ancestors on my grandfather's side came from the tiny northwestern village of Piltene. This photo is of my grandfather's parents, siblings, and grandparents.

with equal venom against everything German and Russian. When the czar's Imperial Guard finally quelled the insurrection, thousands of Latvians were shot, deported to Siberia, or sent into exile abroad.

Papa's mother, Dora of the high cheeks and pulled-back hair, was a devout Lutheran with a penchant for magic. Neighbors came from far and wide to Dora Zingere with their sick and dying, hoping that she would heal them with her white chalk and blue paper and muttered whispers into medicine bottles. Papa's father, the carpenter Fricis, led the family in the Lord's Prayer on Thursday evenings before leading his sick horses to the cemetery for secret mystical healing ceremonies.

Papa, called Willi by his family, was raised on a spiritual diet of strict German Lutheranism—baptism, confirmation, Bible stories, and family prayers—and Dora's healing whispers and chalk drawings. He heard reverent stories from his father of the Russian Orthodox Saint Serafim who was so holy he levitated three feet above the ground when he prayed. And when his cantankerous Uncle Mangels came to visit, he trembled at accounts of the accursed Baptists who, his uncle growled, were murderers and thieves who sacrificed children in secret.

In the red-tile-roofed schoolhouse, Willi learned the Russian language and the endless names of the czar and all his family members. But at night he and his friends dodged the gamekeeper to poach crayfish with homemade nets and skinned frogs as bait. In the summer he worked as a cowherd for a neighboring farmer, his leather-bound feet wet from the cold morning dew, singing to the cows to fend off the loneliness of the darkness before the dawn.

World War I began when Willi was ten years old. The retreating Russians burned Latvian fields and destroyed roads and bridges as the Germans pushed eastward. The heavy taxes imposed by the occupying German army meant little to a boy, but his eyes

This old farmstead in Piltene was built by my great-great grandfather about 1860. It remained in our family until the early 1990s.

sparkled as he told of daring nighttime visits to the miller to grind secret sacks of flour, or fishing drowned rats out of the cream before presenting it to the German tax collector.

One day, after the war was over but marauding bands of soldiers still roamed the countryside, Willi's father got permission to cut firewood from the forest. As Willi drove the wagon to the forest, he heard machine gun fire and a whistling sound, but not until he later followed pools of blood home and found the body of the neighbor boy lying in front of the family's gate did he realize that he himself had driven untouched through a deadly skirmish between Germans and Bolsheviks.

When Willi was fifteen he was apprenticed to a blacksmith on the estate of a German baron. Willi's parents knew that the blacksmith, Mr. Dreimanis, was a Baptist, and they warned Willi not to listen to him or be trapped by his deceptions. Willi proudly boasted, "No Baptist will ever deceive me!" But courtesy forced him to accept the Latvian New Testament that Mr. Dreimanis gave him when Willi came back to the workshop after his Lutheran confirmation.

One Sunday afternoon, Willi followed the sound of music and laughter to the beautiful grounds of the Sakas estate, where a thousand people had gathered to dance and drink and sing. As he leaned against a rock near the edge of the large square, watching the dust swirl through the shafts of sunlight and settle again beneath the feet of the dancers, he suddenly felt a voice speak inside him: "Where will you spend eternity when you die?"

Willi was terrified; he felt as if he were going to die and go to hell at that very moment. He began to run home, but almost out of spite he forced himself to turn around and go back to the square. As he neared the rock again, though, the question returned with increased force: "Where will you spend eternity when you die?"

Willi raced back to his room in a cold sweat and fell down on the floor, overwhelmed by dark fears of imminent death and damnation. Nothing in his upbringing had prepared him for this terrible weight of guilt and dread that now oppressed him. With his face pressed flat against the worn wooden floor of his upstairs bedroom and a nearly physical pain in his heart, he called out to the distant God he had learned about in his confirmation classes, crying out the list of sins that were weighing him down and begging for forgiveness. But still he felt no relief.

For two weeks he continued his desperate prayers, eating little and sleeping only when he could no longer keep his eyes open from exhaustion. Finally, in desperation, he randomly opened the neglected New Testament from Mr. Dreimanis, and read, "If we say that we have no sins, we deceive ourselves, and the truth is not in us."

He burst into tears and cried out, "Lord, I know that I have sinned, and I have confessed my sins to you for two weeks!" Then he read on: "If we confess our sins, he is faithful and just to forgive us our sin, and to cleanse us from all unrighteousness" (I John 1:9, KJV). Finally, the missing piece of the puzzle fell into place. The weight was gone, and he was free.

But God's forgiveness is not man's. And there was still the matter of telling his parents of his new faith. After being baptized in the Baptist church, Willi took a week off and biked the fifteen miles home to his father's farm.

"Mother, you have a new boy!" he said to Dora as he greeted her.

"What nonsense! A new boy? I had enough trouble with you and your brothers. I don't need a new boy," she replied.

"But, Mother, that's not what I mean. I'm the new boy. You won't have to cry over my mischief any more."

His mother was horrified. "What! Have the Baptists deceived you?" she screamed.

"No, Mother, but Jesus has saved me," he replied.

When Willi's father, Fricis, arrived home, the reaction was even worse. He vowed to "beat this Baptist nonsense out of him," and for four days he committed every muscle of his massive frame into physically breaking his sixteen-year-old son's will. But he could not.

I would later hear Papa say many times, "I have endured ten years of misery in my life: one and a half years in the hands of the Soviet Communists, four and a half years in the hands of the Nazis, and four and a half years in refugee camps. But those three days in the hands of my own father were the worst days of my life."

On the morning of Willi's fourth day home, Fricis burst into Willi's bedroom, dragged him to a window, and pointed to the rising sun: "The sun is my witness," he vowed, "that you are no more my son. Go out and never come back again!"

With tears streaming down his cheeks, Willi retorted beneath his breath, "But *God* is my witness . . . he will also be my father."

Father's word was law. At sixteen, Willi was disowned from his family and left to fend for himself. But, as he often recalled afterward, God was a wonderful father during all the long years that followed. His continuing apprenticeship with the blacksmith provided him with food and lodging, and a bundle of used clothing sent to his church from Baptists in America helped him maintain decency and even style during those lean and growing years.

They were growing and stretching times for Latvia, too. With the end of World War I, and after continued and finally successful internal fighting against Latvian Bolsheviks, Latvia declared itself independent in 1918 and cleared its last province of Communist rule in 1920.

The task of building a new independent government, after centuries of foreign domination, was monumental. The land itself was ravaged by war: Latvia's once-fertile fields were filled with trenches, live artillery and mortar shells, and remnants of war. Farm animals and seed had been commandeered by the various armies. And timber, Latvia's age-old source of wealth, was a risky commodity because of the many bullets and shrapnel lodged in the trees.

In the meantime, driven by opposition from his family and old friends, and fellowship with his new family of believers, Willi was growing spiritually. When he was twenty, he was drafted into the military. Here he developed a serious case of mastoiditis, an inflammation of the skull behind the ear, and the army doctors held out life-threatening major surgery as his only hope for survival. He was afraid that he was going to die.

Before the operation, he promised God that he would abandon his promising career as a blacksmith and mechanic and give his life to Christian ministry. Four hours later he opened his eyes in another room and realized that God had saved his life. By the time Willi left for Bible school in Riga after his discharge from the army, both his younger brother and his sister had become Christians, and he had renewed tentative contact with his parents.

After Willi served in the army, he studied for Christian ministry in both Riga and London.

❖

Papa's stories continued as we drove along the hot dusty highways of Arizona and New Mexico, the road before and behind us shimmering and hazy in the sun-baked air. The Latvia of Papa's youth hovered in my mind like a cool, green oasis. Perhaps I slept during the next segment of Papa's life, dreaming of standing barefoot in the cold water, landing a netful of feisty crayfish onto the overgrown banks of *Zvirbulu upite*. Perhaps his stories were interrupted by one of our many wonderfully spontaneous stops along the way, at a rattlesnake farm or yet another alluring tourist trap with a wooden Indian whose face would always look exactly like my Papa's.

Papa and Granny married in Riga on December 3, 1929, and launched into nearly twenty years of ministry in Latvia.

At any rate, the next stations of his life stand out as headlines and old black-and-white photos rather than stories. . . . Papa finishing Bible school in Riga and beginning work with a missionary church in the home of a wealthy merchant in Jelgava. Papa, grown tall and dark, with a long, rectangular face and light, compelling eyes, standing black-robed in front of a group of baptismal candidates. Papa asking for a leave of absence to attend Bible school in England. Papa returning to marry the merchant's daughter, Mary Urban, and devoting himself to building mission stations around the Latvian countryside. English friends encouraging Papa in 1932 to launch the Latvian Faith Mission, which would print and distribute books, tracts, and Bibles throughout Latvia and Lithuania and train young men in missionary work. And Papa's mother Dora committing her life to Christ during a service in Papa's church in Jelgava.

By the time we finally reached Odessa, Texas, Papa had painted an intriguing picture of life as a Baptist pastor in the newly prosperous Latvia of the 1930s. A controversial young leader in the Baptist Union, a comfortably well-off landowner, a contented husband and father of two, and a passionate soul-winner, Papa enjoyed his success and his standing in the community. And there was no better time to be a Latvian than in this short-lived era of prosperity and independence between the wars, with the highest per capita income in the history of the country, the benevolent but strong leadership of the beloved President Karlis Ulmanis, and the highest university enrollment per citizen in all of Europe.

If life had continued as such, surely Papa would have lived on to old age in Latvia. But Latvia was about to go through still another cataclysm, perhaps the bloodiest and most traumatic yet in a long history of bloodshed and trauma.

After six evenings of revival meetings at the Northside Baptist Church in Odessa, the sanctuary was packed on the seventh night with steamy, sweating bodies overflowing the pews onto folding chairs in the aisles and foyer. I sat in the front pew sporting my new cowboy boots, next to two of the boys who had taken me snipe hunting and let me loose on the horse that had tried to decapitate me on a low mesquite branch the night before. The older girl in the pink dress who had given me my first kiss sat two rows back with her mother. The back of my neck burned as I tried to ignore her stare.

The paper programs, folded and waving back and forth in a desperate effort to generate a breeze in the airless space, announced the Reverend Charles Singer speaking from first-hand experience on the evils of Communism. His message was titled "I Saw the Soviet Paradise Behind the Iron Curtain." It was 1966, and the Cold War was in full force.

When Papa stood up to speak, I could see his hands trembling. His Latvian accent, with its wonderfully round, potent vowels, was more pronounced than ever. The crowd strained to hear every word.

"I wish I could speak to you today about the good news of Jesus Christ as I have on the previous evenings of the week. But tonight I have been asked to tell you of my experience of living in Latvia under Communist occupation. Many people ask me if the stories I tell of the horrors of life in a Communist state are true. And this I must reply: I believe that there will never be a tongue or a pen which will fully describe the devilishness of the Soviet Communists as we ourselves eyewitnessed it."

The only sound was the rustling of hundreds of paper programs, fanning the hot air frenetically. Papa continued, his hands gripping the lectern to stop their shaking and his words eloquent in their starkness and passion. As always, his story began with the Russian troops marching into the Baltic states in 1940. Immediately people were arrested, and many were sent to Siberia to slave labor camps from which few came back alive. Thousands of Latvian leaders were murdered in the dark forests for the sole crime of not being Communists. No one was safe.

The Communists nationalized everything: all land, business, and property. Papa's father-in-law Karlis Urbans lost his prosperous clothing business in a few hours—the only thing he could take out was his walking stick. Churches were also nationalized and their buildings were made into theaters, warehouses, gymnasiums, even horse barns. Bibles were loaded onto trucks and taken to paper mills to be remanufactured into wrapping paper. Churches were warned not to give wages to pastors, who were officially "advised" to take up some "productive work." Papa was arrested for selling his car to a Russian air force major before they nationalized all the cars in Latvia. Though he was released, KGB spies were always present in the church services that continued, and many other pastors were falsely accused of crimes and exiled to Siberia, where most died.

"The Soviet brutality climaxed on the night of June 14, 1941, known in Latvian history as 'the night of terror.'" Here Papa missed a beat, and his hands gripped the lectern even more tightly. "On this night, almost 15,000 men, women, and children— 'enemies of the state' such as government officials, intellectuals, and army officers, along with their families—were ripped from their beds, packed into trucks, and transported to the nearest railway stations. By six o'clock that morning they had been herded into cattle cars with barbed wire over the small window openings. And there they stayed for three days and nights without any sanitary arrangements, without food or water. How many of them perished, how many babies and children died, how many lost their reason, only God knows. They were finally sent along the tracks to Siberia—the men to slave labor camps, where most of them died, the women and children to primitive villages in Siberia where many died of starvation and exposure.

"In this awful war," Papa continued, "we had also heard terrible stories of German cruelty. But can you imagine, brothers and sisters, that when the Nazis marched into Latvia less than two weeks later, we wept with joy? And though their intent with Latvia was no more honorable, the dirty work—the killing off of all the best and brightest—had already been done for them by the Communists. After the Russian troops were driven out, we discovered the mass graves of thousands and thousands of our people who we thought had been sent to Siberia, lying plowed under in our own silent forests."

At first, life did indeed seem to be better under the Nazis. Latvian churches were returned and Sunday schools were reopened. Homes and any furniture and possessions that the Communists had not managed to take back to Russia were returned to their owners. But as the Germans established themselves in Latvia, the suffering began again. Jews from all over Europe were brought to ghettoes in Latvia and made to do menial work. Then, finally, they were marched into the forests and shot. Some accounts say that more than 93,000 Jews were lined up three deep at the edges of mass graves and then massacred in the Latvian forests during the German occupation. By the end of the war, only one thousand living Jews remained in Latvia.

Here Papa paused again and patted the sweat from his forehead and palms with his folded, starched white handkerchief, summoning energy to tell of the final Soviet invasion. In 1944, the Russians, strengthened by their American allies, began to push back Hitler's army. Hundreds of thousands of Russians and Ukrainians began fleeing westward into Latvia, trying to outrun the approaching Communists. It was one of the coldest winters on record. At night, in the distance near the railway station, Papa and his family could see the bonfires of the refugees between their tents.

By this time several pastors and their families who had fled other parts of Latvia occupied by the Russians were staying in Papa's home. Papa always refused to retell their grisly stories of Russian soldiers massacring innocent civilians. They all wanted to flee from Latvia to Sweden or another free land, but it was next to impossible. Many Latvians tried to cross the Baltic Sea to Sweden in small boats only to capsize or be captured by the Russians.

"Finally," Papa continued with a deep breath, "on October 10, 1944, my family and I were offered space on a Nazi cargo ship that was headed for German-occupied Poland. We quickly packed our belongings and boarded the overcrowded ship—my wife, my two children, my mother-in-law, and I. In the evening, a few miles out from shore, we looked back and saw our city of Liepaja, burning like Sodom.

"There were more than 4,000 people on our ship along with the cattle and other cargo. About midnight the ship's engines stopped, the lights were turned out, and there was a tormenting silence all over the ship. In our overcrowded hold some women began to scream, but people near them forced them to be still. There were whispers that we were surrounded by Russian submarines, that we would be blown up any minute. My wife and I gave away our lifejackets, which were in short supply, and committed our souls to God. Eventually, though, after what seemed an eternity, the engines resumed and we arrived the next morning in German territory. The next night a Russian submarine torpedoed another ship full of refugees, and many, many drowned."

In Poland they were placed in a slave labor camp, but Papa was able to buy their way out with part of a smoked ham he had carried on his back from Latvia. They eventually made their way by train past the burning cities of Germany to the Austrian Alps, where

When the Communists returned in 1944, Papa, Granny, Granny's mother Elizabeth, and their children Ervin and Lydia (my mother) fled with the retreating German army.

a small Latvian refugee community had settled into four villages. They worked on neighboring farms for scraps of food and begged for what they could not earn, but still they lived on the edge of starvation.

As hard as it was, their continual fear was that when the war ended they might be sent back to Latvia to live under Russian occupation. And the infamous agreement at Yalta between Stalin, Churchill, and Roosevelt gave them good reason to fear. When British troops came to Austria at the end of the war, a group of 40,000 Russian soldiers and their families who had fought against the Communists were camped near the Latvian refugees in an open meadow. One day several hundred boxcars arrived to take the soldiers and their families back to Russia under British guard. Rather than board the trains that would take them back to the Communists, several mothers took their little children and jumped to their deaths in the Drau River. The Latvians knew that they, too, needed to move quickly or also risk deportation.

Word reached them that the United Nations had opened displaced persons camps in Germany where food and shelter were being provided for the refugees. They decided that this was their only hope for escape and survival, and Papa began to forge illegal traveling papers marked with the official-looking rubber stamp of the local Latvian Refugee Committee. Papa organized groups of ten to twenty Latvian families and escorted them with the forged traveling documents through the British zone and into the American zone, where they could travel on without passes to the camps in Germany while he returned for another group. Finally, when Papa learned that the smuggling operation had aroused suspicion and was about to be discovered, he was able to escape with his family out of Austria and into a displaced persons camp in Esslingen, Germany.

They lived in the refugee camp in Esslingen for four years, from 1945 to 1949, with about 6,500 other uprooted Latvians, many of them intellectuals—many doctors, professors, engineers, teachers, lawyers, and politicians. For Papa, this was fertile ground for ministry in the midst of tragedy. In addition to pastoring three churches in refugee camps around Germany, he also began teaching English classes at the university extension. For two years he taught English from surplus U.S. Army New Testaments, even after they received other textbooks, and at the students' request they began having evening Bible studies also. Many Latvian professionals who had previously not sensed a need for God gave their lives to Christ during this time of forced imprisonment.

It was a busy and fruitful time, but it was still a time of waiting and great uncertainty. There were repeated, nerve-wracking medical screenings for immigration permission; their daily rations deteriorated; they were constantly aware of the hatred of the Germans toward them; and the feeling of imprisonment and lack of control over their own lives caused great depression in many. On top of it all, most refugees still did not feel safe from the ever-present threat of further Communist invasion. To add to their personal sadness, my grandmother's mother, Elizabete Urbane, who had accompanied them through so many difficulties during their repeated escapes and stations of exile, died in 1948 and was buried in a small Esslingen cemetery.

Finally, after four years of uneasy waiting, they unexpectedly received a letter from a doctor in California who offered to sponsor their whole family as immigrants to the United States. When they had successfully passed their medical and political screenings, they were loaded onto a train with 800 other refugees and transported to the ship that brought them to America. As they disembarked in New Orleans, a U.S. Army band played to welcome them to the new land. They continued their

In 1949, after more than four years of living in a refugee camp, my family immigrated to the Los Angeles area of California. My mother was seventeen years old.

31

Beginning in 1952, Papa traveled back and forth to Europe to visit refugee camps and immigrant settlements. He formed an agreement with CARE and raised money to send several thousand CARE packages to Christian refugees.

journey westward and finally settled in the doctor's home in Pasadena, just north of Los Angeles.

"And here I stand before you today," concluded Papa, "seventeen years later, a testimony to God's faithfulness. When we landed in America, we were penniless—even the clothes on our back had been sent to us at the refugee camps by friends in America. Our only capital was our faith in God and my English language. With God's help we have used both.

"Soon after our arrival, we began organizing the distribution of tens of thousands of clothing and food packages for needy refugees left in Europe. We were also able to secure sponsorship for more than 600 refugee families to immigrate to America. In 1963, we formalized the work that we had been doing for more than ten years and officially launched the International Refugee Mission to help link sponsors in America with refugee pastors in Europe who needed financial support to continue in full-time ministry. We've now branched out to support refugees, immigrants, and other needy people of twenty-two nationalities in sixteen lands.

"Many of you have had an important part in this ministry through your prayers and financial support. I thank you now on behalf of all who have been helped. And I beg you please to continue to pray for those living in the shadow of oppression everywhere. Amen."

❖

The next day the Impala was ready for the homeward trip. To my cautious relief, the girl in the pink dress did not come to see us off. Just outside of El Paso we ran over a rattlesnake, and in Phoenix the car finally surrendered to the heat, white steam billowing out from under the hood while Papa flapped his new Texan cowboy hat in mute protest.

But all too soon the trip was over, and we had returned from Texas adventures and Latvian dreams to the city streets of my childhood. And the gritty Los Angeles reality of my eleven-year-old life.

It was hard to adjust to real life again after an unforgettable road trip with Papa.

THE STRANGEST KID
ON THE BLOCK

Papa loomed large in my childhood, even during the many times when he was traveling other roads in his increasingly beaten-up Impala. One day he packed up and left on a cross-country preaching trip, raising money for refugee pastors and sleeping in the back of his car. He didn't come home for eleven months.

During his frequent absences, my grandmother was my anchor and the heart of our home. A former prosperous business owner and manager in Latvia, Granny was a kind, warm, and giving force in my life. The daughter of a general in the Russian czar's army, she grew up in the luxury of the court of Czar Nicholas II in pre-Communist Russia, was educated as a teacher in Latvia, and learned nursing in America. She spoke five languages, was deeply committed to her faith, and was never afraid of hard work. Granny largely supported our multi-generational family while Papa devoted himself to his mission work.

Granny worked hard as a nurse, yet she always had time to care for our family and her little dogs. Every morning she fried two eggs for the dogs, making sure to add just the right amount of salt and pepper.

My mother, who had spent her late childhood in Latvia under the alternating, threatening worlds of Communist and Nazi control, and then her

In the 1950s, my mother was an outstanding student in a nursing program in Memphis.

This 1957 photo of my father and me always makes me smile.

adolescence in exclusion and near-starvation as a refugee in Austria and Germany, was an unmentioned participant in Papa's accounts of the tragedy and trauma of the war and postwar years. When she arrived in America in 1949 she was seventeen years old, a bright, pretty girl whose eyes had seen far too much of horror and fear and suffering. Like my grandmother, she attended nursing school. As a young nurse she met my father, Talbert Kelley, seventeen years her senior.

My father, the son of a Missouri politician, was a talented, creative salesman with an abundance of wit, charm, and creativity. His mother Boonie MacArthur was a distant cousin of General Douglas MacArthur, commander of the Pacific Theater in World War II. Boonie also ran a big old boarding house in Memphis, Tennessee, in the 1930s and '40s. It was a place where very poor families rented rooms, shared the household chores, and ate supper together family style. One poor woman boarded there with her odd but talented son who spent all his time playing the guitar. His name: Elvis Presley, later the king of rock and roll.

Like his father before him, my dad had a serious problem with alcoholism. By the time I was three years old, he had abandoned our family, and none of us would hear from him again for more than a decade. My mother, my older sister Linda, and I moved into my grandparents' remodeled garage in Downey, California, where we lived for eight years.

In 1962, when I was seven years old, an evangelist from Texas came for a revival meeting at our First Southern Baptist Church in Downey (later pastored by the young Henry Blackaby). When he gave the altar call after his sermon, Granny leaned down and told me it was time for me to go forward to accept Jesus. Well, it wasn't my idea, but I didn't specifically disagree with her, so I stood up shakily and walked forward with wobbly knees to the loud "amens" of the praying congregation. The evangelist prayed with me and told me afterward that this day would always define my life as a child of God. Several weeks later I was baptized and given a certificate and a Bible to commemorate my immersion. And while this did

Granny and Papa took Linda and me to church every Sunday.

become the orienting Christian benchmark of my childhood, any evidence of a true internal change in my life was hard to find in the years that followed.

Still, Granny continued to encourage me and groom me for church life. During the evening prayer meetings she would lean over and whisper: "Chuckie, I'll give you a quarter if you'll pray aloud tonight." As motivated as any child would have been by that kind of offer, I took the bait. And it didn't take long for me to realize that if I prayed several times, Granny would fork out several quarters, and soon I was doing a booming business.

I will always be grateful that I had several Sunday school teachers who emphasized the importance of Bible memory. I was a quick learner with a pretty good memory, and I thrived on competition. When I was in third or fourth grade we had a memory verse contest that lasted the entire school year. The prize offered to the boy who learned the most verses by heart was a pocketknife that made my heart beat like a tin drum. I decided that I was going to do whatever it took to win that knife. But another boy coveted the knife just as much as I did. Week after week we recited new verses and chapters to our teacher. It was going to be a close contest.

Then I came up with a great idea. I discovered that there was one verse in the Old Testament that was repeated again and again fifty-two times. So I decided to memorize that verse and all fifty-two references. When I stood up and began to recite, my teachers and classmates were stunned. I was immediately declared the winner of the contest and the pocketknife. My championship verse? "And the Lord spoke to Moses, saying. . . ."

However, though I had enthusiastically memorized the Word, literal words were still my nemesis. They sprang from my mind and flooded my head only to stifle and stagnate in a mouth that refused to release them. Stuttering branded my childhood. I was mimicked and mocked. I was sent to speech therapy and psychotherapy. Scolded to think before I talked. But still the words would not flow. Increasingly shy and insecure, I retreated behind my rebellious mouth into my rebellious inner self.

By middle school we had moved with my grandparents into a fourplex in a Mexican neighborhood in downtown Los Angeles, a once-genteel area that was slowly succumbing to the heat and the dirt, its scraps of lawn growing slowly smaller and dustier and increasingly hidden by an endless variety of junked cars. As middle school progressed, I grew more and more rebellious. Though I went to church every time the doors were open, I grew resentful and angry. I actively tried to talk my friends out of any belief in God that they might have harbored, arguing that the Bible was contradictory and the church was full of hypocrites. I began skipping school, lying, cheating, and smoking.

In 1968, Granny sent Linda and me to the Billy Graham Crusade in nearby Anaheim. To show our patent antipathy for the proceedings, we sat near the top, smoking and making snide comments while Ethel Waters sang "His Eye Is on the Sparrow." I have no idea what Billy Graham said.

When the altar call was finally given, Linda had a brainstorm. One year older than me and also a confirmed rebel, she had already taken one year of French and felt fluently superior to the monolingual throngs surrounding her. "I know what we'll do," she whispered excitedly. "We'll go down and say that I'm your cousin from France, and I want to become a Christian!" I never needed any persuading for a prank, so we wound our way down to the crowds congregated near the platform as the audience sang "Just as I Am." When a counselor approached us, I introduced Linda as my French cousin Raquel who had been touched by the sermon, all punctuated by Linda's artful *bonjours* and *s'il vous-plaits*.

"You wait right here," said the woman helpfully, "I know someone who can speak French. I'll get her right away."

We dissolved into disrespectful giggles as we raced to the other end of the crowd to try it again. This time two men asked if they could help us. Linda trilled "*Je ne sais pas*" and "*oui, oui*" as I made my stock introduction, but then one of the men looked at us closely and said, "She's not really from France, is she?" I continued to assure them that she was, but Linda broke down laughing and unmasked us.

These perceptive men separated us, and the first one gave me a penetrating stare: "How about you? Do you want to become a Christian?"

"Oh, I'm already a Christian. I go to church a couple times a week. My grandpa's a pastor."

"But have you asked Jesus into your life?"

"Oh, yeah, lots of times."

"But if you died tonight, would you go to heaven?"

Suddenly this question brought me up short. I could no longer laugh this serious man off or make a caustic answer. I melted away into the crowd and eventually managed to meet up again with Linda, but I was shaken up. I knew I had no assurance with which to answer that question.

Several weeks later my sister and I were sitting in our Sunday school classroom at Westmoreland Chapel, a small offshoot of the Plymouth Brethren that was two blocks from our home. Our teacher was Bill Nuckles, a middle school teacher and basketball coach. He was a former Marine who had survived Pearl Harbor and had turned the bars in every port upside down before he became a Christian. He did his best to engage our group of junior high school students in a discussion about the Bible passage we were studying. But Linda and I were in high form that morning, and we led the others in giving Mr. Nuckles our most apathetic and resentful looks, refusing to answer his questions or even acknowledge his existence. Finally he had had enough. Slamming his Bible shut, he stood up and growled in a low and trembling voice: "My dog has more respect for people than you do." And he stormed out.

Though I couldn't show it in front of the others, I knew he was right. I later apologized to Mr. Nuckles for my behavior, and he invited me to go with him on one of his weekly visits to the Christian Serviceman's Center at Camp Pendleton Marine Base north of San Diego. The center was packed with young Marines about to be shipped off to Vietnam, all frightened and homesick and desperate for hope. Mr. Nuckles sat down next to one eighteen-year-old Marine who said he had been in the service for seven months. With a handkerchief and a grease pencil, Mr. Nuckles drew the young man diagrams he had learned in his Navigator training: "God is here, you are here, and you need a bridge to connect you." When he asked the Marine if he wanted to give his life to God, he said yes, and Mr. Nuckles prayed with him as I watched. Somehow I sensed that this was no place for my usual cynicism.

As Mr. Nuckles struck up the next conversation, he paused midway through his explanation and said, "Actually, this is so simple that my friend Chuck here can tell you the rest of the story." White-faced, I managed to stutter through the words I had just heard Mr. Nuckles say, summoning them from the recesses of a mind still steeped in habitual sarcasm and doubt. "This is you, this is God, this is heaven, this is hell, this is sin . . ." As Mr. Nuckles continued, this young Marine also gave his life to God as I watched.

That night, on the long drive back to my home, Mr. Nuckles made a suggestion that began to change my outward life, just as what he was showing me during these visits to the Christian Serviceman's Center over the following months would begin to change my inner life. "Chuck, I've noticed you stutter a bit," he began.

Kind of an understatement, I thought, and automatically went into my blocking mode.

But he went on and I listened in spite of myself. "I had a student who was a stutterer, too. He learned to control it by figuring out what sounds he was having trouble with that day or that hour and thinking ahead to avoid saying words that had those sounds in them. It took concentration, but he did it. He's still a stutterer, but you'd never know it."

I was asleep by the time he pulled into the driveway of the fourplex where my family lived. But the next morning in Sunday school, I listened to what Mr. Nuckles had to say. And when I answered his questions, I found to my amazement that I could steer my words away from the sounds that were giving me trouble that day and restructure my intended sentence by substituting words that meant the same. He had given me back my voice, and soon I would find the words that it needed to proclaim.

❖

It was 1969. I was into my ninth grade year at school, and though I was learning to disguise my stuttering, my old habits were still unchanged. In November, when our report cards were to be issued, it was clear to several of my friends and me that we would be failing more than one of our classes and would be in big trouble if those report cards ever reached our homes. So I stole enough blank report cards for all of us and forged new ones with more favorable results. In the meantime, my mother, who had learned that I could not be trusted, was routinely going through my notebooks when she found some of the extra blank report cards. She panicked, convinced that her son was headed for juvenile delinquency and jail, and asked my grandfather to give me the whipping of my life.

When she confronted me with my crime and told me that my grandfather was waiting for me, I was terrified. Papa, a firm old-world adherent to the school of corporal punishment, had given me my share of spankings during my childhood years. But now, given the seriousness of the offense and the steely glint in my mother's eyes, I truly feared what might be in store for me.

I was shaking as I walked into his living room on the other side of the fourplex. He was waiting for me there with his little dog beside him.

"Your mother has told me of some things you've been doing," he began. "Tell me about it."

I was surprised, confused, and put off guard. *He wants to talk about this? He's asking for my story?* This was not what I had expected at all. In a rush I told him everything that I had done.

"What prompts you to do this?" he asked.

"I—I'm not sure. I guess it's partly my friends." I continued to try to explain the confused, dark morass inside me that made me do what I did.

"Why don't we ask God to help you?" he asked. Still amazed by this kindness and acceptance that Papa was showing me in the face of my grave trespasses, we knelt. And I prayed with great sincerity—for the first time since my early childhood—that God would change my life. When we stood again, Papa hugged me and sent me off without my spanking.

My mother, who had secretly listened to the conversation as she waited impatiently on our side of the fourplex, could not believe that her father had not done what she had asked, and did not for one moment buy my story of repentance and conversion. So she herself gave me the whipping of my life. It was the last spanking I ever received.

Later that evening, in my own room, I knelt again and prayed alone: "God, I give you my life to change it."

This proved to be my point of no return. Papa's love and acceptance had melted my defenses and modeled Jesus' love to me, the culmination of a long string of steps that had been leading me back to God. I not only stopped lying, stealing, ditching school, and smoking, but I also started telling my friends about the Lord. And I began looking outside myself and my own private world of misery and disappointment to a bigger world with deeper griefs and truer hopes.

In 1970, when I was fifteen years old, my mother and father began corresponding again after twelve years with absolutely no contact. My father, who had never paid any alimony or child support, had kept his whereabouts a secret to avoid arrest. Soon my mother told Linda and me that she and my father were thinking of getting back together. We were so excited at the thought of being a family again, even with a father we didn't know.

One evening in March I answered the phone to hear an unfamiliar voice saying, "Chuck, this is your dad." We talked for a while, and he confirmed that he was coming to Los Angeles in the next week to see us. Linda and I both told him how much we were looking forward to seeing him again before we hung up.

The next day I told as many of my school friends as I could that my father was coming home. I was overjoyed at the idea of being part of a normal family.

But he never came. Days later my half-brother from my father's previous marriage called my mother to tell her that my father had been found dead of a massive heart attack in his hotel room in Mississippi. The coroner's report placed the time of death within thirty minutes of our telephone call with him.

My mother screamed and let the phone fall as I walked dazedly into the kitchen. "Dear Lord, I thank you," I said, recalling the Bible lesson I had learned the previous week that we are to give thanks in everything. Then I began to cry.

Papa was on a ministry trip to Texas when he heard the news. He immediately called me and assured me with the wonderful verse in Romans 8:28 (NASB): "And we know that God causes all things to work together for good."

The next few days we spent all of our free time looking at old photographs and talking about my dad with affection and fondness. There is no doubt in my mind that God gave Linda and me a great gift: conversation with our father on the day he died, after twelve years of silence, and a memory of him that is washed in love and forgiveness.

Shortly before I fully turned my life over to Christ when I was fourteen, Granny decided that I should begin going to the Church of the Open Door in downtown Los Angeles. COD not only had a wonderful pastor, Dr. J. Vernon McGee, but it was also known for its popular youth ministry. I objected, still hating church and declaring it boring and irrelevant, but that didn't stop Granny.

Photo courtesy of the Church of the Open Door

We were quite a sight when we walked into the candle-lit room, packed with a group of fifty kids sitting on the floor. I was tall and skinny, ever so proud of my black leather jacket and sunglasses. She was short, chubby, and wore "old lady" clothes and shoes. To my embarrassment, Granny stayed, sitting primly on a chair in the back of the room.

As the evening progressed, though, my sense of embarrassment shifted to intrigue. The kids in the group looked normal, but they didn't act normal. They sang enthusiastically, shared their hearts with one another, and prayed for their friends. Most importantly, a seventeen-year-old student, Herb Reese, took an interest in me. He looked beyond my insecurities and asked me questions about my school, my family, and myself. It felt wonderful.

I returned the next week without my grandmother. I was disappointed that Herb wasn't there that Sunday, but within a few minutes another student, Gregg Cantelmo, reached out to me with equal sincerity. I was hooked. Within two months I was deeply involved in the life of the youth ministry and the church.

This was a vibrant, growing church with two main emphases: teaching the Bible and world missions. During my high school years the church hosted many major missions conferences with guests such as Brother Andrew, the famed smuggler of Bibles into Eastern bloc countries; Cameron Townsend, the founder of Wycliffe Bible Translators; Bill Bright, the

I will always be grateful that my mother and grandparents forced me to learn how to play the piano. This photo was taken in 1971, the evening I performed my first original song for my family. It was an average song, but a great memory.

founder of Campus Crusade for Christ; and Corrie ten Boom, the concentration camp survivor and elderly hero of *The Hiding Place* who continued to travel around the world to tell people about God's love and forgiveness.

My new friends in the church's large youth group—like typical teenagers—tended to roll their eyes at yet another missions meeting, but I strangely could not get enough. I sat on the edge of my seat as missionary after missionary described the needy lives they had encountered, and their stories joined the tapestry already woven in my mind by my grandfather's accounts of Latvia.

In August of 1971, I joined a team of fourteen other high school students led by our church's youth pastor, Jim Klubnik, to travel to the Pai Pai Indians, an indigenous group of people living on a dusty plateau several hundred miles south of California's border with Mexico. We traveled at a snail's pace for hours in the backs or on the cab tops of our pickups, packed in with our sleeping bags and suitcases and equipment, dust swirling up around us and coating us with a gritty film of gray. We went with the goal of providing a Vacation Bible School for the children: we played games with them, told stories, sang songs, and presented the story of Jesus. At night we slept outside in our sleeping bags, amazed at the distinctness of the stars in the broad Mexican sky.

As the time for us to leave drew near, the village chief came to watch our program, and he invited us to present our message at his home. That evening, after our youth pastor presented the gospel to the assembled villagers and I played "Just as I Am" on our old-fashioned pump organ, the chief was the first to walk forward and profess to give his life to Christ.

We were surprised at what God had done. Here we were—fifteen kids and a youth pastor playing with children, but God had bigger plans. We were able to extend our stay long enough to help them build a simple church before we returned. And when we arrived back in Los Angeles, I was changed. The tapestry of stories and experiences was taking shape and form, and I finally knew that I wanted to give my life to proclaiming the news of Jesus and teaching the Bible through missions.

The following autumn, as a high school senior, I led my first missions trip. I organized a group of high school and college students to drive down to Tecate, Mexico, during Thanksgiving vacation. During the day we held children's events, and in the evenings we presented evangelistic programs. That was the first of many trips that year. Groups of youth from the church went into Mexico nearly every other weekend, often with sports teams to bridge the cultural barriers and establish rapport. Not surprisingly, we found that our specialized American football and basketball teams dominated, but our volleyball team was crushed—a good lesson for us and firm insurance that this would not be a ministry of condescension. Though my family was supportive, I financed the trips by my two part-time janitorial jobs at Westmoreland Chapel and the Church of the Open Door.

During my senior year of high school, I began to struggle with fundamental doubts about the truthfulness of Christianity. How could I know there really is a God? Is the Bible really inspired by God? If God is good, why is there so much evil in the world?

There were not very many people I felt comfortable speaking with about my questions, but the same young man who had been so friendly to me that first day I came to church offered to meet with me once a week to discuss Christianity and philosophy. For the better part of a year, Herb and I met every Sunday morning at 7:00 at the old Biltmore Hotel coffee shop in downtown Los Angeles. It was magnificently appointed with rich walnut panels, thick woolen carpeting, and remarkable art. Many Salvador Dali pieces adorned the walls, giving Herb and me the impetus to discuss how modern art reflects and informs modern culture.

A history major at UCLA at the time, Herb was especially interested in introducing me to the writings of Francis Schaeffer, an American pastor-philosopher who had established L'Abri, a study center in the Swiss Alps where questioning sojourners from all around the world could visit to discuss the deeper issues of life, reality, and meaning. Together we worked through Schaeffer's most famous books—*The God Who Is There, Escape from Reason, He Is There and Not Silent,* and *Genesis in Space and Time.* Though I wasn't mature enough to grasp everything he wrote, I was deeply impressed and adequately assured that it is indeed intellectually credible for one to believe that only in the triune God of the Bible are there answers to the important complex questions of our day.

Over the years, these age-old questions have resurfaced from time to time. And each time I recall with a sense of profound satisfaction that I didn't simply make an emotional decision to follow Jesus. It was a choice that made a great deal of sense.

In 1973, as I was preparing to graduate from high school, my grandfather asked me if I would like to go to Europe with him. He and the board of the International Refugee Mission were concerned about choosing his successor, and since my indication the year before of a call to ministry, my grandfather was grooming me for an eventual transition. He contacted a faithful supporter from Texas, Jake Diel, for the funds for my trip, and after a wide-eyed flight on a 727 to Frankfurt, Germany, Papa and I were "on the road" again together— in the first-class carriage of an old-fashioned train pulling slowly out of the Frankfurt train station.

When Papa took me to Europe for the first time in 1973, my worldview was enlarged forever. This photo captures me going for a walk on the city wall of the medieval town of Nordlingen, Germany.

Papa had organized this European trip to give me an overview of the work of the International Refugee Mission. We began in Cologne, Germany, where my jet-lagged, neo-Californian eyes first glimpsed the glories of an older world: the soaring double spires of the gray-stoned Cologne Cathedral, the narrow cobblestoned streets lined with noisy pubs, and through it all the legendary Rhine River, weighted from its passage beneath the mythical Lorelei crag and the medieval Mausturm. We attended a Latvian folksong festival in the cathedral, the beauty of the exiled music haunting as it echoed in the distant heights of the grand old church. This was my first encounter with the Latvian community in exile and the Latvian language as a real form of communication quite independent from my grandparents.

In England we met with the IRM European Committee and my great uncle Ernest, Papa's younger brother, and his wife, Dr. Ruth Zingers. Uncle Ernest and "Dr. Ruth," as Papa always called her, had been missionaries to India for twenty-two years. Now semi-retired, they had a thriving ministry among expatriate Indians and Pakistanis near their home in Birmingham, where Dr. Ruth treated many poor immigrants free of charge and told them about God in Hindi and Urdu.

From England we traveled to Italy, which was memorable for me as the place where I gave my first sermon, in a tiny Italian Gospel Mission church in a village in southern Italy. That day my grandfather complained of a sore throat and told me that I would need to preach that evening. I had given talks and short messages before, but never a sermon – and never before a group of pastors, never through a translator, and certainly never in front of my grandfather!

After my initial panic and guilty feelings of suspicion at Papa's "convenient" sore throat, I began to think more clearly. During my janitor's jobs I had gotten into the habit of listening to any one of my five sermon tapes from a dynamic young preacher named John MacArthur. I realized that I had surely listened to each of them at least twenty times and, if I really tried, could probably repeat any of them verbatim. So in the few hours that remained before my ordeal, I scribbled down an outline from memory. And that evening, an eighteen-year-old, fresh-faced high school graduate stood up before a church full of seasoned Italian pastors to preach on "How to Know God's Will for Your Life."

They were a gracious and forgiving congregation. After the service I noticed that the people were greeting one another with kisses, so as an elderly lady walked through to shake my hand I bent down to kiss her on either cheek. She beamed, and I leaned down to kiss the next woman in line. Soon I became aware of a group of pastors gathered off to the side, howling and bent over with laughter. Eventually someone gently informed me that men were only supposed to kiss other men, and vice versa. I regretfully surveyed the pastors' daughters lined up in my receiving line and lamented my loss of innocence.

We also participated in several baptism services while we were in Italy, church-wide celebrations of a publicity and pomp that I had never experienced in America. After a special service at the church, the pastor walked through the heat of the Italian summer Sunday with the baptismal candidates dressed in long white robes to the shores of the Mediterranean, where a crowd of curious onlookers in bikinis and Speedos soon gathered around the assembled congregation. Here, with the blue water lapping at his feet, the pastor would preach an evangelistic sermon before leading the candidates into the sea for immersion. Afterward everyone was invited back to the church for a big celebratory feast of purely Italian proportions and excellence.

In Paris we stayed at the home of Granny's brother, George Urban, formerly a Latvian Supreme Court justice. Now an exiled pastor, Uncle George had established a Russian-language Christian magazine called *Prisiv* ("The Call") that had been smuggled into the Soviet Union since the 1930s and sent to Russians in seventy-two countries. Interestingly, most of the couriers were Russian military personnel who could smuggle copies of *Prisiv* into many different parts of the Soviet Union.

Perhaps the most memorable personality I met on this trip was Princess Helen Wiazemski, Uncle George's secretary and the wife of the former captain of the guard for the Russian czar. She herself was a member of the Russian aristocracy who had grown up in the czar's court in the Hermitage. Princess Helen had been a gifted opera singer and pianist and a student of Rachmaninoff; before World War I she had sung in all the capitals of Europe to Rachmaninoff's accompaniment. Since I had learned to play several Rachmaninoff pieces while studying classical piano as a child and youth, I peppered her with questions about the famous composer.

Still every bit a princess though stooped and arthritic, Princess Helen took the day off work to show me around Paris. "Chuck," she said, "today I vill show you ze Palace of Versailles." And together we slowly trooped through the accoutrements of French aristocracy as she reminisced about a long-gone childhood amidst the glories of the Russian court.

This final stop was a fitting end to our trip, for it positioned us with our focus toward the east. Traveling to Latvia, to the country that my grandfather and Uncle George and Uncle Ernest longed for, was still unthinkable and impossible. But meeting these people who, like my grandfather, were still devoting their lives to the people behind the Iron Curtain, gripped my passion and my imagination and would not let me go.

IS THE PARISH MY WORLD, OR IS THE WORLD MY PARISH?

It was the steamy summer of 1976. Gerald Ford and Jimmy Carter were running for president as America celebrated her bicentennial. An Israeli commando squad made a daring raid to rescue 103 hostages that had been hijacked by Palestinian terrorists in Entebbe, Uganda. A young pony-tailed Romanian gymnast named Nadia Comaneci captured the heart of the world from the mats of the Montreal Olympics. And I was in Europe on a summer missions trip between my junior and senior years of college.

This was my second European summer since enrolling in Biola College in La Mirada, a Los Angeles suburb. In 1974 I had gone to France with Unevangelized Fields Mission to help missionaries with literature evangelism and remodeling a youth camp. Later that summer I went to Monte Carlo to visit Trans World Radio, where I was introduced to Russian and Ukrainian leaders responsible for broadcasting the gospel behind the Iron Curtain. Many of these leaders had just returned from the International Congress on World Evangelization in Switzerland, and they spoke enthusiastically of the consensus they had reached there with other evangelicals and the document they had just signed that would later play such an important role in my life. They expressed amazement that the USSR had actually permitted a few pastors to attend, though they had to stay in isolation from the other delegates.

Now, in 1976, I was back in Europe, sweating through the hottest summer on record since 1727. I began in scorching Florence, Italy, where Papa was conducting a conference for his mission's most active arm, the Italian Gospel Mission. After Papa left I stayed behind to volunteer wherever I was needed, putting my unlimited Eurail pass to good use in seizing every opportunity to travel and gather new experiences, including teaching the Bible to middle-school students at summer camps in southern Italy, publicizing a new Campus Crusade outreach to university students in Rome, attending international conferences and Bible classes in Belgium and Austria, and teaching Bible studies at Operation Mobilization's Bible-smuggling base in Vienna. Near the end of the summer I traveled to England to work in a little

A group of Biola students on our 1974 mission trip, including Bob Rasmussen, later the best man in our wedding.

Baptist church outside of Manchester as a volunteer youth and worship leader.

Throughout the summer, I was drawn to reading books about ministry behind the Iron Curtain, and while I was in England I read Brother Andrew's *God's Smuggler* for the third time. Once again I was struck by his faith and his daring, and as my time in England drew to a close and I prepared to return to Amsterdam for my flight home, I realized that I had a once-in-a-lifetime opportunity to try to meet this man who had had such an impact on my imagination.

I traveled to Holland early, put my luggage into storage at the train station in Amsterdam, and set off on a woefully uninformed search for Brother Andrew. The only address I had for him was the post office box and village name that he listed in his book. I scoured the maps in the train station for Ermelo, the name of the village, but it was nowhere to be found. Finally I found a ticket salesman who had heard the name and could direct me to the appropriate train.

As I stepped off the platform in the tiny village of Ermelo, I began asking the passersby if they spoke English; all shook their heads and kept walking by, eyeing me warily. I randomly chose a direction on the narrow pavement. "Lord, please lead me to a phone booth," I prayed. I stopped and looked around. There, directly in front of me, was a trademark green Dutch telephone booth. But once inside with a phone book in my hands, I had no idea where to look. At a loss, I looked under "B" for Brother. "A" for Andrew? Nothing. "O" for Open Doors Ministries? Again nothing. I didn't know his real name.

I stepped out of the phone booth into the hot midday sun and prayed again: "Lord, please lead me to a post office." When I looked around to find my bearings, I realized that I was standing in front of the steps leading up to the Ermelo post office. I walked the steps as if they were holy ground.

Inside there were long lines, dozens of people with arms full of letters and packages. As I took my place at the end, I once again prayed: "Lord, lead me to Brother Andrew. Please help me." Within a minute a postal employee dressed in white approached me at the end of the line and said, in perfect English, "May I help you?" By this time I had nearly ceased to be surprised, so surreal—so miraculous—these answers had become.

He walked to the counter and came back with a handwritten note: "You'll find Brother Andrew at this address," he said.

"How do I get there?" I asked.

"There's a cab right outside," he replied and motioned through the windows to a taxi cab idling on the street I had just left.

I thanked him in amazement and numbly walked down the steps outside to the cab. The address it delivered me to was right next to Brother Andrew's house, the headquarters of Eastern European Bible Mission, today Hope International, directed by Hank Paulsen. I told Hank my adventures and my desire to meet Brother Andrew and take Bibles into Latvia. "Andrew's not available right now," said Hank, a six-foot-eight Dutchman. "But while you're waiting, I can show you around here."

It was an exciting tour. Hank explained the internal workings of Eastern European Bible Mission and Open Doors, and introduced me to the carpenters who redesigned the vehicles used by the Bible smugglers. I soaked in the information and the commitment of those who worked there.

Finally, Hank took me to Andrew's offices and told me to wait in the tiny library. Eventually, a small, unassuming man with kind eyes walked in to where I was waiting. "Hi, I'm Brother Andrew," he said with a pronounced Dutch accent, shaking my hand warmly. He sat with me and asked questions as I told him about my Latvian heritage and my interest in taking Bibles into Latvia.

"Chuck, we'd love to have you join us," he said when he had heard my story. "We have no one going into Latvia. We're going into Poland, Czechoslovakia, Hungary, Bulgaria, but we don't have any people with contacts in Latvia."

I raced back to Amsterdam, and the excitement infused me throughout the long trip back to Los Angeles. When I reached my grandfather's study, I swallowed my news long enough to give him a detailed account of all of my summer adventures. He was an eager and interested listener. Finally, when I had finished, I cautiously broached the subject of my hope. "Papa, I met Brother Andrew," I began.

"Who's he?" he asked, sensing the new note in my voice.

"Brother Andrew. You know—he wrote *God's Smuggler*! He asked me to work with him to take Bibles into Latvia. I really want to go. I feel I should go!" My enthusiasm could no longer be contained.

"Ah," he said, standing and walking to the window, "he would have you risk your life by smuggling Bibles into Latvia. Don't you realize that the KGB would like nothing better than to arrest Charles Singer's grandson for just such an offense? I am out of their reach now, but you would be walking back into their trap and they would seize the opportunity. No. I cannot permit it. By no means. It is out of the question."

"But Papa—"

"No, that is final," he thundered. "It is out of the question. Go back and finish school." He turned his back and busied himself with the papers on his desk.

Utterly deflated, I trudged out of the room. I knew that there was no use arguing with Papa. I was still a member of his household, and his resolve dominated and outlasted all of ours. With a heavy and deeply disappointed heart, I unpacked my bags and began to prepare unenthusiastically for my senior year of college.

I had always wanted to marry someone like my grandmother. She was my ideal woman—considerate, kind, warm, and giving, she stood on a pedestal in my mind that no mortal female could approach. But then, sitting cross-legged on the floor of my choir director Loren Wiebe's living room at a Biola Chorale Christmas party during my freshman year of college, I met Nancy Heidebrecht. She had big brown eyes and a magnetic, sparkling smile—she was considerate, kind, and warm . . . and studying to be a nurse, just like Granny. I was smitten!

During our spring choir tour I finagled my way into occasionally sitting next to her on the bus, and I was impressed with the depth of her personality and her devotion to her family. On our free evening in San Francisco, I asked her to go with me to Ghirardelli's Chocolate Factory, where we indulged ourselves in the world-famous hot fudge sundaes

I was amazed when Nancy agreed to go with me to the Andraé Crouch and the Disciples concert.

and a spectacular San Francisco sunset.

Back at Biola, when gospel stars Andraé Crouch and the Disciples came to campus for the spring concert—our college's safe, "danceless" version of the spring prom—I borrowed my mother's turquoise '63 Thunderbird, rented a white tux, and relished Nancy's company for a three-hour praise concert. And when Andraé told us all to join hands for the final song I could have swung from the rafters.

But when I asked Nancy for another date, she politely said no. A second time. And a third time. And a fourth. Until I finally got it through my thick head that she really wasn't interested in spending any more time with me.

College freshmen males are nothing if not resilient, and I soon moved on. For safety's (and variety's) sake, I usually made it a policy to be asking two or three girls out at any given time. By the end of my senior year, these tactics had given me the decisive edge in an informal contest among my friends for having taken the most girls out on dates during my college career. My proud total of forty-two was impressive numerically, but only two of those represented serious girlfriends.

During those years, my job as the youth pastor of a small Southern Baptist church in Paramount, California, gave me ample opportunities to invest and test the principles I had learned as a high school student at the Church of the Open Door. I continued leading summer mission trips to Mexico. Some were more memorable than others: during the first trip I led as a youth pastor, at the ripe old age of twenty, we had to make seven separate trips back across the border to the emergency room for various and sundry misfortunes among the group.

All through my four years in college I loved to bring people along and include them in ministry, and at any given time seven or eight friends would be helping at the church with the junior and senior high youth groups or singing in and directing the choir. The pastor also generously provided many opportunities for me to preach, usually another of my infamous warmed-over John MacArthur classics.

Of course, in the meantime I was also pursuing my studies in world missions, with emphases in cultural anthropology and communication. But somehow school never managed to rank very high on my overflowing list of priorities. I was more interested in sports, music, student government, my youth ministry, and, of course, girls.

As time passed I began running into Nancy more frequently at the library, and she unfailingly greeted me with a friendly smile. Near the end of the spring semester of my junior year, as I was plowing my way through research for a term paper, she responded to what must have been a desperate look in my eye by offering to type my paper. And so I unexpectedly spent many of the next spring evenings in Nancy's apartment with her and her roommate Lynn Luttrell as they laboriously worked through my paper on Lynn's

manual typewriter. I managed to insist on periodic breaks for the three of us, cajoling them away for fun-loving walks through the nearby park.

Finally, under the pretense of a thank you gesture, I cautiously asked Nancy if I could take her to Universal Studios in Hollywood. She had recently separated from her boyfriend of several years, and when she agreed, I borrowed my pastor's '59 MGA Coupe, she packed a lunch of fried chicken, and we spent a whole stolen Saturday together, playing and laughing like children.

But then, far too soon, school was out and I was off to Europe. Determined not to surrender any slight headway that I had won, I wrote several letters to Nancy and Lynn with "prayer requests from the mission field," guessing rightly that this would keep

Nancy and I posing with "Jaws" at Universal Studios.

me in her mind without putting any unwanted pressure on her. And several weeks after I came back to the United States, Nancy called my house to see if I had returned.

We went to a park together, and I remembered again why I had left for Europe with this woman on my mind. By our next meeting, I had resolved to end the uncertainty and distractibility in my life. I sat on the sofa in her living room and fixed her with my most intense stare. "Nancy, I really like you, but I don't want to play any dating games any more. I want to know now if you are interested in having a serious relationship with me."

Poor Nancy was stunned. She had expected to entertain a returning missionary, a brother in Christ, and here she was suddenly confronted with an overeager college boy pressuring her to say yes to preparation for a lifelong commitment.

"Uhh, Chuck, uhh, thank you, I'm, um, honored," she stammered, "but I need some time to think about this. Can you give me three days to pray and think before I give you an answer? And I think we shouldn't see each other during that time."

The three days seemed interminable to me as I chastised myself for my impetuousness and imagined again and again how I could possibly repair the hard-earned bridges I had just burned. When Nancy and I met again at the end of the stipulated time, my hands were sweaty and I could hardly find a word that would come out without stuttering. But she was lovely and calm and kind as usual.

"I've been thinking it over," she began. "I didn't expect to feel this way, but as I prayed, I kept realizing more and more characteristics in you that I really like. I guess what I'm saying is that I'm ready to commit to a relationship."

And so began our courtship. That fall we traveled several times up the California coast in my souped-up 1970 Chevy Nova to visit her parents. We attended several of Papa's mission prayer meetings at my grandparents' home in Los Angeles. We worked together with the youth group I led. And we began, inevitably, to talk about marriage. On one of the long eight-hour drives to her

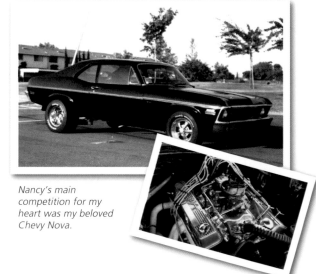

Nancy's main competition for my heart was my beloved Chevy Nova.

parents, we pulled off at a picturesque turnoff high above the crashing, golden Pacific and I asked her to marry me.

After a hearty holiday meal at Nancy's Uncle Dan and Aunt Eleanor's house, I could restrain myself no longer. I charged into the room where Nancy's father was taking his post-Thanksgiving-dinner nap, and as he rubbed his eyes and tried to place a name with my face I asked him for his daughter's hand in marriage. Fortunately he recovered his sleep-stolen senses and graciously agreed, and that afternoon we made the announcement to her family. I was blissful.

Nancy's father, Rev. Harry Heidebrecht, performed our wedding in the Evangelical Free Church of Fremont, California, where he was pastor.

Nancy graduated with her degree in nursing in January and moved to Fremont to work in a nursing home and plan our wedding while I completed my last semester at Biola. And in June of 1977, seven days after my graduation, we were married.

After our honeymoon, we packed up our car and a U-Haul trailer and I once again began the long trip to Texas, this time to seminary. I had long dreamed of going to Dallas Theological Seminary, where so many of my mentors and well-respected professors had attended. But my grades had never been stellar, and since I was no longer forging report cards, Dallas Seminary had denied my application.

But I come from persistent stock, and when Southwestern Baptist Theological Seminary, the world's largest evangelical seminary in neighboring Ft. Worth, Texas, accepted my application, I decided that it would be a good starting point. When we arrived in Texas, we drove straight to the Dallas Seminary campus, where I parked our loaded car and trailer outside the administration building and walked into the admissions office.

"Hi, I'm Chuck Kelley from Los Angeles. My wife is sitting outside with all of our belongings, and we're driving to Ft. Worth, where I've been accepted at Southwestern. But where I really want to be is here. Is there anything we can do?"

The admissions officer had the grace to smile at my brazenness. "Why don't you take one semester of classes at Southwestern and see what you can do with your grades," he said kindly. "If you can prove yourself there, we'll see what we can do about you coming here."

He was as good as his word, and so, it proved, were my grades, and after the first semester I transferred to Dallas Theological Seminary.

Nancy worked nights as a nurse at a hospital, and I sold organs and pianos on commission at a Sears store until I took over the paid position as junior high youth pastor for a group of more than a hundred junior highers at Pantego Bible Church in Arlington. Again, the challenges and rewards of hands-on ministry often overshadowed my formal studies, but my time in seminary was nonetheless an intensive learning period. Soon after my arrival, the invitation of one of my favorite professors inspired me to begin a habit of setting up a lunch appointment with a different professor each week. It was during these brown bag sessions in their offices or the seminary snack room that my most in-depth and lasting education took place as I grilled them about the content of our classes, future studies, faith, and life questions in general.

One sunny winter day, I treated Dr. John Walvoord, the seminary's renowned president and theologian, to a simple lunch at a nearby diner. While walking back to the campus, he taught me a lesson on vision and leadership that I'll never forget. As we passed an old Greek Orthodox church, he said, "You know, Chuck, that church will be ours some day."

"Really?" I replied. "Has the seminary purchased the church?"

"No, we haven't even begun negotiations. But the seminary is growing and we need to expand our property, and that includes the church."

I was surprised.

"But that's not all," Walvoord continued, pointing to another large building owned by a computer company. "That will be ours, too. We'll establish a leadership development center there."

Again I asked, "Oh, has the seminary bought that?"

"No, not yet. But we will."

Within fifteen years, Dr. Walvoord's predictions came to pass. The old church was purchased, remodeled, and turned into a marvelous student book store. And the computer building is now the Center for Christian Leadership, a place that has provided invaluable pastoral training to thousands from all over the world.

I will always be grateful for professors like Elliott Johnson, Bob Choun, Howard Hendricks, Haddon Robinson, Ron Blue, Charles Ryrie, and Don Regier. The lessons I learned from them over sandwiches and coffee continue to resonate in my life today.

As my seminary studies drew to a close, the pressure to chart our future course began to mount. For years it had been tacitly expected that I would succeed my grandfather as the leader of the International Refugee Mission. In fact, I invested two years of my life writing my master's thesis on "The History and Present Ministry of the International Refugee Mission."

But Papa was still actively leading the mission in his late seventies, opening new mission fields and serving as the unifying figurehead of the organization, and after years of operating on his own he had difficulties finding a place for me to minister with him. Nor was he very interested in discussing future directions with me. The fact that he never told me what he thought of my thesis was painful.

So Nancy and I decided that perhaps a better introduction to working with IRM would be to begin on its primary mission field in Italy with people I had worked with before. We were willing to raise support, go to language school, and move to Florence. But this plan also encountered Papa's opposition. As I began to interview with churches for pastoral positions, church boards were understandably concerned when I explained that I would need to leave any position as soon as my grandfather died or decided to retire.

Finally I was forced to realize that this limbo was an untenable position for me and Nancy, who was expecting our first baby. I wrote a letter to Papa explaining the decision I had made to go ahead as God was leading me, even if it meant that I would not work with IRM, and then I threw myself into the interview process. Fourteen churches responded positively, and inexplicably, as Nancy and I prayed over the list, the last one in line—in Oregon, of all places—slowly inched up in priority. Finally, when the formal invitation and time for a decision arrived, we were surprised to be in agreement that First Baptist Church in Corvallis, Oregon, would be our destination.

Peter was two months old when we moved to Oregon to work with First Baptist Church of Corvallis.

Fresh from seminary, brimming over with ideas, and a proud new father of a baby boy, Peter, I arrived in Corvallis in July of 1980 in the familiar position of youth pastor, eager to bring my unique perspective and experience in overseas missions to my work in the local church. But a rude awakening awaited me. "Missions work is for missionaries," the senior pastor informed me in no uncertain terms soon after my arrival. He made it clear that pastors who were interested in active global ministry would be frowned upon. Again I felt the door to missions slamming in my face.

Much later, during a youth Bible study in which we talked about the work of smugglers taking Bibles into Eastern bloc countries, I began to cautiously tell the youth group about my meeting with Brother Andrew during that hot summer of 1976. They were amazed at the thought of someone they knew actually having spoken to a famous missionary-smuggler and being offered the chance to work alongside him, and I couldn't help feeling that we were robbing these young people by confining their Christian vision to the walls of our church. John Wesley's famous quotation—"I look upon all the world as my parish"—had been a favorite of mine since seminary, but now it had become a defining question for my ministry: Was the parish my world, or was the world my parish? Still, when one of the youth wondered aloud that evening if God would still answer my longing to serve him overseas, I immediately replied, "I don't see it." Local parish work seemed to stretch out ahead of me like a long narrow tunnel.

But I continued to learn, and I loved youth ministry. I had already discovered that music and sports were powerful languages to communicate the gospel and Christian values to youth, and I pursued both with abandon. We formed a rock band called "Prism," a fittingly raucous combination of amateur and professional musicians that practiced in the proverbial basement in our home and performed at youth outreaches and retreats.

We rigged up an adjustable basketball hoop in our driveway that hosted many a dunk-a-thon and special basketball marathons to raise money for youth camps. And I met regularly with small groups of young men for in-depth discipleship and study.

I soon began to detect a sense of isolation and competition among the evangelical pastors of the area, and simultaneously a strong need within myself for contact with other youth pastors who were giving their lives to the same pursuits as mine. Gradually I got to know several youth pastors in the area, and soon we were meeting monthly for prayer and encouragement. In 1981 we formed the Corvallis Youth Workers Fellowship, a network that built bridges among youth workers and provided the infrastructure for organizing citywide youth activities, outreaches, and retreats.

One man at First Baptist who had a profound impact on my life in those youth ministry years was George Waldo, eighty-five years old to my twenty-five, a horticulturist and retired professor who had developed the marionberry and the Cascade strawberry. A deacon in the church, he was the only man who responded to my announcement in church of an early-morning men's prayer meeting, standing alone in the rain outside the locked door when I arrived five minutes early to let him in. We continued to meet each week for a year, just the two of us, praying for an hour before he treated me to breakfast at Sambo's. During breakfast, where I always watched in amazement as he poured at least half of the salt shaker contents on his fried eggs, we talked about life, history, marriage, childrearing, sex, and the marionberries thriving in our backyard. He prayed for me and my ministry faithfully, and I learned more from him than from anyone else during those years of ministry in Corvallis.

Gradually, however, as I grew older, I found myself more interested in talking to the parents of the youth than to the youth themselves. Further, though my pastor was not supportive of my multicultural interests or interdenominational activities, he did give me ample opportunities to preach. Though some of my early sermons were characterized by extensive stuttering, I fell in love with sermon preparation and I sensed that the people really were blessed when I preached.

So in 1984 I accepted a position as senior pastor of a Mennonite Brethren church in neighboring Salem, the capital of Oregon. An ideological leap for us from our mainstream evangelical roots, serving at Kingwood Bible Church exposed us to the full grit and glory of Mennonite theology: hands-on, practical forgiveness, reconciliation, and peace. Though I strained against this emphasis at times, an excellent teacher in the person of a retired pastor in our church took me under his wing and became a life mentor for me. Arno Wiebe, forty years my senior, became the Paul to my Timothy, continually encouraging me to develop my gifts and my Christian mandate to bring people together, regardless of denominational lines.

The lessons I learned here in cooperative ministry confirmed the call that I was sensing from God to build bridges across lines of denomination and distrust. But a restlessness within me continued to betray my longing for an active part to play in God's work beyond the boundaries of my parish.

Papa and Mom were proud to be at Kingwood in January 1984 on the first day of our new ministry. Nancy has been an amazing wife, mom, and pastor's wife.

Dr. Arno Wiebe, a veteran pastor with fifty years of experience, was an important life mentor for me. He served as my associate pastor in Salem.

A typical scene in my office at Kingwood: I have always been a lover of books and computers, and my life has always been inundated with too many papers.

This 1987 family portrait is my all-time favorite picture of Peter, Phillip, Scotty, Nancy, and Karen.

From Lausanne
to Latvia

I looked out over the congregation as they sang the opening hymn on this Sunday morning in early April of 1989. It was the last day of my first full year as senior pastor of the First Baptist Church of Corvallis. It had been a good year, I thought to myself as I surveyed the many familiar faces. A good and a difficult year. Nancy sat near the front of the church with our band of squirming, Sunday-scrubbed children: eight-year-old Peter, his younger brothers Scotty and Phillip at six and five years old, and little three-year-old Karen. How Nancy managed to stay so serene and beautiful with that wonderful, wiggly bunch of Kelleys I would never know.

I had returned to this church as senior pastor determined to expose the congregation to a missions worldview and to lead by example, and my acceptance of the position had been dependent on my request for three weeks of missions travel each year. Within two months of arriving at First Baptist, I was flying east to Washington, D.C. to participate in Leadership '88, a conference for young Christian leaders and evangelists interested in missions. Sponsored by the United States Lausanne Committee, this conference brought together one thousand people under the age of forty and allowed us to sit under the teaching and preaching of older spiritual leaders such as Ted Engstrom, Leighton Ford, Bill Bright, Luis Palau, and Richard Halverson in an intentional passing of the visionary baton of global ministry to the next generation.

I was surprised when I was invited with a small delegation of participants to a special meeting in the Eisenhower Executive Office Building led by Senator Richard Lugar of Indiana on the state of religious freedom in the Soviet Union. Before the meeting we were given a special tour of the White House, complete with a brief appearance by President and Mrs. Reagan and their little dog Rex.

As we were walking from the White House to the Eisenhower building next door after our encounter with the president, I stopped at a phone booth and called home.

"Hello," answered Nancy.

"Hi, honey!" I replied enthusiastically. "Guess where I am? At the White House. I just saw Reagan and I'm headed for a meeting with a senator...."

She didn't let me finish. "I don't care where you are! Talk to Phillip!"

She called our third son to the phone. "I don't want to talk to Daddy!" I could hear him yelling in the background. "I don't want to talk to Daddy!" Eventually he came to the receiver, in time for me to persuade—or threaten—him into listening to his mother.

I'm not sure who has the bigger sense of humor, the Lord or Nancy. Certainly Nancy has not been one to allow me to glory very long in the glow of the spotlight. And the Lord has been creative over the years to keep me in my place.

After my reality check, I returned to the conference. The organizers had chosen the Lausanne Covenant as their foundational framework, a remarkable document forged fourteen years earlier in Lausanne, Switzerland, by 2,300 evangelicals representing 150 countries and all branches of the Christian church. These leaders came together to seek clarity and consensus on many of the controversial questions of the Christian world in the second half of the twentieth century. They tackled critical issues such as the relationship between evangelism and social concern, unity and diversity among Christians, the belief in the uniqueness of Christ that was being challenged by a growing acceptance of other religions, religious liberty and human rights, and the relationship of the gospel to culture.

What emerged from these prayer-intensive work sessions was a fifteen-article document, edited by John Stott, that affirmed the supremacy of God's word as good news for the entire world, stating that world evangelization requires "the whole church to take the whole gospel to the whole world." The articles further explained the central points of foundational Christian belief that all in attendance could wholeheartedly embrace, backed up by multiple Bible passages. Great care was taken to make this a clear articulation of solid, Bible-based, orthodox Christianity, not another watered-down, modernized version of the gospel. Then each of those 2,300 leaders in attendance signed his or her name to the covenant in public agreement and commitment to work together toward the evangelization of the world. (See Appendix E for the Lausanne Covenant.)

Nearly a decade and a half later, I was overwhelmed by the power and simplicity of the covenanted articles in the Lausanne Covenant, and by the public commitment that it represented. That week in July of 1988, when our organized sessions were over, I played tourist in the U.S. capital, walking the Washington Mall from the Capitol Building to the Lincoln Memorial and visiting several Smithsonian museums and the National Archives. There I took my place in line to file past the glass-covered copies of the Magna Carta, the Declaration of Independence, and the Constitution. I could not read much of the old-style script of the texts themselves, but I was drawn again and again to the names that filled the final pages of these dangerous statements of intent and commitment. As these men wrote out their signatures—some large and with a flourish, some with a modest, compact, unassuming style—they knew that they were putting their lives on the line. I didn't recognize most of the names, but the documents they had sealed with their signatures had had a profound impact on our history.

Where have I put my name? I asked myself. The answer echoed back: *Nowhere. Nowhere.*

By the time I flew back to Corvallis later that week, I had made several decisions. I knew it would be a controversial course in a Baptist church that expected strict biblical exposition, but I was going to teach the Lausanne Covenant. We needed a mechanism to unite us for the future that was larger than our church, our programs, our buildings, and our small Oregon world. We needed a biblical statement of faith, strategy, priority, urgency, repentance, and commitment to see the world as God sees it, through the lens of his creation, sacrifice, and grace. And we needed to personalize the process and focus on the power of names, on the serious step of making a public commitment by signing our names to a document greater than ourselves.

So, as I had determined, fifteen weeks of Sunday evening services during this first year at First Baptist Church had been taken up with an article-by-article study of the Lausanne Covenant. To become a common vision for our church, we needed to understand it thoroughly and claim it intelligently, so we had spent those evenings studying the statements, challenging their assumptions, questioning their legitimacy, and looking up all the supporting verses. There were those who opposed our association with this document, claiming that it was not "Baptistic" and we needed no document but the Bible to base our lives on. But I still believed that those who truly studied the Lausanne Covenant would agree with me that this was a commitment, in today's language, to stand firmly on biblical truth alone as we tell others about Jesus.

First Baptist Church was an old church with a history and desire to reach out beyond its own walls, but it was a stretch for this established congregation to embrace all of my vision and enthusiasm for global ministry. Still, this church has been continually involved in ministry in Latvia since 1989.

Now it was April 5, 1989. As the offering was being taken and our four children joined the stampede to children's church, I glanced at Nancy for the reassuring smile I always sought before I stepped to the pulpit. Today was the culmination of this process that had spanned nearly the whole first year of my pastorate here, a moment of truth in the formation of our church's vision for itself and the world.

"You've seen in your worship folders that the title of my sermon today is 'Missions, Commitment, and Me'," I began as I stepped forward with my sermon notes. "I'm basing my sermon on the instructions given to us by Jesus that have come to be known as the Great Commission. This is recounted in each of the Gospels, but today I'll read to you from Matthew 28:18-20 (NIV): 'Therefore go and make disciples of all nations, baptizing them in the name of the Father and of the Son and of the Holy Spirit, and teaching them to obey everything I have commanded you.'

"This year, as we have repeatedly talked about missions and our role in winning, building, and sending people for Christ, several people have asked 'Why all this fuss about missions? If we haven't reached the world yet with news about Jesus, we're never going to, so why bother?'

"I would like to answer with some startling facts that I hope will not leave you apathetic. During the ten seconds it took me to ask those last questions, twenty-six people died — that's 2.6 people each second. Two of them were Buddhist, two were Hindu, five were Muslim, seven were Christian in the broadest definition of the word, and eight were agnostic, atheist, or animist.

"Of the more than 12,000 ethnic groups in the world—the 'all nations' Jesus specified in his command—1,800 groups have had almost no Christian witness, and 1,200 entire ethnic groups representing hundreds of thousands of people have never encountered the good news of Jesus Christ.

"There are approximately one million full-time Christian workers in the United States, giving us about one worker for every 230 people, but there is less than one Christian worker for every one million Muslims. Nine percent of the world's population speaks English as a native language, but 94 percent of all ordained pastors in the world minister to that minority. Only 4 percent of all American Christian giving is spent on efforts to reach the 94 percent of the population that does not live in the United States. Chuck Swindoll claims that Americans spend more on chewing gum than on world missions, and more on dog food in fifty-two days than on world missions in one year.

"What do these statistics tell us about our commitment to disciple-making? Jesus told us that if we love him, we will keep his commandments. A commitment is a *promise* to do something that God has commanded, and then the fulfillment of that promise— actually *doing* it. It is the choice to keep moving ahead, regardless of hardship or failure or discouragement. It is a conscious decision to do what Jesus told us to do.

"Today we have a holy opportunity to make a public commitment to follow Jesus' Great Commission. Like our American forefathers who publicly signed their names to a document they believed in, we have the chance today, as members of this church, to sign our names to a statement that we have studied and proofed as an expression of God's heart for the world. Signing our names today to the copy of the Lausanne Covenant at the entrance of the church will be an expression of our commitment to pray, to give, to go, and to send for the cause of world evangelization."

I glanced briefly at Nancy again as I continued.

"We have in our culture a prevailing fear of commitment. There will always be fear, but the desire to commit to something greater can transcend that fear. I admit to you today that I am afraid, but I want to be held accountable to Jesus' command. I am afraid, but I want our church to have a focus greater than buildings, programs, and history. I am afraid, but I feel this is an accurate expression of the heart of God, and it unites us with Christians around the world for God's work. I'm afraid of failing, but I'm willing to risk for God to use me to accomplish his purpose for the world.

"If you are prepared to join with me to make this commitment, will you stand with me, please, and read together our statement of commitment printed on your bulletin:

"'We, members of the church of Jesus Christ . . . believe the gospel is God's good news for the whole world, and we are determined by his grace to obey Christ's commission to proclaim it to all mankind and to make disciples of every nation. In the light of this our faith and our resolve, we enter into a solemn covenant with God and with each other, to pray, to plan, and to work together for the evangelization of the whole world. . . . We make public our covenant by signing our names to a copy of the Lausanne Covenant. We call upon others to join us. May God help us by his grace and for his glory to be faithful to this our covenant.

"'Amen. Alleluia.'"

And then hundreds of us walked down the aisles to the front of the church to sign our names to an artist's copy of the original covenant. We were now visibly accountable, to one another and to those original signers from around the world, for Christ's commandments and for our brothers and sisters in all nations.

I have finally signed my name, I thought as I wept. *Amen. Alleluia.*

Summer had arrived in Corvallis, and with it an invitation for me to fly to Manila, the Philippines, to attend Lausanne II on the fifteenth anniversary of the original conference. Very few pastors had been invited, and I had only squeaked in by specifically requesting an invitation from one of the organizers, Ted Engstrom. It didn't take long for me to be confronted about my presence. Soon after my arrival, a Methodist bishop from India asked me why I had been allowed to attend as a mere pastor.

"I'm a pastor who's interested in missions," I replied.

"Oh, I understand," he replied. "The real reason you were invited is because you're an American who can pay the full price of tuition. That helps us internationals who can't."

Initially offended and angry at his analysis, I slowly realized that he was probably right. But I still felt that I—and other pastors—belonged at this conference that was expressly committed to mobilizing the local church as its main vehicle of world evangelization.

Under the theme of "proclaiming Christ until he comes," Lausanne II was an exciting meeting of more than 4,000 missions leaders from around the world. I met and spoke at length with missionaries serving in many different countries, and what began to emerge for me was their common struggle to raise enough money to support themselves and their work overseas. We had seen this at home with one of our own church members whom we had been trying to fund for service in Belgium with Greater Europe Mission. He had been raising money for years, but he was still considerably short of the $60,000 in annual support that was required.

"Times have changed," several seasoned missionaries told me, shrugging their shoulders. "We have become faceless names for most of the churches that support us. When we come home on furlough, we have to spend all of our time traveling to a multitude of churches just to barely maintain our support base. So we never have time to develop a relationship with a church that will solidly back us with their finances and their prayer. We end up exhausted from the time that was supposed to renew us, and churches are unenthused about budgeting money for people they don't know."

Their discouragement and fatigue were palpable. As I heard more and more such stories, I began to question the premise that we had been operating on for so long in our missionary endeavors. And as I walked to a session one day in the fragrant heat of Manila, I suddenly felt overwhelmed by a need to pray. "Lord, show me a new way, a way to communicate your good news that won't cost $60,000 each year for a foreign missionary. Please show me."

On the first day of the conference, I had eagerly scanned the nametags for anyone representing the delegation from the Soviet Union. As our church's missions perspective had solidified through our contact with the Lausanne Covenant, I had felt more and more strongly that I should try to return to Latvia on an official missions trip from our church. Unfortunately, the only Latvian pastor I had known had died, and we needed an official invitation to receive a visa. Finally, in a convoluted roundabout, Pavils Bruvers, a Latvian dissident in Germany and an old friend of my grandfather, arranged for a Baptist pastor he knew in Riga, Latvia, to send me and several students an invitation to Riga for later that summer. The formal telexed invitation from Pastor Ludviks had arrived the month before, inviting us to be his guests during August of that year, and though we had already bought our airplane tickets, I had still not met or spoken to him. I had heard that he would be part of the Soviet delegation to the conference in Manila, and now I eagerly awaited his arrival.

About 4,000 leaders from more than 180 nations descended upon Manila for these historic meetings, making them more internationally representative than the Olympic Games.

The chairman of the congress, Leighton Ford, encouraged us to "take the whole gospel to the whole world."

Musicians from all over the world led wonderfully inspiring worship.

I met three interesting Latvians in Manila: Almers (left); the Rev. Janis Vanags, pastor of the Saldus Lutheran Church; and musician Gunta Jukumsone. Vanags soon became the archbishop of the Evangelical Lutheran Church of Latvia. Gunta served as Almers' interpreter. Photos courtesy of Almers Ludviks

Eventually we were informed that the sixty-eight-person Soviet delegation had been detained by the KGB in Moscow, where they had had to sleep on the old wooden pews of Moscow's only Baptist church for three days before they were allowed to fly out. When they finally arrived, tired and rumpled, word circulated that only sixty of their group were known pastors and Christian leaders, and the remaining eight were apparently KGB agents. A friend finally pointed out Pastor Ludviks to me, and I approached him with my hand outstretched. "Almers Ludviks?" I asked. He looked at me seriously, almost sternly, without replying. I was taken aback. "I —I'm Chuck Kelley. You sent me an invitation to visit you next month in Latvia."

It soon became clear that his English was about on par with my nearly non-existent Latvian, but fortunately other Latvian delegates, Gunta Jukumsone and Viljams Shultz, spoke English and occasionally served as interpreters. Otherwise our conversations were very basic, but still meaningful. For the next seven days we were inseparable as we soaked up the heady atmosphere of the conference and began to dream together about our upcoming trip to Latvia.

Almers Ludviks was born in the Latvian port city of Ventspils in 1956. His father, Zanis Ludviks, was pastor of the Ventspils Baptist Church for forty years and had been a friend and colleague of my grandfather in the Latvian Baptist Union fifty years earlier.

As a child, Almers remembers his father being repeatedly summoned by the KGB to appear before the Special Department of Religion in Riga to account for the illegal Sunday school and youth meetings that he provided in his church. Each time his mother cried as the family huddled together and prayed, wondering if his father would return. But each time, against all expectations, Pastor Ludviks came back. During one summons he overheard a KGB interrogator saying, "That Pastor Ludviks is like Satan—we can get nothing from him."

Once during Almers' early childhood a returned Siberian deportee came to Pastor Ludviks at night, showing him a letter from an old friend of his, also a pastor, who was still serving a sentence in Siberia. The letter asked Pastor Ludviks to help the deportee escape to Sweden. Something about the situation made Almers' father uneasy, however, and he told the man that he was in no position to help him. He later learned that the KGB had forced the pastor in Siberia to sign the letter; with no choice, the pastor had prayed that God would give Pastor Ludviks the wisdom to recognize the trap.

Almers' older sister took him with her to illegal youth meetings, and when he was fourteen he gave his life to Christ. By the time he was fifteen, their youth leader had been assessed repeated penalties by the KGB for his leadership of the group; finally, when he was warned that he was about to be arrested and sent to prison, he reluctantly stopped. With no other leadership available, Almers stepped in. The group met on Saturday nights, in a different home each week to avoid discovery. But it was ultimately futile to hide, for the KGB had collaborators in every group of society. Soon KGB agents were coming to the school regularly to interview Almers about his Saturday night activities.

"What do you do in these meetings?" they demanded.

"We pray and we study the Bible. That is all," he answered.

Suddenly they changed their tactic: "We know. We know that is all you do." They were very polite, very reassuring. "Almers, you are a good boy. We want you to work for us. Where do you want to study? Do you want to be an officer in the Army? You just tell us what you want and we'll make it happen. All you have to do is sign this paper to show you'll work with us."

When Almers insisted that he was not interested, they merely smiled confidently. "Take a week or two," the leader said. "We'll come back and see what you're thinking then." When they returned, Almers surprised them by steadfastly refusing to cooperate with them.

Still the KGB visits had served another purpose, and Almers' teachers were now more aware than ever of his suspect status as an active Christian. His Latvian literature teacher routinely gave his painstakingly crafted essays failing grades. "These are not your thoughts" she scrawled in politically correct red ink across the tops of his papers. Years later she would come to Almers to apologize for her prejudice against him and his faith.

During his late teens, Almers organized and played drums in a rock band with some of the other youth who met at the illegal Saturday meetings. As the band practiced in the church one late, cold December night, a group of girls walking home from a basketball practice at the nearby school heard the muffled sounds of a hard rock jam session and traced it to its unlikely source in the Baptist church. They peeked quietly in through the windows to get a closer look and were amazed at the intensity and volume of the young musicians. One of the girls named Vija was intrigued enough to come back for the Christmas service. And there on Christmas morning, from the balcony where he had arrived early, Almers first saw his future wife as Vija walked in.

After he finished school, though, Almers was drafted into the Red Army for his obligatory two years of military service and sent to Brest, on the Bug River in Belorussia. There he became good friends with a devout Catholic Lithuanian, and together they began listening to Christian radio broadcasts from abroad. After they had listened for

Almers served in the Soviet army in Belarus. Here he is acting in a propaganda film about how the great Soviet army crushed the evil Nazis. Almers portrayed a German soldier who later was killed in action. The Latvians were always made to play the Nazi roles. Photo courtesy of Almers Ludviks

awhile, his friend could no longer keep quiet. "Almers, we have to tell the other guys about God!" But when they began to tell the other soldiers about their faith, they were quickly labeled spies and separated, and Almers was sent to another base to be re-educated with court-martial cases and alcoholics.

During his first muster at the new base, the commanding officer paced up and down the lines of soldiers. "Anyone who is not a Communist, step forward!" he barked. Almers stepped forward from the line and stood at attention. The officer stood next to him, boring into him with a cold eye. "Anyone who is a Christian, step forward!" he barked again. Again, Almers stepped forward. The officer stared at him a moment longer, then burst out laughing derisively. "After one year here, you won't believe in God anymore! Dismissed."

Months later, this officer's driver became ill and Almers was assigned to take his place. One evening, the officer came out to the car to find Almers reading a newspaper. "Why are you reading a newspaper?" he demanded. "I thought you said you were a Christian!" When Almers explained that being a Christian didn't mean isolating oneself from the world's news, the officer continued to ask more questions about his faith. Eventually, he apologized to Almers for his taunts about his faith. "I didn't realize that this was what Christians were like," he said.

When he was discharged from his service in the army, Almers began to study engineering at a branch of a technical university in Ventspils. Throughout his time in the military, Almers had been struggling with God and God's purpose for his life. Again and again it felt like God was telling him to become a pastor, but he chafed against it. Finally, though, after his return home, he realized that he could no longer run, and near the end of 1978 he accepted his full-time calling as a pastor. After his marriage to Vija in 1979, he began attending monthly preaching lessons at an underground Bible school in Riga. Together with fifteen other students, they were secretly taught homiletics and New and Old Testament at Matthews Baptist Church in Riga.

In 1980 Almers and Vija accepted their first pastorate in the small town of Piltene, where my grandfather was born. It was a good training ground in the daily life of a pastor, but it was an old congregation matched with a very young pastor and his wife, and it was a sometimes lonely life. During these Piltene years, Almers took a three-year correspondence course from the KGB-infiltrated Soviet Union Baptist Association in Moscow. Despite its unhealthy political alliance, there were good teachers among the faculty who helped provide a theological framework in the absence of any other opportunities for formal training.

Almers preaching at Matthews Church.

In 1989, Almers was ordained in the Matthews Church by Bishop Janis Eisans, Alfreds Petersons (former Agenskalns pastor), and Peteris Egle (former bishop).
Photo courtesy of Almers Ludviks

From 1984 through 1987 Almers and Vija pastored a Baptist church near Liepaja, and now since 1987 he had been the pastor of Agenskalns Baptist Church in Riga, a large and growing congregation whose building had been confiscated and transformed into a television studio during the Khrushchev era.

My first impressions of Almers in Manila were of a serious man, soft-spoken and contemplative, with wire-framed glasses and slightly receding brown hair. He seemed an unlikely person to have impetuously issued an invitation to a complete stranger and his companions to come and stay in private homes of church members, something that had not been done among Christians in Latvia since the Soviet occupation. In fact, I do think there were times in Manila when he wondered about the wisdom of his rash act. But as I grew to know Almers more intimately over the following days and weeks, I began to realize that his subdued exterior hid a bravery forged in the fire of adversity that comes from living publicly as a Christian in a hostile environment. And as we dreamed of the possibilities of our upcoming time together in Latvia, I began to warm to him as a trusted and steady companion on a journey that would prove to be far longer and more adventure-filled than either of us could imagine.

GATES OF BRONZE AND BARS OF IRON

CHAPTER 5

The year 1989 was a very interesting time to visit the Soviet Union. Everything was changing; nothing was certain. But spiritual doors were opening all over this crumbling empire.

The cavernous Moscow airport echoed its emptiness as we deplaned our Aeroflot flight and walked nervously toward customs. Ours was the only flight arriving at that hour, and the humming, busy sounds of an international airport were noticeably absent here. When we collected our suitcases they felt unusually heavy, as if the illegal Bibles, theology works, and humanitarian supplies we were carrying were pulling them down with the guilty weight of contraband. The memory of my trip through Soviet customs lines four years earlier was still acutely imprinted on my mind: strip searches, interrogations, and minute scrutiny. As we joined the end of the nearest line, thoughts of discovery were uppermost in our minds.

It was August 1989, a time of international upheaval and uncertainty. Earlier that summer, the world had watched in disbelief as Chinese tanks rolled over students camped beneath their handmade Goddess of Democracy in Tiananmen Square. Solidarity leaders in Poland had won a resounding victory in their country's first free elections since World War II. And conflicting reports were emerging from within the Soviet Union as well. The Baltic states were beginning to awaken from their decades of Soviet occupation, testing the boundaries of *glasnost* with huge "calendar demonstrations" commemorating historical taboos such as the mass deportation of Latvians to Siberia in 1941 and the secret pact between Hitler and Stalin that ceded Latvia to the Soviet Union in 1939. Latvia's daring reformers were pushing the limits of Soviet patience beyond anything it had yet encountered, and the official response wavered between unexpected tolerance and severe repression.

With this tense political situation, we couldn't help fearing that the Moscow authorities might use extra diligence in their search of our luggage when they realized we were flying on to Latvia. Bible smugglers had reported a variety of consequences for discovery, from confiscation and escort out of the country to several days of imprisonment and interrogation. My heart was pounding as we inched forward in our line.

My mind went back to what Mike Parker, one of the two college students accompanying me, had read to us while we were still in Germany, waiting for our Moscow plane. A friend of his had sent him a note with the reference for a passage in Isaiah, which Mike had looked up the night before we left: "I will go before you and will level the mountains; I will break down gates of bronze and cut through bars of iron. I will give you the treasures of darkness, riches stored in secret places, so that you may know that I am the LORD, the God of Israel, who calls you by name." (Isaiah 45:2,3; NIV) The customs line moved forward another few feet. *Bars of iron, darkness, secret places . . . .*

We still didn't know what God wanted us to do on this trip. First thoughts of a sports outreach had failed when our 6-foot 10-inch basketball player had gotten injured and had to cancel. Mike, a former junior college football All-American candidate who had played at Oregon State University, was limping badly with a cast to protect an injured ankle. Our exuberant dreams back in Manila with Almers of open-air evangelism seemed wildly rash as we looked at the stern faces of the customs officials ahead and felt the gray oppressiveness of the Soviet atmosphere.

Suddenly, the man waiting behind us—a Russian, a stranger to us who we never saw again—leaned forward and whispered over my shoulder in heavily accented English:

"Excuse me. You must have another form. Over there. Before you go through. Very important. Over there." He gestured to a writing table stacked with official forms.

As we stood to the side to fill out the missing paperwork, our line continued, and from our vantage point we could see behind the partition where several broad-shouldered matrons were inspecting the suitcases. One pulled out a sweater, draped it over her arms and chest to check its size, and laid it aside with a contented grunt on the confiscated pile. Another rifled through carefully folded clothing, removed a bar of chocolate, took a bite, then tucked it back in the suitcase by the bottle of perfume that she had just squirted on her wrist. We knew that our luggage wouldn't stand a chance against their scrutiny. As we painstakingly printed our names and passport numbers on the required forms, we prayed again the Smuggler's Prayer: "Lord, when you were on earth you made blind eyes see. Now please make seeing eyes blind. Do not let the guards see those things you do not want them to see."

By the time we were finished and ready to rejoin the line, we were surprised to find that we were among the last passengers left. As we moved toward the customs desk with our suitcases, we heard a burst of laughter from a television screen to the side. The laughing guard called several others, and as they joined him they waved us through with a dismissive jerk of their heads. Hardly believing our good fortune, we hurried through with our unopened luggage, still heavy with Bibles and other contraband. As we passed, we looked back at the guards crowding around the screen, now pointing and laughing raucously. It was a video game, perhaps one of the first to enter Moscow, confiscated from the luggage ahead of ours. God had clearly leveled this first mountain and broken down the gates of bronze. We were excited to see what other miracles he was planning to perform.

Two dynamic university students joined me on this journey to Latvia: John Henderer (left) and Mike Parker.

Before we left Corvallis, we filled out prayer sheets for our home church to give them a better idea of how they could pray for us. Mike was full of optimistic enthusiasm: "Let's ask them to pray for thousands to come to Christ!" he urged.

"No, no, Mike," I said. "That's unrealistic. This is the Soviet Union we're talking about. We can't give them—and ourselves—inflated expectations. We'll only be disappointed." I remembered the restrictions of my Latvian trip in 1985 only too well— the overwhelming official scrutiny; the perpetual plainclothes KGB officers following me and electronically bugging my hotel room, my phone, and my taxi cab; the all-pervasive propaganda; and the drab, oppressive despair of the people.

We bounced numbers back and forth, and finally, with Mike's reluctant agreement, we wrote that we were praying for ten people to make a decision to follow Christ. Now, as we traveled from a brief stop in Riga on to Tallinn, Estonia, I hoped that we had not been too optimistic with even that low number. For the sake of Mike's faith and of John Henderer's, the other college student with us, and for the church at home that was following us with prayer, I fervently hoped that God would grant us the privilege of seeing ten people profess faith in Christ.

Estonia is the Baltic state to the north of Latvia, also an unwilling member of the Soviet Union in 1989, and we had been invited to participate in a Youth for Christ evangelistic youth concert there. When we arrived, however, I was told that the seminar I'd been asked to teach on cults had been canceled. In an effort to salvage a reason for our

detour to Estonia, I mentioned to the concert leaders that our All-American football player had a dramatic testimony he'd be willing to share. And so it was that Mike Parker found himself on stage between Sheila Walsh and Scott Wesley Brown, two stars of the Christian music world, in the filled-to-capacity 6,000-seat Lenin Cultural Hall and Sports Palace of Tallinn, Estonia,

At the time Mike was not accustomed to speaking before large crowds, but he did a tremendous job of sharing his personal testimony at the Youth for Christ Festival in Tallinn, Estonia, in August 1989.

telling the crowd through an Estonian interpreter about his life before and after meeting Jesus.

"I grew up in a military family, and my parents divorced when I was fourteen," began Mike. "After the divorce I hopped from one foster family to another, trying to find love and acceptance. I started looking for it in all the wrong places—sex, taking and selling drugs, fighting, stealing, and breaking into homes. I dropped out of school.

"But I was good at football, and I finally got a scholarship to a renegade junior college in southern California. Most of the players were like me—in trouble with the police and any other authority figures in our lives. By this time I was taking so many drugs that there are weeks of my life that I do not remember. I drank whole bottles of whiskey at one time. Our drug deals were carried out at gunpoint, and I slept with a knife under my pillow.

"But amazingly, I could still play football, and our team won the national junior college championship. I was named a preseason junior college All-American, and one magazine listed me as one of the best players in the nation. Still, at the peak of my popularity, my life was miserable, haunted by fear and anger, and achingly empty.

"After my sophomore year I was recruited by teams around the country, but I chose to go to Oregon State University. Within a few weeks of my arrival there, my life exploded. Several of my closest friends from high school and junior college were arrested for selling drugs. Other friends were killed in drug-related shootings. I knew that it was a matter of time before I would be shot or arrested. I began to question the meaning of life.

"As I began asking if there really was a God, I noticed posters around campus advertising the speaker Josh McDowell giving a series of talks called 'The Great Resurrection Hoax: Did Jesus Really Rise from the Dead?' Inside I told myself that if Jesus were not really who he claimed to be, and if God were not real, then I would live my life just as I had been, no matter what the consequences.

"But there was something different about this speaker's life—there was a peace that I didn't have and had never known. And as I kept going back to those meetings, talking with staff members of Campus Crusade for Christ and reading the Bible, I began to encounter God—the God from Psalm 116 who 'heard my voice and my supplications. Because He has inclined His ear to me, therefore, I will call upon Him as long as I live.' (NKJV) When I read those words, I fell down on my knees and cried to God for hours, confessing every sin I could think of. The room became very bright, and I heard a voice saying over and over again, 'I love you, I love you, I love you. I forgive you, I forgive you,

I forgive you.' I felt like my soul was being washed clean. For the first time in my life, I felt loved unconditionally. And my anger at the world seemed to melt away.

"As I stood up I knew I was a different man. My life had been changed. That was five years ago, and I am still wholeheartedly following this amazing God. And I'm here to tell you today that God's limitless love and forgiveness will change your life, too, no matter where you've been or what you've done."

As Mike limped off the stage in his cast, the audience was hushed and still. And when Scott Wesley Brown later invited those who wanted to accept Jesus to come to the front of the auditorium, the crowds streamed forward. Over four nights, more than 1,000 came forward to commit their lives to him. We were seeing the treasures of darkness, the riches stored in secret places!

As we drove the five hours back to Riga in the cramped car, it was hard to temper our enthusiasm. But I reminded Mike and John that Latvia's situation was entirely different. Estonia's proximity to Finland had allowed a freer climate to prevail than anything that we would find in Latvia. We needed to adjust our expectations again, and remember our cautious hopes for ten new believers in Latvia.

When Almers met us again in Riga, though, we were still bubbling over with the news from Estonia.

"Almers," I said, "do you think we will have the opportunity to do open-air evangelism here in Riga? Is it possible?"

Almers was skeptical. "Nothing like that has ever been done here before. Only the government can give that kind of permission, and we try to stay as invisible to the government as possible."

But he was willing to try, and to his amazement, permission was granted. With the official way paved, Almers scrambled to organize a program. Within days, he had lined up musicians, printed posters, and broadcast radio commercials advertising the first-ever "legal" open-air evangelism in Latvia since the Communist takeover in 1944. In this prevailing political climate of anticipation and anxiety, with Latvian citizens alternating between standing in bread lines and marching in calendar demonstrations, nobody could predict either the official or public response. So we waited, prayed, and wondered whether anyone would come.

The poster behind me advertises the outreach in the park with a concert by Vards. I was proudly wearing a handmade Latvian tie given to me by a friend.

Mike's walking cast piqued the crowd's curiosity while his simple and direct testimony touched many hearts.

For two glorious evenings I preached and my first Latvian friend, Viljams "Bill" Shultz, interpreted. My grandfather was sitting in the second row with relatives.

Three nervous young pastors—me, Almers Ludviks, and Ainars Bastiks— sat in the front row while the musical portion of the program began.

The day of the meeting arrived, and we set up our simple equipment in front of the open-air theater in the city park. It was a slow and sultry August evening. Couples sat together on the park benches and children gathered to stare at us as we placed speakers and chairs on the platform. As the hour drew near we looked at each other, eyebrows raised. Would they come?

Slowly, gradually, the park seemed to be filling up. Or was it just my imagination? No, there were certainly more people milling around and sitting on the green benches in front of the platform, looking around expectantly. Talis and Ingrida Talbergs, the Latvian husband-and-wife music team, began singing and playing, and more onlookers gathered. Mike and John gave their testimonies, and still more filtered in. Then the youth choir from the Matthews Baptist Church began to sing. By the time it was my turn to speak, we had a definite crowd on our hands—a conservative count placed it at six hundred.

I looked over at the sponsoring pastors, Almers Ludviks and Ainars Bastiks, sitting in the front row with me, brave young men in their early thirties who had never done evangelism outside of their church before. They were white-faced and trembling. As I stepped forward to speak, Ainars leaned over and whispered hoarsely, "Chuck, please preach short. We don't want them to leave."

I could feel the anticipation and curiosity rising from the crowd as I began.

"I am a Latvian. My mother was born in Jelgava. My grandfather comes from Piltene. But I'm also an American. My father was born in the United States. I was born in California. I'm a Latvian-American. But most important, I'm a Christian. Tonight I want to tell you why. But first of all, Latvia needs to know that there is a God, and he is the king of Latvia."

The crowd was silent, absorbing every word. My eighty-five-year-old grandfather, who had just flown in to Riga to join us, sat in the second row, hardly daring to move at this amazing thing that was happening. I knew the pastors were praying, even as their eyes scanned the audience for the inevitable KGB agents. They would be there without a doubt. We knew that many others had come that evening out of a heady curiosity at this brazen thing happening in the park, yet another new example of free assembly and expression after years of repression. Whatever the motivation, we were grateful for this chance to present them with our potentially life-changing message.

As I reached the end of my talk, my courage began to waver. *Now would be the time,* I thought, *to ask for action, to ask these people to make a decision to follow Jesus. But we know the crowd is laced with informers and KGB agents. Can I ask them to take such a risk? And what if no one responds?* Still, I knew it was the only thing to do.

"Tonight, if you have realized that God needs to be the king of your life, to take away your sin and make you a new person, I'm going to ask you to pray silently with me as I lead you. Lord God," I prayed, "I know that I have sinned. Please forgive me and come into my heart. I want to love you and follow you for the rest of my life. Amen."

I gulped and continued. "If you prayed that prayer with me tonight to accept Jesus Christ into your life as your Lord and Savior, could you raise your hands high so we could see them and pray for you?"

And then, with no hesitation, hands shot up all around the park. The audience held them high, some beaming, some with tears streaming down their faces, more than half the crowd reaching up in testimony to God's grace and power.

We all rejoiced, the Latvian pastors, the musicians, and our tiny band from America. Papa couldn't contain his joy. When he got back to his Riga hotel he called Nancy, who was back in Oregon getting ready to go to church. He excitedly described what God had just done. And within the hour, Nancy shared the joy with the praying congregation back in Corvallis.

It was an exciting time in Latvia. The next day we spoke at a small church, and forty people gave their lives to Christ. On the following evening we held another open-air meeting, this time with a youth choir and a Latvian testimony, and many more made public decisions to follow Jesus.

We also met with the vice mayor of Riga, presenting him with an official letter of greeting from our mayor in Corvallis and inviting him to our meetings. After we had given him our symbolic gifts, we formally asked, on behalf of the Agenskalns Baptist Church, for the return of their church building. In 1961, at the height of the oppressive Khrushchev regime, this

The Agenskalns Baptist Church had been confiscated by the government and transformed into a television studio. The cross was removed from the tower and replaced by an antenna.

church that Almers was now pastoring had been forced out of its building, which was taken over by a television studio. Since then the 400-member congregation had shared space in a building with another large Baptist church in Riga.

"I cannot do everything," the cordial vice-mayor said, "but I will do something."

Years later I learned that a few months before our visit, Almers and a Lutheran pastor, Juris Rubenis, had written a letter to Presidents Reagan and Gorbachev that was hand-delivered by a Latvian delegate, Pastor Modris Plate, during one of their famous summits. The letter commended the *glasnost* process and informed the two leaders of the need for the state-controlled TV station to return the church to the congregation. Within a few days the KGB summoned Almers to their Riga headquarters. They informed him that for some mysterious reasons, people in very high positions in Moscow had told them to begin the process of moving the TV station and that the congregation was going to get the building back. It was to be the first church building in the Soviet Union to be returned by the state to the people.

The transfer had been hindered by one delay after another, but within three months of our visit, Agenskalns Baptist Church was officially notified of the pending return of its building, nearly thirty years after its seizure.

In a personal highlight of this trip, my grandfather and I were given permission to travel to Jelgava to worship in the church he pastored in the 1920s. There I met more cousins than I ever knew I had, and was able to watch several of them turn their lives over to Christ as Papa preached again in Latvian from his old pulpit. After the service,

I was very pleased to be in Latvia with my grandfather at such an important time in world history, and he was thrilled to preach again all over the country.

stooped old men and women, most of them younger than Papa's eighty-five years, came to shake his hand, kiss his cheeks, and talk of the old days.

From Jelgava, Almers took Papa and me on an illegal pilgrimage back to Papa's birthplace, back to the Piltene of green rolling hills and fresh crayfish and deep forests. Papa's brother Heinrich still lived in the wooden farmstead built in 1860 by my great grandfather and his father, the house where Papa's mother Dora told her stories by firelight and whispered her magic healings. We stood together at the graves of my great great grandparents, we walked beside the clear waters of the stream running near the homestead, and Papa retraced the path he had taken away from the house after his father had disowned him and banished him for his faith.

By the time our eighteen-day stay in Latvia was over, the Latvia of my childhood imaginings had finally assumed form and substance, flesh and blood. Now more than the danger and darkness of my youthful daydreams, it was the people who formed the compelling images in my mind. People like Almers, this soft-spoken young pastor who was leading his homeless church with little theological education but with a firm and brave resolve to follow God, wherever he might lead. People like my fourth cousin who insisted that I take one of his rationing coupons—good for one bar of soap every three months—to show the people of America the poverty that the Soviet system had imposed on Latvia. Or Anita, a chemist and the best cook in the church, who took her week of vacation to cook food procured for us from the black market, food that she could never have bought or eaten herself on her meager 240 rubles-a-month salary.

And above all, I could not forget the hundreds of people who had so eagerly committed their lives to following Christ during the unprecedented open-air evangelisms. Would the churches have the resources and the courage to open their doors to these eager new seekers?

Our homeward trip through the Moscow airport was a joy-filled one. The Bibles and theological works had been successfully delivered, as had the humanitarian aid. God's truth had been proclaimed and spectacularly received. As in my earlier trip to Latvia, God had made blind eyes see and seeing eyes blind. And in my heart burned a vision for mobilizing others to stand with the Latvian churches in this time of new freedoms in their country. I was confident that God's promises would continue to hold true behind the Iron Curtain: "I will go before you and will level the mountains; I will break down the gates of bronze and cut through bars of iron. I will give you the treasures of darkness, riches stored in secret places, so that you may know that I am the LORD, the God of Israel, who calls you by name."

SURPRISED BY HOPE

We returned to the peaceful Willamette Valley to report to our church and begin drawing up plans for a sister church relationship between First Baptist Church in Corvallis and the two Baptist churches in Riga.

But Latvia was far from peaceful. On the morning of August 23, 1989, the day after we left Latvia, two million Latvians, Lithuanians, and Estonians converged on a 370-mile stretch of highway that connects their three countries from north to south. Beginning at a Lithuanian castle beneath a hot August sun, snaking past the Freedom Monument in Riga and ending around an Estonian castle in the north, they joined hands to form what was probably the longest human chain in history—"The Baltic Chain"—to protest the fiftieth anniversary of the secret Molotov-Ribbentrop pact that had illegally annexed the Baltic states to the Soviet Union. Black ribbons, flags, hand-lettered signs of protest, and candles lining the chain testified to their outrage.

The aging Soviet Union was slowly imploding, pushed along by a vanguard of intrepid Latvian reformers and their compatriots in the other Baltic states of Lithuania and Estonia. They engaged in a skillful and daring dance with Moscow toward independence, stretching the limits here and giving a little there, a policy of patience and persistence they described as "one step at a time." They—as all of the millions who gathered on that hot day in August along the "Via Baltica" (Baltic Way)—knew that they were risking everything in the confrontation, but Gorbachev's *perestroika* had opened the door to the outside world just a crack, awakening them from their political slumber of decades, and many felt there was no turning back. For the first time in half a century, Latvians began to feel like Latvians again, and they hoped they were ready to pay the price of freedom, whatever that might be.

Latvia issued a ten-year commemorative stamp of the Baltic Chain in 1999.

In June of 1990, just after the official vote by the Latvian Supreme Senate to begin the transition toward independence, I returned to Latvia at the invitation of the Latvian Baptist Union to plan a citywide program of evangelism for the following year. Our church, excited to be participating in ministry in this suddenly important part of the world, had collected six extra suitcases of humanitarian aid that I had carried with me. But as John Carty, a college student who had accompanied me, and I drove into Riga from the airport, the city appeared surprisingly quiet for a touted hotbed of revolution. Our driver explained that since the election of the new senate and the subsequent vote for independence, the people had turned back to their work and their gardens, content to let the democratically elected representatives plot their future. And with the Soviet-imposed economic blockade in full force, their gardens had become increasingly important: the Russian ruble had experienced a drastic devaluation, food prices had soared, and the average monthly salary had remained static at somewhere between twenty and fifty U.S. dollars. Long lines for all basic commodities were commonplace; for gasoline it was common to wait five hours. It was a curious lull in the process of protest, a summertime apathy of fatigue and absence that would affect our entire stay.

We soon learned that those who had invited us were out of the country, taking advantage of the newly relaxed travel rules—Almers, on a short stay in America as a guest of the American Baptists, had visa difficulties that prevented him from returning at the appointed time; and Ainars, the other Baptist pastor in Riga who had signed our official invitation without making a note of the dates, was visiting in Germany along with the new Baptist bishop. As we tried to set up meetings and begin our planning, we ran into multiple roadblocks, with no one in authority to speak for us or with us. Finally, in frustration, I holed up in my room with my Mac Plus computer and pounded out a detailed strategic plan for an evangelistic crusade modeled on the Luis Palau crusade in Salem in 1985, my only previous experience with citywide evangelism. We presented this document to representatives of the Latvian Baptist Union and then left it behind for them to give to their leaders when they returned. And then we boarded the plane to return home, hoping that this trip would not have been wasted time.

❖

With the end of summer came also an end to the temporary season of rest in Latvia. An increasingly independent-minded Latvian government began pressing the limits of its sovereignty, establishing customs offices on its eastern borders to check the flow of exports to Russia. Hardliners in Moscow convinced Gorbachev to tighten his grip on the rebel republics, and in September the Black Berets stormed and occupied the building of the Latvian state prosecutor to prevent it from falling into republican hands. Originally formed as a special riot militia, the Black Berets had become the mercenary arm of the Latvian Communist Party. In early November they joined with uniformed Soviet marines to take over the governmental offices in Latvia's resort city of Jurmala.

The atmosphere in Riga was noticeably changed as we drove into the city from the airport that cold November of 1990. Within two weeks of returning home from my last visit, the Latvian Baptist bishop had written to invite me to come again to plan in earnest for what they were calling "Hope '91." I took advantage of my remaining ten days of annual mission travel to come to an altered Latvia. There was a sense of inexorability in the air, of something about to happen. Ominous Black Berets were conspicuous in the city. Citizens closely monitored and discussed reports of the fall of the Berlin Wall and developments in Czechoslovakia's Velvet Revolution through the increasingly uncensored media. To prevent any further coups by the Black Berets, Latvian citizens had erected barricades around the Parliament Building. Buses, trucks, and tractors were driven in from all over the country to reinforce the barricades, which were plastered with profound patriotic statements, poetry, and coarse profanities.

This prevailing intensity also marked our planning meetings, which were long, focused, and grounded in concentrated prayer. During the evenings and on Sunday, Mark Hubbell, Oregon's director of Prison Fellowship who had accompanied me on this trip, and I were carted all over Latvia to preach in churches and prisons. Mark preached sixteen times in five prisons and devoted himself to the development of the newly appointed Prison Fellowship and Latvian Christian Mission prison workers.

Mark Hubbell shared the gospel with numerous prisoners and guards.
Photo courtesy of Mark Hubbell

The highlight for me was the evangelistic event held at the Cultural Palace in Riga on November 17, just one day before the celebration of the seventy-second anniversary of Latvian Independence Day. As the reformers prepared for another high-stakes calendar demonstration outside, 150 Christians met in the morning for training as evangelistic counselors. That evening, after Mark Hubbell gave his testimony and I preached an evangelistic message, many came forward to give their lives to Christ. And long after the rest of the audience had filed out into the cold November night, counselors were still huddled around the arena in groups, praying with those who had come forward.

The next day, on Latvian Independence Day, thousands gathered around the Freedom Monument to lay flowers at its base, light candles, and pray. For the first time, I also knelt at the monument to pray passionately for the country of Latvia. At midnight crowds and candles still surrounded the monument, lighting the freezing air with hope.

❖

At the beginning of December the Black Berets staged nine explosions in Riga in an attempt to simulate chaos and justify Soviet military intervention. In response, Latvians from all walks of life took to the barricades; surprisingly, every fourth person on the barricades was a non-Latvian Russian resident of Latvia, those who many had assumed would feel a stronger loyalty to the Soviet Union than to their adopted country.

But the citizens of Latvia were uncommonly united in their determination to defend their newfound freedoms. Bonfires and barricades became the symbols of their resistance.

On January 2, the Latvian Press Building was occupied by the Black Berets and all non-Communist newspapers were shut down. On January 13, skirmishes between Soviet military troops and demonstrators trying to protect the television and radio tower in Vilnius, Lithuania, resulted in the deaths of fourteen people and more than six hundred civilian injuries, some of whom were rolled over by Soviet tanks. And on January 20, in an attempt to occupy the headquarters of the Ministry of Interior in Riga, Black Berets opened fire on civilians in a park, killing two unarmed policemen, a television cameraman, and a thirteen-year-old boy riding his bicycle.

But despite the casualties, the attempted putsch was not successful. Boris Yeltsin, who would later become president of Russia, made an impassioned speech to Russian soldiers to refrain from shooting Soviet citizens in the Baltic republics. And the Latvians' evident resolve to fight bullets with stones if necessary proved victorious. The hardliners in Moscow pulled back their troops. And Western democracies began to strongly advocate the case of the Baltic republics in the world arena.

We arrived back in Riga in May of 1991 to a people living on the threshold of revolution. The atmosphere was electric with expectation. We had come with a team of evangelists, musicians, and teachers to present the long-planned Hope '91, a week-long evangelistic crusade with a mini-school for Christian workers. Representatives of European, Baltic, and Soviet news services were intensely interested in the events and participants of Hope '91, and we immediately became the center of a swirl of media attention.

We soon realized that we were perceived as part of an inswell of Western influence riding into Latvia on the swift tide of revolution. Many Latvians caught up in the revolutionary fever were reaching out indiscriminately to all things Western, ready to adopt all of our cultural trappings and paraphernalia wholesale. We were interviewed daily, quoted widely, and heralded as representatives of the West. It was a heady time and a dangerous opening for demagogues and charlatans, and we soon realized how important the decades of prayer leading up to this event would be in keeping us grounded and focused.

Before our arrival in Riga, we had gathered together at the Solåsen Training Center, an old villa on a steep fjord in Sweden dedicated to instilling missionary vision in emerging spiritual leaders from all over the Soviet Union. Here the entire team had spent hours in prayer, worship, communion, and cultural orientation before boarding the plane for Latvia.

Photo courtesy of Solåsen

At home in Corvallis, Mike Parker was leading our church in a round-the-clock prayer vigil for the success of Hope '91. And Almers welcomed us at the airport with the hopes of his father, who had prayed for five decades for this moment in Latvian history when the word of God could be publicly proclaimed. This history of prayer proved to be an essential and solid bedrock for us in the days of feverish activity and media scrutiny that lay ahead.

The Latvian executive committee had prepared long and hard for our arrival. At the large downtown post office, a sixty-foot golden banner announced the dates for "*Ceriba '91.*" They had rented the cavernous Sports Arena, a dark, dingy, dirty old building with hard wooden benches, filthy bathrooms, and hardly a functioning light bulb in the hallways. Our counselor training would take place in the giant cloak closet with barely three lights burning. But the committee had filled the main hall with flowers and hung another gigantic golden banner across the stage, a Christian fish symbol with an adjoining American and Latvian flag to symbolize our cooperation. Ten thousand copies of the Hope '91 songbook lay stacked and ready, a compilation of fifty hymns and contemporary songs that was the product of a core of highly committed musicians who had dedicated themselves to translating the Western songs into Latvian.

In the country at large the Black Berets stepped up their harassment, attacking customs outposts throughout the Baltics and swooping indiscriminately to kill and kidnap. But the ponderous pendulum of the Soviet Union's history had already turned against them, and there was a prevailing sense that their time was near its end.

On the evening of Sunday, May 19, the participating churches and ministries gathered together at Golgotha Baptist Church in Riga for a celebratory service of prayer and dedication. And on the morning of Monday, May 20, Hope '91 officially began.

❖

During the half century of Soviet occupation in Latvia, church activities had been officially restricted to Sunday morning church services and choir practices. These they had pursued with a diligence that often left Western visitors breathless: their choirs and musicians were spectacularly talented and well trained, and their church services were long and focused. But other traditional areas of church life had been forcibly neglected: evangelism, outreach, children's and youth ministries, and pastoral training. Now that new freedoms were in reach, the church leaders felt inadequately prepared for the challenges and opportunities, and they had put together a list of topics in which they wanted further training.

These became the blueprint for the Hope '91 mini-school, held each day of that week in May from 10:30 until 3:30. On each of these days, more than 400 pastors and lay leaders from around Latvia gathered at the three Baptist churches for practical teaching in pastoral counseling, preaching, women's ministries, personal evangelism, current theological issues, youth ministry, Christian education, and prison ministry. The instructors represented churches, seminaries, and twelve ministries from North America and Europe, and they were amazed at the students' eagerness and aptitude.

But the central purpose of this week in May was still the nightly meetings at the dark and derelict Sports Arena. The deluge of publicity had done its work, and night after night the 4,500-seat hall was filled to capacity. Our young masters of ceremonies began each program with a welcome and a roof-raising Latvian rendition of "Majesty," our theme song for the week.

The Latvian pastors had chosen the unifying topic of hope as our focus, and each evening was directed toward a different segment of the population: hope for the family, hope for the elderly and handicapped, hope for the intellectual skeptic, hope for the future, hope for youth, and Christ our hope. It proved to be a rousing and highly relevant theme for this week perched on the brink of independence.

The Hope '91 evangelist was Steve Russo, a professional drummer from the United States with a dynamic message expertly suited to the theme of hope. During Friday evening's session geared toward youth, Steve quoted Psalm 100's "Make a joyful noise unto the Lord, all ye lands," then sat down at his drum set and played a spectacular drum solo that brought all 4,500 audience members to their feet in an overpowering standing ovation. This was an invigorating new form of sacred music that seemed to capture the excitement of the times and of the Christian message that many in the young crowd were hearing for the first time.

Each night, after the testimonies and the music, the message and the invitation, hundreds came to the front of the hall to pray with counselors and commit their lives to following Jesus Christ. Those who came forward in response to this once shunned and dangerous message represented a remarkable cross-section of Latvian culture, including students, firebrand reformers, middle-aged bureaucrats, and members of parliament.

As the week progressed and the crowds remained standing room only, we began to realize that the children's program we had prepared would probably not be adequate. During the course of inviting people in the streets to the Hope meetings, members of our team had encountered a children's drama troupe from North Carolina performing on a street corner in Riga. They were impressed with the quality of the presentation and the soundness of the message, and we agreed to ask them to perform for Saturday's children's program. They were able to provide us with a script of the performance one day in advance, and Estere and Bill, two of our amazing interpreters, worked through the night to translate the American slang production into a Latvian script for simultaneous translation on the day of the performance.

On Saturday morning, more than two thousand squealing, wound-up children crowded into the Sports Arena, wriggling and wrestling on the hard wooden benches. As I looked at the rows of bodies from the front of the arena it seemed that the very wood had hatched and sprouted wings into thousands of vibrant, vibrating butterflies. But when the program began they settled quickly, delighted at the well-trained Latvian children's choir and the young soloist singing "Jesus Loves Me" in Latvian. And when the drama troupe came on stage, all two thousand were spellbound by the powerful story of Jesus' love and sacrifice.

At the end of Steve Russo's invitation the hall was amazingly quiet. And then the children began coming forward, children raised from birth to know no God, indoctrinated through every medium that touched their lives to serve the state and reject all superstition, streaming toward the front to respond to the gift of Jesus' love. More than seven hundred of the children came to the front of the hall that morning to give their lives to Jesus. We wept as we met them.

Three months later, on August 19, 1991, the KGB and the vice president of the Soviet Union staged a coup in Moscow, kidnapping Gorbachev in the process. Although it ultimately failed against the compelling image of Boris Yeltsin towering above the tanks that surrounded the Kremlin and exhorting the Russian soldiers and citizens to resist, its effects were dramatic. Latvia declared its total and immediate independence on August 21, ending the transitional period of independence and catapulting the country into the little-charted waters of democracy and—for a time—near-chaos. And it signaled the eventual death knoll of the once all-powerful Soviet Union.

In many ways, Hope '91 was a cross-tie on this track to freedom. It occurred in the center of a firestorm of obsession in Latvia for all things Western, and much of its initial pull may truly have been an undiscriminating embrace of anything American-made. And to be sure, we made many mistakes along the way. We later learned that representatives of the cults—the Hare Krishnas and Moonies and others who were expertly taking advantage of this obvious openness—were circulating among the legitimate counselors after the Hope sessions to convert and claim those who came forward to accept Christ.

But through it all, the solid bulwark of generations of prayer for this week in May of 1991 protected us—and those who came to hear our message—from our own inadequacies and mistakes. A formal evaluation in the late 1990s commissioned by the Latvian Baptist Union pointed to Hope '91 and the Hope campaigns that would follow in 1992 and 1994 as the most important factors in Latvian church growth in that first decade of freedom. Eighty-five percent of the students enrolled in the Latvian Baptist seminaries in 1994 and 1995 gave their lives to Christ during the Hope campaigns of 1991 and 1992. Others who are now leaders of ministries with nationwide influence also publicly professed Christ for the first time at these outreaches. The mini-school equipped the Christian pastors and leaders who attended to reach out beyond their walls in the new era of religious freedom. And many ordinary citizens of Latvia entered the difficult years of chaos and crisis that would follow independence with a true hope that could not be shattered by the disillusionment associated with unrealistic expectations of democracy and capitalism that would crush many of their neighbors and friends.

I also returned to Corvallis with a changed heart, challenged by the changed lives and the turbulent times we had experienced. And as I saw the impact of the message we had brought on members of parliament as well as children, I began to formulate aloud a question that had been bouncing around in my brain for some time now: Does God want our church to influence a nation?

Evangelist Steve Russo, a former professional drummer, surprised and thrilled the crowd when he played a drum solo during Youth Night at Hope '91.

Every night hundreds of people came forward to indicate that they were interested in following Christ.

The Latvian music ensemble 'Maranata' played often and well.

In 1991, it was very inexpensive to advertise major events at the train station and in front of the post office. People came to the Sports Arena by the thousands.

A group of Hope '91 leaders waves farewell to our team. Tears were flowing freely on the bus.

Photos by Rihards Kocins

WHO WILL BUY
A LIGHTHOUSE?

The fellowship hall in the First Baptist Church of Corvallis was packed. The potluck dinner had been excellent as usual and more than a few of us had overindulged—as usual. But Mark Hubbell, our amateur auctioneer and regional director of Prison Fellowship, was merciless. As he made his way to the front of the crowded room and adjusted his microphone, the contented crowd slowly quieted to hear his words.

"We all know why we're here tonight, folks. Besides enjoying some great food and fellowship, we need to get our friends Almers and Vija and their children back to Latvia. When they went to pick up their round-trip Aeroflot tickets, they were told that they're only one-way. That means that the money we raised before won't cover their return trip. So tonight one of our church members, Bob Wilson, an industrial arts professor

Bob and Ethel Wilson worked together for several weeks to make more than twenty lighthouses. These were sold to pay for the Ludvikses' transportation costs.

at Oregon State University, has donated thirty of his handmade masterpieces, these tiny working lighthouses."

From the rows of models in front of him, he held up one for the crowd to see: a metal lighthouse model as large as his hand, painted bright white, with a white revolving beam in its tower.

"We need to raise $3,300 tonight. That means we need—" here he paused to scribble down some numbers—"$110 per lighthouse. Folks, let's have an auction! Do I have a bid?"

I consciously willed myself not to cover my face with my hands in dismay, but I was aghast at his boldness. One hundred ten dollars for each lighthouse? Surely our people would feel they'd already surpassed the required bounds of generosity in their support of the Ludviks family. I scrunched down in my seat, expecting a first bid to eventually come in at $10—maybe.

Finally, from the back of the room, Jim Muldoon, a retired teacher, stood up: "$110! I'll buy one!" he called. The room exploded with applause. As he made his way forward to collect his lighthouse, a woman on the other side stood up as well: "I have a bid—$110! Let me see my lighthouse!"

I was speechless, but I realized I needed to think fast. I had been preaching about leading by example, so I stood up and called out: "We'll buy one, too!" I had no idea where the money would come from, but I was beginning to see that God didn't seem to have a problem with that when we trusted him.

Within ten minutes all the lighthouses were spoken for, some with good-natured bidding that exceeded the $110 needed, and the Ludviks family had their tickets home. Vija, who had attended the banquet unaware of any plans for an auction, was stunned by what she had seen. In ten minutes' time, this secret worry that she had been carrying in her heart for months had been eradicated. On her way home that night, she clutched in her hands one of the little lighthouses, given to her by one of the buyers, Dave Willis, as a memento of the auction and a reminder of God's rich faithfulness.

The story of the auction really began much earlier, when the First Baptist Church of Corvallis and the Agenskalns Baptist Church of Riga agreed to launch a sister church partnership in January of 1990. Initially much of the relationship consisted of us sending much-needed humanitarian aid—aspirin, children's clothing, coffee, baby bottles, yarn,

In 1990, two very different churches formed a partnership that lasted for many years.

and fabric—and church supplies such as Sunday school curriculum, paper, pens, books, and discipleship materials. Our church members followed the political situation in Latvia closely and prayed specifically for the members of our sister church.

Since our first meeting at the Lausanne II Congress in Manila in 1989, though, Almers and I had also been dreaming of bringing him to the United States to attend seminary. In the spring of 1990, Almers came to the United States as a guest of the American Latvian Baptists. During this brief visit he was able to sit in on leadership meetings at our church, visit adult and children's Sunday school classes, and get a sampling of American church life. Our church members welcomed him with open arms, eager to have a chance to meet this man whose name they had been hearing for more than a year. They took him clothes shopping for his family, sat and talked with him over coffee, and invited him home to dinner. For our congregation, it was a powerful taste of missions brought home—being able to actually take our missionary partner to lunch put a real human face on the distant theoretical and financial discussions that usually seemed to typify our missions dealings.

After Almers returned to Latvia, we began to ask what the next logical step should be in our sister church partnership. Our church had been so inspired by Almers' visit that we started to talk about bringing his whole family over for a year, giving him an opportunity to get more theological training at Western Seminary in Portland and his family the chance to live with our church family for a year.

People in the church were excited about the idea, but the venture was a formidable one. We were in the middle of a building project, raising money to turn our old sanctuary into a gym and youth activity center. Our general and missions funds were always struggling, their financial heads above water, but just barely. And as we sat down to make an estimate of how much we would need to raise to bring the Ludvikses to Corvallis for a year, the conservative $20,000 estimate we arrived at seemed a nearly insurmountable amount.

Still, we went ahead and formed a Latvia Committee of interested church members who were eager to brainstorm the possibilities. Chaired by Joan Tice, they sat down at their first meeting in the winter of 1990 with a single sheet of paper in front of each of them, a stark black-and-white report of estimated itemized expenses for a family of four for one year. Airfare to get them here and back. Food. Housing. A car. Gas. Insurance. Medical expenses. Clothing. Those were the basics, and there was no getting around them. While they were discussing the sobering statistics, committee member Shirley Henderer spoke up.

"You know, we've been talking about renting the Ludvikses a house or an apartment, but I just realized that there might be a better way. You know that my dad just died. The house he was living in is just a block from our house, and it's empty now. That would mean we'd have a furnished house that the family could live in for a year, rent-free!"

The idea caught and jumped like a wildfire.

"That's great!" broke in Carole Wille excitedly, "That takes care of the house, but why stop there? Maybe we could do the same thing with some of these other categories. Our church has great resources—I just bet someone has some food to donate, maybe even the use of a car. We simply have to give them the opportunity!"

The committee agreed to draft a letter to send to the church members, explaining what was needed, how the first of those needs was being met, and asking for more creative contributions. The letter struck a profound chord in the congregation, for within ten days of its issue the Latvia Committee had received cash and in-kind contributions that more than covered the $20,000 needed. Lanny Zoeller donated half a beef. Jeff and Jenny Smith loaned the Ludviks family a credit card to pay for their gas expenses. Mark and Deb Hubbell received permission to loan the Ludvikses a car they were keeping for a friend of theirs who was doing a mission project in China. Dr. Gellinger and Dr. Johnson agreed to care for the family's teeth without charge for a year, and Dr. Castillo provided their medical care for free. Other offers poured in for home-canned fruits and vegetables, children's clothing, and household items. And the cash gifts more than covered the costs for health and car insurance and airfare.

The Latvia Committee was flooded and ecstatic. The process of creatively asking a profound question—What can *I* give?—had suddenly made this a project that everyone owned. Sunday school classes eagerly jumped on the bandwagon. During the next months of preparation, classes descended on the Henderers' lovely three-bedroom home to clean, spruce, and decorate. One class volunteered to do the yard work for the house, tending the large orchard in the back and planting a flower bed in front with red and white flowers to mirror the Latvian flag. Another did a top-to-bottom spring cleaning till the house shone. Still others collected clothing for the closets and decorated the home for a family: pictures and plaques on the walls, a beribboned pink bedroom for six-year-old Renalda and a sports-filled room for eight-year-old Reinis. And the hard-working members of the Latvia Committee continued to fuel the rest of us with their enthusiasm as they minded the details, drew up lists, and made final preparations for the Ludvikses' arrival in August of 1991.

❖

The Agenskalns congregation blessed the Ludviks family as they headed for America. Some in the church feared that they wouldn't return to Latvia.
Photo courtesy of Vija Ludvika

Back in Latvia, Vija Ludviks was unconvinced by reports of our preparations.

"Chuck, you are just telling us a story," she would say to me repeatedly during my Hope '91 visits. "I will pinch myself and then I will see that this is all a dream."

But as the plans became increasingly concrete, even Vija began to believe it would happen. On August 19, 1991, Almers and Vija and their children boarded a plane bound for the United States. Not until they reached New York, as they were jostled and buffeted about by the pressing crowds at JFK, did they hear of the coup in Moscow that day by the KGB and other hardliners. As they boarded another plane for their flight to Oregon and watched the immense city disappear into the night beneath them, Vija wondered if she would ever see Latvia again.

I was worried also as Nancy and I waited for them at the airport in Portland. This was a political move that none of us could have anticipated, and I was frightened about its implications for Latvia and the Ludvikses. But when we spoke to Almers after he landed he was strangely unconcerned.

"Chuck," he said in his still faltering English, "when we left Riga, someone in my church received a prophecy that I would return at the end of this year to become a pastor again at Agenskalns Baptist Church. That is why I am not worried about this." The failure of the coup two days later proved that Almers' calm was well grounded.

Nancy and I drove the tired Ludviks family out of Portland. As we drove farther out of the city, past tall stands of Douglas fir and green fields dotted with sheep, Vija could not contain her wonder. "She thought that America was all cities—New York, Los Angeles—like we see in the movies!" Almers translated.

When we drove through the quiet neighborhood and up to the one-story wooden house that would be their home, the children's eyes were wide. The Latvia Committee was there to welcome the family, with the refrigerator and cupboards full of groceries, flowers in a vase on the table, and the house gleaming. Vija walked through the house as if in a trance, fingering curtains and peering disbelievingly into cupboards. "It is still a dream," she murmured repeatedly in Latvian. Later, when her English was better, she would say, "Everything about the house that first day said, 'We love you!'"

Vija is tall, a former basketball player in the Soviet sports dynasty. Her mother's family had owned a small farm, but during Stalin's reign they were labeled bourgeois landowners and deported to labor in Siberia. When Vija's father came to visit a friend in Siberia after his discharge from the Red Army, he met Vija's mother and stayed to marry her. One brother was born and died in the never-ending struggle against the Siberian cold and hunger; by the time her parents were released to begin their long and arduous journey back to Latvia, her mother knew that she was pregnant again.

Vija was born not long after her parents reached Ventspils, Latvia. Her family's background was Catholic, but she had never been taught the meaning of their nominal faith. By the time she reached grade school she was active in the Pioneers and Komsomol, Communist youth organizations, and in high school she traveled with her basketball team around Latvia and even to Moscow. Vija's curiosity about the unlikely Baptist rock band she heard after a basketball practice prompted her to attend a Christmas Day service at the Baptist church, and Almers and an acquaintance she saw at the service that day invited her to come to a Bible study during the winter holidays. She seized at the opportunity to finally learn something about Christianity, and soon afterward she was baptized by Almers' father in the Baptist church as a believer. In 1979 she and Almers were married.

Now, half a world away, Vija's American dreams had become reality. Those first days in America were wide-eyed hours of learning for Vija and the children. Carole Wille invited the family to her house on a hot August afternoon for lemonade and a splash in the pool with her children, punctuated by sign language and long silences. Several women invited Vija to join them as they canned peaches, beans, applesauce, and other products of abundance from our fertile farming valley. Vija, who was used to the necessity of home canning in Latvia where there was nothing on the store shelves, was amazed that people in bountiful America would spend time canning. When we took her shopping in grocery stores she looked around in disbelief at the prodigious amounts of food. She later went back to videotape the store for her mother. "But where are all the people?" her mother wrote back.

The neighborhood where Almers and Vija lived was also home to more than ten families from our church, and every morning a group of women met to walk together. Each day they swung by to pick up Vija for their walk, and she soon began to feel more comfortable with their open, laugh-out-loud ways. She was amazed at the other neighbors who greeted her as she walked by—in Communist times in Latvia, neighbors were always viewed as potential enemies. As she grew to know more and more people in her neighborhood, from our church and from others, she often said, "This must be just like heaven."

Reinis and Renalda soon found friends as well in their new elementary school. In Riga they had attended an Estonian school, so when they arrived in America they were fluent in Latvian and Estonian; by Christmas they were also fluent in English and were the best spellers in their classes. They reveled in having rooms to themselves for the first time in their lives, and in watching Saturday morning cartoons on the home's color television. One thing the children did miss, though, was Latvian food. Oregon's seafood and the well-meant casseroles of the church ladies were too much for their meat and potato palates, and Vija always had to cook again for the children after they had been invited out for dinner.

Life in a new land and language was not without its unexpected humorous moments. As Vija laboriously learned her first English words and phrases, she was told that when people called the house for Shirley's deceased father, she should say, "He's passed away." One determined caller, however, could not seem to understand Vija's unusual intonation of that simple phrase, insisting again and again on speaking to Mr. Bullock. Finally, in exasperation, Vija shouted, with all the clarity she could muster: "He's DEAD!" Apparently the caller got the message.

Although there was a language barrier in our church services, the Ludviks family felt right at home. It was unusual for them to see someone at the front of the sanctuary leading worship, and the more contemporary songs were new to them. But the hymns and the basic format of the service were familiar and comforting. Vija said, "It felt like we were visiting relatives."

Almers was also kept busy. Back in Riga in May at the evening meeting following the closing of Hope '91, as we had sat in the smoky restaurant exchanging official gifts and reliving the highlights of that remarkable week, Dr. Jim Sweeney, vice president of Western Seminary in Portland, Oregon, stood at his table to speak.

"It has been my great honor," he said, clearing his throat, "to spend this week getting to know you all, and especially Ilmars Hirsch, the president of Latvian Baptist Seminary, which has recently reopened after fifty years of forced closure. Ilmars is a brother and a friend. And I am now proud to announce to you that Western Seminary and Latvian Baptist Seminary have formed a sister seminary partnership."

Our little crowd erupted in applause, while I sat at my table and wept. I had not known this would happen, this partnership, and it had been done entirely without my prompting or facilitation. This vision of international partnership for God's glory was taking flight, and it was beautiful. I leaned over to Almers sitting next to me and said, "I could die right now having lived a meaningful life."

Now this new partnership had opened up a scholarship position for one Latvian student to attend Western Seminary each year, and Almers was its first recipient. While Almers' English had improved it was still halting, so I was his tutor as he immersed himself in his graduate classes. We spent many, many hours together working through his textbooks and preparing his papers. And as his English improved he became increasingly independent and confident in his studies.

Almers was also the honorary associate pastor of Corvallis First Baptist Church, so he had the opportunity to serve with and observe our staff, sitting in on board meetings, studying our church constitution, and participating in the many details of American church life. When pastors from the community met for interdenominational prayer, Almers was there with us.

Perhaps most influential for Almers during his stay in America was his exposure to missions. For so long in Latvia, international outreach had been a closed book. All church work was concentrated within the walls of the church building. Now suddenly Almers was being bombarded with the outward perspective that being an active member of a missions-minded church requires. He was asked to speak at a missions conference at Western Seminary, he listened intently to the other speakers, he read missionaries' newsletters telling of the struggles and opportunities. And he began to develop an understanding and a passion for Jesus' Great Commission commandment.

Both Almers and Vija were eager students of the principles and practicalities behind our children's and youth ministry programs, two areas that they recognized to be the core and future of their newly liberated church ministry. Vija asked questions and took copious notes on all facets of our children's ministry. Carole Wille invited her to come to her Child Evangelism Fellowship classes, and Vija soaked it all up like a sponge.

Vija had already been a Sunday school teacher at Agenskalns Baptist Church in Riga, where attendance had been rapidly growing. It was a time of spiritual revival in Latvia, enhanced by Hope '91 and the new political situation, and when she left there had been more than two hundred children regularly attending classes taught by six or seven teachers. Many of the children were not from Christian families. As the teachers met to discuss their classes, they had begun to dream about how wonderful it would be to be able to teach these children about God on days other than just Sunday, and they had started to pray about the possibility of starting a Christian school. But without any model to base it on or resources to work with, they had felt stymied.

On one of her morning walks with the

Almers and Vija enjoy a fun afternoon at the Oregon coast with Kay Gingerich and Carole Wille (far right). Photo courtesy of Kay Gingerich

women of the neighborhood, Vija confided her dream of a Christian school in Latvia to Carole. Carole was immediately enthusiastic and suggested taking Vija to meet friends of hers who worked at Santiam Christian School, an independent Christian school located north of Corvallis on a former military base. Vija immediately hit it off with Diana Long, a friend of Carole's and an elementary teacher, and with the elementary school principal, Steve Potter. Before long, Vija was making regular visits to observe classes and talk with teachers and administrators, and her dream was growing in scope and intensity. When she spoke to me about the possibility, I'm ashamed to say that I tried to strongly discourage her. "It's just not feasible, Vija," I remember saying. "You're biting off more than you can chew."

In retrospect I can see that it simply didn't fit into my vision, so I automatically dumped cold water on it. Fortunately, Vija was not so easily discouraged. And I was about to learn—as I would repeatedly—that when you expose people to a God-given vision, they will naturally receive and want to pass on an outgrowth of that vision that may look very different from the original.

Vija proved to be a natural networker and visionary. Steve Potter caught her enthusiasm and eagerly promoted it in the Santiam Christian Elementary School, and the children began collecting and donating school supplies for Vija's dream. When it was time for her and Almers and the children to return to Latvia, they took the two suitcases they had come with—and 150 boxes full of school supplies collected by Santiam Christian School students, clothing for orphans, and construction supplies. And signed in friendship and anticipation was an agreement for a sister school relationship between Santiam principal Steve Potter and Vija's still non-existent school back in Riga. Soon after their return to Riga, Agenskalns Christian School was born in the basement of the Baptist church.

One year after their return, Almers and Vija resigned the pastorate at Agenskalns to start a new congregation in a recently returned church building. Combined with the growth of the school's enrollment, this necessitated a move for the young school. Torolds Barbins, a Latvian-American from Cleveland, donated money to buy a building for the school—ironically, the headquarters of a bankrupt bridge-building company with a recently remodeled corporate culture center, gym, kitchen, and dining facility. Named after his late father, a Latvian Baptist pastor, George Barbins Christian School was founded.

At the beginning there were many struggles—it was difficult to find qualified Christian teachers, for Christians had not been accepted into the Communist higher education system. Their principal of choice was elected into the government, so Vija reluctantly wore the principal's hat for the first three years of the school's existence. Today, however, they are fully accredited and twenty-one teachers educate one hundred twenty-six students in twelve grades, the largest privately funded school in the country. As other private schools in Latvia founder and fail, the George Barbins Christian School continues to enjoy an outstanding reputation, attracting many students from non-Christian homes for its academic excellence and committed faculty.

Ten months after their arrival in Oregon, the Ludviks family returned to an independent Latvia. Almers had finished his year of graduate studies at Western Seminary with a new vision of the local church's role in reaching out to the world. Vija was full of enthusiasm and ideas for teaching children the good news of Jesus, both through Sunday school and through her dream of a Christian school. And our congregation at Corvallis First Baptist Church would never be the same.

We had invited this family to give Almers an opportunity for further education and his wife and children the chance to live in America, but we had not anticipated how it would change us. Until their visit most in the congregation had listened to my reports about Latvia, contributed when asked, and followed the political situation from afar, but they had never been personally invested. Now, through this family that we had come to love, with whom we had laughed and eaten and cooked and walked and gardened and dreamed and prayed, through them we had learned to love the people of Latvia. Now we read the news from Eastern Europe with concern and understanding, we prayed with specificity and passion, and we continued to train our resources and thoughts on the needs and possibilities of this small, potential-laden country, the bridge between East and West, home of the people we loved.

I'll never forget the Ludvikses' final Sunday at church. Vija and Renalda dressed in Latvian national costumes and sang and danced to Latvian folk music. Photo courtesy of Vija Ludvika

A Tough Assignment
In Tough Times

T he day the Parkers arrived in Riga in 1993 from Oregon's green Willamette Valley it began to snow. And until they left eight months later the snow was their constant companion, gentle flakes that soon congealed into hard and dirty heaps, mounded in blackening masses beside roadways and gray apartment buildings, icy and perilous and bitterly cold.

Mike Parker and his wife Stephanie had accepted Agenskalns Baptist Church's invitation to reciprocate the visit of the Ludviks family to Oregon. In 1992, when I originally presented the invitation to our church in Corvallis, there were a few vocal dissenters among the congregation. After all of our experiences with Latvia in the past three years, some members continued to feel that the church's main focus should be the local mission field, not some far-off country with its own homegrown problems. Still, after several hours of intensive discussion, the congregation unanimously voted to send the Parkers to Latvia, in cooperation with Agenskalns Baptist Church and Western Seminary. Sending out missionaries from a local congregation to another congregation overseas was an unprecedented step in our Baptist circles. No mission board was involved. The Parkers would be supported by their home church and like-minded friends.

Newlyweds Mike and Stephanie were logical candidates for this venture. They had met as student leaders of Campus Crusade for Christ on the Oregon State University campus, and after graduation had begun working with the youth at our church. Mike, who had accompanied me to Latvia in 1989, had a burning desire to take his faith to the world's farthest corners. As a child of military parents who divorced when he was fourteen, he had moved thirty-two times in his first twenty-nine years, so his roots were

*Mike and Stephanie Parker in Riga
in the winter of 1993-94.*

shallow and he was ready for adventure. Stephanie, the product of a strong Christian home in the red canyons and high deserts of central Oregon, was prepared to go with him. Tall and striking, Stephanie was an accomplished equestrian with a passion and drive that led her to excel in everything she tried. And each was firmly committed to following where God led.

Mike and Stephanie accompanied the teams to Latvia for Hope '92, and then stayed for two months following the outreach to see if they could form a vision for what they might have to offer to the church in Riga. But as the rest of the team flew away, elated with the successes of the conference and the mission accomplished, the Parkers felt a cloud of darkness settle on them. The struggles of everyday life in the Latvia of 1992 set in, a Latvia consumed with the rigors and dangers of daily survival.

Almers immediately fell ill and had to be hospitalized, making it necessary for Mike and Stephanie to stay with another family with whom they could barely communicate. One day, as they made the forty-five-minute walk with Vija to the hospital to take food to Almers, they came upon the scene of an accident caused when two drunk pedestrians had walked into the path of a car. One was decapitated instantly, his blood staining the snow and running away in rivulets like a crimson fan; the other body lay face down, bloody and broken in the road. When the ambulance arrived, its drivers were also drunk.

One kicked the corpse in the road, while the other laughed as he picked up scattered body parts.

As they reached the hospital, a military Jeep screeched to a stop in front and uniformed soldiers jumped out, machine guns in their hands, pushing Vija and the Parkers aside and disappearing into the hospital. Tentatively, Mike, Stephanie, and Vija also entered the hospital and made their way to Almers' room, not sure of what they would find. But Almers lay as he had for days in the filthy room, huddled in the bed with his overcoat bundled around him against the cold. Still no competent doctor had examined him or prescribed anything helpful for his severe sinus infection. Wind blew through the unrepaired cracks and holes in the concrete walls. Vija gave him the food that he would otherwise not receive, and then they made their way outside. On the way out the soldiers again pushed them aside, jumped into the Jeep, and squealed away.

From the hospital they walked to the church where Mike, a relative newcomer to traditional church life, had been thrust into the position of leading services during Almers' illness. Outside the church they found a long bundle wrapped in old cement bags—a body, apparently dead for some time. An elder explained that he had gone to visit Almers at the hospital, and while he was there he had discovered the body of a pastor from the countryside who had come to the city for treatment. He did not know how long the pastor had lain dead in the hospital room, but he had offered to take his body back to his home in the countryside to bury him. Wrapping the body in a hospital bed sheet, he had walked the long, icy way back to the church with the unwieldy bundle on his shoulder.

And so it continued. Still, after two months Almers and Mike and Stephanie felt strongly that God had given them a vision for helping the church in Riga, specifically in the area of youth ministry. So Mike and Stephanie returned to the United States to devise a plan with our church and Western Seminary of how best to go about it.

Together with their professors at Western Seminary, they created a four-year master's degree program in intercultural studies that would include nine months in Latvia and three months in the United States each year. Then they enrolled in the seminary and began to raise money. And in October 1993, after two semesters of intensive intercultural and missiological studies, the young couple returned to Latvia. To the snow.

❖

Like their two months in Latvia the previous year, the first four months of this stay were a time of darkness and difficulty for them. Determined not to be pushy, dominating foreign missionaries, they lived simply like their Latvian friends and waited to find their niche in the Agenskalns congregation. Unlike many foreigners at the time, they had no house and no car. They lived on a Latvian budget in a simple, two-room apartment on the fourth floor of a bleak, Soviet-style cement block house. When they had running water, Stephanie washed their clothes in the bathtub.

Afternoons were occupied with shopping on foot, standing in long lines on the icy sidewalks and cobblestones to fill their pantry and tiny refrigerator: bread from the bakery, apples from the apple stand, cheese from the dairy store, and a hopeful but often unsuccessful search for good meat from sometimes a half-dozen different meat shops. Their diet—like that of most Latvians of that time—consisted mainly of potatoes, cheese, cucumbers, onions, apples, and bread. An occasional unexpected find of meat was cause for celebration.

Each morning they picked their way carefully out to the distant tram stop, hoping that a tram or bus would come by within the next hour to take them several miles closer to the church, where again they would navigate the icy sidewalks for the remaining twenty-five-minute walk.

At the church they met with their language tutor for a Latvian lesson, painstakingly studying the Latvian language with its precise phonetics and seven grammatical cases. An important part of their training as planned by their professors at Western Baptist Seminary was also the cultural component, so their tutors took them to museums and music performances, showed them the fine architectural features of downtown Riga, and told them the old pagan legends and folksongs of Latvia, of magic oaks and mystical forests and gods in the sun.

It was easy for Stephanie to fit into the church's strong musical heritage. A gifted and trained musician, she joined the choir, a step that also helped her language acquisition. Mike's musical prowess, on the other hand, was similar to that of most football players, but his desire to more deeply understand all things Latvian prompted him to take weekly piano lessons. He practiced a half hour each day.

The church building, which thirty years earlier had been confiscated by the Soviets and turned into a television studio, had been recently returned and was in need of extensive renovations. A crew of unemployed men was working on the repair in exchange for a midday meal—a steaming bowl of potato or beet soup—and Mike and Stephanie ate lunch with them each day after their lessons. In the afternoons each met with a group of four or five youth in discipleship groups, or Mike met with area pastors for Hope '94 planning sessions while Stephanie began the daily search for food.

They hoped to develop a strategy for youth ministry with the Latvians, but it seemed an uphill battle. While many were grateful for and supportive of their presence, some were suspicious of outsiders in the Latvian church, the residue of decades of oppression and secrecy that had defined church life during Soviet occupation. The sudden freedom had encouraged the church to cultivate a near frenzied pace of activities, making the schedules of leaders and church members a non-stop tangle of choir practices, mid-week services, prayer meetings, youth group meetings, and building renovation that left little time for anything new. So Mike and Stephanie kept praying, loving, and trying to learn as much as they could about Latvian ways and life in the church. And each night they returned to their apartment to the screams of the Russian woman next door being beaten by her drunken husband, and the sound of neighborhood dogs barking through the night.

These years of 1993 and 1994 were times of deep despair for many in Latvia. The unease and depression that Mike and Stephanie felt were given statistical weight by the United Nations' grim 1998 report on Latvian Human Development, which highlighted the years of 1993 and 1994 as the rock bottom of Latvia's post-Communist backlash. The radical removal of the socialist system at the end of 1991 had left the Latvian economy sprawling, and every facet of society was in chaos.

Inflation had skyrocketed along with unemployment. Suicide and chronic alcoholism among men had more than doubled. The infant mortality rate rose to crisis levels, and abortions were at an all-time high, with 68 abortions per 100 women in their childbearing years and 1,400 abortions for each 1,000 live births in 1993. Parents struggling with their new economic and social woes abandoned their children to orphanages at a much higher rate than ever.

Inadequate pensions for retirees left them unable to pay even their most urgent bills—rent, food, clothing, medicine—and stories abounded that winter of elderly people found dead in their homes, frozen or starved to death because their meager allowance had not been enough to cover the rising prices of heat and food. Mike and Stephanie stumbled into several frozen bodies in the streets, middle-aged men and women whose escape from hopelessness into alcoholism had hastened and publicized their death.

Violent crime in Latvia rose steeply to its highest point ever in 1993, with robbery, murder, and rape at all-time highs and the number of crimes involving firearms tripling. Organized crime grew all across the former Soviet Union, and a wave of explosions in cafes and stores in Riga and other cities spread fear through any who refused to bend to the extortion of the Mafia. The official population of prostitutes in Riga grew to 10,000, but the unofficial numbers of girls and women who were imported from other parts of the former Soviet Union and controlled by the organized crime bosses were much higher.

New banks sprouted and died routinely, prompting a high-stakes gambling game among those brave enough to invest and pull out at the last possible moment before bankruptcy. Latvia led the entire Baltic and Nordic region in traffic fatalities, most of which were caused by drunk driving.

Everyday life was uncertain, fearful, and dark.

As Mike and Stephanie struggled to cope with these overwhelming external factors, they also began to grapple with difficult personal issues. Stephanie, who had grown up in the wide open spaces of central Oregon, felt stifled and claustrophobic in the noisy, polluted, people-filled city. By nature outgoing and confident, she became insecure and longed for the familiarity of home and family. And she grew increasingly alarmed as Mike, who was thriving on life in this foreign culture, began dreaming of pushing even further east, into Mongolia and beyond, the more remote and inaccessible the better. They spent hours together in prayer during these months, questioning the fit of their marriage when their hearts' desires were so far apart and begging God to intervene and change someone's heart.

❖

Before they had left for Latvia, a missionary couple on home leave from Taiwan had told them a story that continued to echo in Stephanie's mind during these difficult months. Like Stephanie, the woman had been a horsewoman. The process of giving up her horse as she prepared to go overseas had been very difficult, but an older missions veteran had told her: "God has given you this passion for a purpose. Pack your breeches and boots and wait for God to be faithful." She had followed the advice with a shrug, but she had ended up riding with the Taiwanese Olympic equestrian team. And she had passed the same advice on to Stephanie.

One snowy day several months after their arrival, when the discouragement had settled in deeply, a young girl who had attended one of Stephanie's Bible studies from the previous year presented Stephanie with a creased street map of Riga that was marked with an "X". "I remember that you talked about your horse last year," she said. "There is a horse barn not far from where you are living. This map will help you find it."

On their next free day, Stephanie collared Mike and, map in mittened hands, they went in search of the horse barn. Not surprisingly, they were soon hopelessly lost, riding a bus that was obviously traveling in the wrong direction. At the end of the line, Stephanie rifled through her pocket Latvian dictionary to try the words "Horse barn, please" on the puzzled bus driver. He eventually understood, and in a string of confusing Latvian made them understand that they should stay on the bus. Eventually they left the crowded streets of Riga behind, and finally, in the middle of a snow-covered field, the bus driver stopped the bus and motioned for them to get out.

As the bus drove away, Mike and Stephanie looked around at vacant fields and an empty road, swept clean by a biting polar wind. Far ahead a stooped, old countrywoman hobbled down the side of the road, hunched under the weight of age and her cloth-handled shopping bags. Their hearts sank, and Mike began wondering how they would ever get back home. "Please, God," Stephanie prayed aloud desperately. "Please send us someone who knows English and who knows where the horse barn is." Even as she prayed she realized the improbability of meeting someone who could speak English this far out of town.

Still, determined not to give up, Stephanie quickened their pace to catch up with the old woman. As they drew near, Stephanie smiled and tried out her new words: "Please, horse barn." The old woman paused and smiled a toothless smile as she shifted her heavy bags. "Oh, you must be from America," she said in accented but clear English. "I work at the horse barn. I'll take you there."

In amazed disbelief they followed her up the road to the horse barn, a luxurious facility that contained three indoor rings, 150 splendid horses, and the Latvian Olympic equestrian team. The old woman introduced Stephanie to Sandra, a member of the team who spoke some English, and she and Stephanie soon arranged to meet again for a lesson.

The next time, equipped with her breeches and boots from home, Stephanie had no difficulties in finding the barn, and her performance during her lesson proved to Sandra that she was already a skilled horsewoman. After several meetings, Sandra asked if she would like to come to watch the team practice the next morning.

When she arrived, Sandra handed her the reins of a spectacular Latvian Warmblood. "Please," she said. Stephanie assumed that she wanted her to hold the reins for some reason, and she stood still, savoring the proximity of the wonderful horse. Soon Sandra rode back over: "Please, ride this horse." Still in disbelief, and hampered by a vast language barrier, Stephanie clambered onto the tall horse in her unwieldy snow boots. She let him trot a few paces and then stopped, but again Sandra rode over: "Please, ride this horse."

Finally, Stephanie put the majestic horse through his paces, taking him in circles, walking, trotting, cantering, and reveling in his precise responses and exquisite training. When she was finished, the team members who had been watching burst into vivacious discussion. Finally Sandra again approached and responded to a question that Stephanie hadn't known existed: "Yes, we would like you to come on Wednesdays and Fridays at 10:00 am to ride with us."

Stephanie's love for horsemanship allowed her to build relational bridges with members of the Latvian Olympic team.

For Stephanie, this was an undreamed dream come true, and, in the middle of a dark and lonely time, a much-needed reminder of God's great love for her. She and Sandra became good friends, and in stumbling Latvian and English, with the smell of horse sweat and leather as backdrops, they talked about life and the country of Latvia and its suffering people.

But the snow remained. The dirty frozen heaps at the roadside grew daily taller and the cobblestones became more icy and treacherous.

Knowing that the fourth month is often the critical time in the adaptation to a foreign culture, Nancy and I had scheduled a visit to Mike and Stephanie in February of 1994. And there, in the damp, gray, cold of their Riga apartment, punctuated by the scuffles and cries of the Russian couple next door, we huddled with them for three days of intense intercessory prayer.

In retrospect, they separated their eight months in Latvia into the four months of frustration and the four months of fruitfulness. This midpoint in the bleak coldness of late January and early February proved to be the crucible for them as they gradually began to sense a thaw in opportunities that had seemed frozen for so long. Soon they were meeting regularly with the youth leader, Ausma, a busy mother of three small children who led the youth in addition to working twelve hours a day as a translator and interpreter for a Swedish company.

Together with Ausma and the seventeen young

Mike and Steph rejoiced when Nancy and I delivered them a suitcase filled with their favorite foods, snacks, and spices. We also spent time with Ausma Ece and others who ministered to youth at Agenskalns Church.

Nancy and I also guest taught at the newly established George Barbins Christian School.

117

people who attended regularly, the Parkers developed a program they called "NURPS," a Latvian acronym that translates into "Come and See for Yourself." Modeled on programs that Mike and Stephanie had studied and led in the United States and modified to fit the Latvian cultural context, the youth program organized a core group of leaders who were assigned responsibilities based on their spiritual gifts. After intense meetings of prayer to support the new outward-directed focus, NURPS opened its doors on March 3, 1994. And within weeks, youth between the ages of sixteen and thirty were coming from all over Riga to "see for themselves" this new and unusual event that was happening each week in the basement of the Agenskalns Baptist Church.

The word was out, and on this cold Wednesday night just before 7:00, the Agenskalns area of Riga was alive with the sound of young voices and booted feet tramping in the packed snow. They came alone and in groups, by foot and by bus, converging on the odd-shaped cement church building, an aging amputee that had barely survived Soviet occupation with its peeling paint, chopped-off steeple, and cement-blocked facade that had formerly held beautiful, arching, stained-glass windows. They crossed through the large wrought-iron gate and into a neatly kept garden, over a swept walkway and then down the steps into the basement, where at the end of a cold hallway more voices called out to greet them. And here was a long, narrow room with a single row of bare bulbs hanging from wires down the center of the room, two coat racks already buried with worn coats and homemade gloves and scarves, a mountain of book bags heaped up beside them. The room was bare of decoration and dimly lit, but there was something here—a momentum, an excitement—that these young people had never felt before.

In one corner, a group of budding young capitalists was discussing their latest exploits of high-stakes, short-term investing in the banks with this week's highest interest rates. Jekabs Bikis, always in the middle of the group with his tales of entrepreneurial adventure, was one of the core group of leaders who had already been here for an hour or more, reviewing the evening's program, praying, and making things ready.

Finally, at 7:00, Ausma and Mike invited the youth to find seats on the three-legged stools set up in rows facing them, and when the group was settled the official program began.

After a welcome and brief announcements, one of the youth leaders stood and led the group in a short opening prayer. Then the music and worship team gathered around the old piano to lead the youth in Latvian praise songs. Music is an essential part of Latvian culture, and the young people loved the new songs they learned from the overhead projector and the single, tinny piano.

As the notes of the last song faded, Ausma introduced the drama team, and a young man carrying a large bag walked to the front. As he was shown being ambushed, beaten, and robbed, some who had grown up in the church began to recognize the story of the Good Samaritan. But as the skit continued, it seemed for many not so very different from life on the streets of Riga. Eventually, after several of his own people passed him by, it was the hated Samaritan who extended help to the broken man. The group was silent when Mike finally got up to speak.

"Tonight we're going to be talking about reaching out beyond our comfort zone," said Mike. "Obviously, several years ago this would have been dangerous, maybe even unthinkable. In the Soviet Union, people who reached out often got cut down. But today Latvia is a different place, and I believe God is calling us to be people who live beyond our own borders of comfort, people who build bridges to others. Think for a moment about who that might mean. Who is outside your comfort zone? Who is God asking you to reach out and touch with his love? Your neighbors? Kids in your school? People you work with? Your mom and dad?"

He paused. "How about Russians?" A murmur rippled through the room.

"Why Russians?" called out one young man on the left. "All of Latvia's suffering is because of them. Why should we reach out to them?"

"Latvians have suffered because of the Soviet Union, that is true," replied Mike, "but many, many Russians have also suffered. Most Russians were not oppressors. There are 500,000 Russians living here in Riga right now, and many of them are struggling with Latvia's new citizenship and language requirements. Yet this is their home, too. Many of them were born here. It is time to reach out and forgive. And to ask for forgiveness."

It was a hard message. The team knew before it presented this evening's program that it would be a controversial one, but they felt it was one that needed to be given. As Mike continued presenting Jesus' parable in the Latvian context, Ausma and Stephanie and the other leaders could see some heads slowly nodding. He was getting through.

After about twenty minutes, Mike closed in prayer and Ausma stood to explain the four different Bible study groups that would meet for the next hour: one for seekers, one for new Christians, another in-depth study for more mature Christians, and a topical study. With a scraping of stools and a massive, laughing shuffle of bodies, the roomful of young people separated itself remarkably efficiently into four groups, and for the next forty-five minutes they devoted themselves to serious study.

Finally, at 9:00, cheerful noises from the hospitality crew in the kitchen called the groups back into the main hall. After a last praise song on the hard-working piano and a closing prayer, the kitchen crew emerged with loaded trays of standard mass-produced Soviet china, bright orange teapots and cups with big white polka dots, steaming with weak black tea. The plates piled high with cookies and special Latvian *Laima* chocolate were soon emptied, but the discussion remained animated until shortly before 9:30, the hour when the last bus left the Agenskalns area.

With startling speed the stools were suddenly empty, the tangle of heavy coats and scarves sorted and donned, and good-byes were said. And those who had tasted the NURPS message, those who had come and seen for themselves, were tramping up the concrete steps and disappearing into the cold night air.

But Ausma and Mike and Stephanie were learning that they would be back again next week with new questions and more of their friends. And once more the basement would be buzzing with life and anticipation.

The snow had only been melted a few weeks when Mike and Stephanie left Latvia to return to Oregon on June 3, 1994. In the weeks that followed their departure, NURPS continued to grow to an average attendance of over one hundred, a testimony to the strong leaders they had trained and the effective structure they had developed.

But for Mike and Stephanie, the leaving was bittersweet. Although they had formed lifelong friendships and were still compelled by the need and potential they saw, they had decided that they would not continue the four-year commute between Latvia and America as they had planned. The physical and emotional strain of living in Riga in these difficult times had taken their toll on them, and they desperately needed rest. Mike still dreamed of tribes in Mongolia and Central Asia, while Stephanie felt an overwhelming pull to home and family, to the land and her horse. And their prayers to God to change one of their hearts had seemingly gone unanswered. Exhausted and discouraged despite their objective success, they were their own harshest critics.

What none of us could anticipate was God's surprising answer to the combination that seemed at this moment to bring such heartbreak. And how their decision to "prematurely" return would prove to be the catalyst for far greater bridge building than any of us had imagined.

WHERE IN THE WORLD
IS TURKMENISTAN?

"You've been praying for seventy-five years to evangelize Russia," thundered the usually mild-mannered Swede to his wide-eyed Russian audience, "and with your new religious freedom you finally have the opportunity. If there's ever been a time to go to Siberia, it's now. But you," and here his voice became slow and pointed, "you want to go to Sacramento!"

The unlikely prophet's name was Ingemar Martinson, former president of the Slavic-Swedish Mission, the oldest of all missions focused on the Soviet Union. Ingemar, a longtime friend of Brother Andrew, had been blacklisted for years in the Soviet Union for his organization's participation in a wide range of covert ministries behind the Iron Curtain, including Bible smuggling and the smuggling and publication of underground reports from Soviet prisoners of conscience. In 1980 he founded a training center in Sweden in an old villa on a fjord to quietly invite and train small groups of Christian leaders from around the Soviet Union, an effort that has given birth to many new ministries around Eastern Europe and the Russian-speaking republics in the last twenty years.

I confess that I cringed at Ingemar's audacity when I heard him addressing the Russian congregation in Riga in 1990. Here he was, a Westerner in front of a church that had just emerged from three-quarters of a century of religious persecution, scolding them for not wanting to pursue voluntary hardships in this new era of freedom. It did seem a bit much to ask.

But as I continued to listen to Ingemar over the following months, his vision and passion for the missionary opportunity presented by the Soviet Union and its breakup became increasingly persuasive. And finally, in November of 1992, during the plenary session of Hope '92 in Riga, before a group of Latvian church leaders, his words finally penetrated my heart with a force and a permanence that were impossible to ignore.

At Hope '94 Ingemar Martinson shared his deep conviction that Latvians are called to bring the gospel to the Samaritans of their lives. Estere Roze was the interpreter.

"I am teaching today from Acts 1:8," began Ingemar that morning. "Jesus said to his disciples, 'You will receive power when the Holy Spirit comes on you; and you will be my witnesses in Jerusalem, and in all Judea and Samaria, and to the ends of the earth.' (NIV)

"This was a radical statement for Jesus to make. For his Jewish disciples, Jerusalem was a natural mission field for the good news. But Samaria was home to the hated Samaritan, an enemy and most certainly an unwanted ministry target. And the ends of the earth were radically beyond anything that touched their daily lives as fishermen and tax collectors. We can be grateful that the early Christians did not let these barriers of natural aversion and distance stand in the way of their evangelism.

"But I stand here today to tell you that you are in Jerusalem now. And you have a Samaritan, an unwanted ministry target. Your Samaritans are the Russians, those whom you despise for the last decades of oppression that they represent. And the ends of the earth are the many obscure groups of people who have been forced to learn Russian over the last difficult years.

"Just as God used the Roman Empire, which was evil in its intent, to disseminate a universal language, to conquer the world with the Pax Romana, to create a network of roads and trading centers and a familiar infrastructure so that the good news of Jesus Christ could be spread with the greatest efficiency and effectiveness far beyond the borders of Israel, so can God use the Soviet Union and its aftermath. 'What man meant for evil, God has used for good.' Here, united by one common Russian language, you have 300 million people representing 148 different ethnic groups, 42 of which are

Muslim, 6 Buddhist, others animist. They have all been forced to learn the same language and operate under the same economic, educational, and social systems.

"You in Latvia naturally want to posture yourselves toward the West, but you must realize that you are uniquely situated by God as a gateway, as a bridge to the East. You must recognize that you have a language and a cultural framework forged in the suffering of Soviet domination that allows you to travel to Uzbekistan or Kazakhstan or Turkmenistan and step off the plane and immediately know how to function in that Muslim country. And you arrive at a fraction of the cost and without the cultural baggage associated with a foreign Western missionary or the controversial reputation of the average American."

Most of the Christian leaders in the audience shuffled their feet or looked uneasily down at their hands. These were hard words for Latvians to hear in 1992, when their daily lives were consumed with survival. Yes, they were newly free from the constraints of Soviet domination, but, as I was often told, "You can't eat freedom!" Hopes that freedom would bring about the instant wealth of the West were being bitterly dashed on the twin rocks of skyrocketing prices and a devalued currency.

By the time Ingemar had finished that morning, though, his message had finally reached me. I sat stunned, tears streaming down my face, my notebook and pen forgotten in my lap. *Latvians using the Russian language to take the gospel to the Muslims—what a perfect, God-made redemption of years of suffering. And another way for our sister church partnership to rise to a new level, working together to fulfill Christ's Great Commission.*

That night I gingerly broached the subject to Almers as we sat together in his tiny living room, reviewing the events of the day.

"Almers, I've been thinking. I believe God wants to use Latvians to take the gospel to the Russian-speaking Muslim countries. What do you think?"

There was a long pause. He wrinkled his forehead and rubbed his hands through his brown hair. "Oh, Chuck, Chuck," he said, shaking his head slightly. "I don't know about you."

"Well, what do you think?" I persisted.

"I don't know. I need to think about this . . . and pray about it," he said, with his typical caution.

I took this to be an extension of the unease and lack of enthusiasm I'd detected from the other Latvian leaders earlier in the day, and decided that I'd probably never hear anything about it again. So I was surprised when, as we sat together the next evening, Almers brought up the subject again.

"Chuck," he said, with a grin, "you're *traks*, you're crazy."

"I know," I grinned. "And so are you."

He smiled, paused, and then continued. "I've been praying about it and I think you're right. I'll go to Turkmenistan if you'll go with me."

I jumped off the chair. "That's wonderful!" I cried. "Let's go!"

This time it was my turn to hesitate a beat. "Where's Turkmenistan?"

❖

Water is a Turkmen's life, a horse is his wings, and a carpet is his soul.

Turkmenistan is a sand-blown, oasis-veined desert country in Central Asia, one of the five Russian-speaking Muslim republics of the former Soviet Union. The traditional home of the fierce, nomadic tribes of Turkmen, it is bordered by Iran and Afghanistan to the south, Kazakhstan and Uzbekistan to the north and east, and the Caspian Sea to the west. Like Latvia in Europe, Turkmenistan's territory has served as a bridge and battleground for Asia's invaders and marauders, being penetrated and often conquered through the centuries by such historic luminaries as Alexander the Great and his

Macedonians, Genghis Khan and his Mongol warriors, diverse khans and shahs from Persia, and Peter the Great's Imperial Russian troops. Camel caravans traveling the fabled Silk Road between Bahgdad and Xi'an passed through the scorching Karakum Desert, the lush Amu Darya Oasis, scented with wild licorice, and the volatile, earthquake-ridden Kopet-Dag range of Turkmenistan, bringing wares and ideas and religions—including Zoroastrianism, Buddhism, and Islam—from across Asia and the Middle East.

The Turkmen themselves were a warring, feuding, fragmented network of clans, living in carpet-hung *yurtas* pitched in the desert sands next to their flocks. Notorious as mercenaries and robbers of caravans, their golden, desert-bred Akhalteke horses—proud descendants of Alexander the Great's favorite mount Bucephalus—were their most prized possessions. The forced collectivization that accompanied the Soviet takeover of Turkmenistan in 1924 sent these horses to state-run stud farms, and effectively crippled the nomadic way of life. The ensuing years of the Turkmen Soviet Socialist Republic brought about an influx of experts from Russia and Ukraine, a growing agricultural economy, and tremendous economic potential from Turkmenistan's position as the world's fourth largest producer of natural gas. Since the government declared the end of Soviet rule in 1991, Turkmenistan, with a population of 4.2 million, had been establishing its identity as an independent, nominally Muslim state. In the capital city of Ashgabat, 60 percent of the 400,000 inhabitants are Turkmen, and the remaining 40 percent are a colorful mixture of Russian, Azerbaijani, Uzbek, Iranian, or Tatar.

President Saparmyrad Niyazov, the Moscow-controlled Communist party boss before 1991, managed to maintain control of the country after the breakup of the Soviet Union. When he was re-elected to a ten-year term in 1994 by a 99.9 percent margin (the election was boycotted by outside election monitors), he changed his name to Turkmenbashi, "the leader of all Turkmen." His leadership style follows in the dark footsteps of Vladimir Lenin, Mao Zedong, Saddam Hussein, and other despots. In 1999 the Turkmen Parliament made him president for life, and now Turkmenistan overflows with Turkmenbashi's statues, portraits, and monuments. Streets, cities, schools, and children are named after him, along with the only state-produced brand of vodka.

Almers had suggested this particular Muslim melting pot because a Latvian member of Matthews Baptist Church in Riga named Aigars had already moved there, taken a job in a telephone company, and was considering becoming a Turkmen citizen.

When I returned from Latvia in November of 1992, I reported to the church in Corvallis this new vision that God had given us of Latvians using the Russian language to bring the gospel to the Muslim republics of Central Asia. Internally I cringed during my report, knowing that there could be some criticism of this new direction. A few church members had felt that we'd gone overboard with our focus on Latvia, and now I was dreaming of Muslims even farther away? Amazingly, the immediate response was overwhelmingly positive. Still, I braced myself for later criticism.

On the following Saturday, I was sitting at my desk at the church working on the next day's sermon when a congregation member named Coral Zoeller came into my office. She looked a little upset, and I assumed that she was probably unhappy with something in the church. I braced myself.

"I've come to talk to you about your plans for Turkmenistan," she began. "Last night I had a dream about Muslims." She paused and looked down at her trembling hands. "You need to know that I have difficulties with Muslims. I work with them at the university and they frighten me. But after this dream, I know that God wants me to help them. My mother has left me an inheritance. As you know, she was supportive of missions all her life, and Lanny and I feel it would be an honor to her memory to use a portion of her estate to help you, Almers, and the others go to Turkmenistan. Do you know how much you will need for the trip?"

I struggled to regain my composure. "I . . . I think we'll need about $3,000 for everything.

Tears filled her eyes as she reached for her checkbook. "That's the amount I thought I was supposed to give. Mom would have loved this project."

Lanny and Coral Zoeller (right) and her parents Earl and Roberta Weilmeunseter. Photos courtesy of Coral Zoeller

Nine months later, in August of 1993, our bags were packed for Turkmenistan. Christian ministry in a Muslim country can be a risky endeavor. In Turkmenistan in 1993, it was illegal to speak openly about Jesus Christ or to encourage others to believe in him. No missionary activity was tolerated. On the Sunday morning before our departure I preached from John 15 about the world hating the followers of Jesus, and for the first time I publicly stated my acceptance of the risk that this trip might cost me my life. That morning, overcome by my professed willingness to give my life for the gospel, an aging ex-convict in the audience who had spent forty years in the federal penitentiary gave his life to Christ. Our church saw once again, as they simultaneously sent me off to Central Asia and welcomed a repentant sinner in Corvallis into the family of God, that a global vision can have a life-changing impact on the person in the pew.

That first trip proved to be a scouting trip. Our team consisted of three Latvians—Almers; Ainars Bastiks, pastor of Matthews Baptist Church; and Raimonds Locs, a seminary student—a Swedish missionary and evangelist, Kenneth Berqvist; Roger Draves, a Conservative Baptist mission leader with extensive experience in Eastern Europe; and me. As we sweltered in the scorching heat blowing off the vast Karakum Desert and savored the famous Turkmen watermelon, we spent a great deal of time in prayer and tried to learn as much as possible about the small group of believers in Turkmenistan—fewer than twenty people, by all estimates.

And as temperatures soared above 120 degrees in the shade, Almers and Ainars baptized a young Turkman co-worker of Aigars in a lake of the green Kopet-Dag Oasis that cradles the city of Ashgabat. This was a profound event: Because of the financial support of a sister church in Oregon, Latvian pastors were able to go to Turkmenistan to baptize a young Muslim convert, saying to him in the common and once-hated language of Russian: "You are now a member of our churches in Riga until there is a church for you here in Turkmenistan."

It was truly a holy moment.

For Almers, this experience proved to be a turning point in his vision for missions. When we returned to Riga, he eloquently presented an account of our trip to his church board, articulating the significance of this new church member to the mission of the Agenskalns Baptist Church.

To our surprise, Ilmars Lams, the rather reserved chairman of the board, began to weep. "In the early 1960s," he said, "I was serving in the Soviet army as a guard on Turkmenistan's border with Iran. For two years I stood at my post, looking out over the barbed wire for eight hours every day, watching the Turkmen people in the fields with

TURKMENISTAN 1993

It was our privilege to bring the first copies of the Gospel of Luke in the Turkmen language into Turkmenistan. Roger Draves is in the center and Kenneth Bergqvist is on the right.

These young ladies (right) would not allow me to photograph them unless they were serving a man, in this case the Muslim mullah (left) who showed us how he prayed. The woman in the center photo spent three months making this carpet that sells for twenty dollars.

129

their horses and their sheep. They seemed so wild. My heart went out to them, and I often prayed that God would send someone to tell them about Jesus. But I never would have believed that God would send my own pastor."

❖

With the support of the Agenskalns Baptist Church, Almers kept this missionary vision alive. They adopted the fledgling group of believers in Turkmenistan as a sister church and, in spite of their own repair and rebuilding projects on their returned building and the continued struggle for daily survival in Latvia, the church in Riga was able to raise several thousand dollars by 1994 to help support a new church in Ashgabat.

In early 1994, when Mike and Stephanie Parker were nearing the end of their stay in Latvia, Almers informed them that it was time to return to Turkmenistan for a pastoral visit with their young ex-Muslim church member. Mike and Stephanie were thrilled at the opportunity, but the $1,200 they would need for visas and airfare seemed an insurmountable obstacle. The youth group at the Agenskalns church began to pray with them for a miracle.

Before long Mike received a phone call from Luke Hendrix, a youth pastor he'd met months before at a church in Prineville, Oregon. "Mike, after I told the parable of the talents to our youth group, I gave each of our fifty kids a one-dollar bill and told them to use them wisely as talents from the Lord. Some of them pooled their money to start a concessions stand for the boys' football games and made several hundred dollars; others got together to buy a permit to log a few cords of wood to sell, and they made a couple hundred dollars. We'd originally planned to buy you a video camera, but we're wondering if you have any other more pressing needs for the money?"

Mike told him about the upcoming Turkmenistan trip.

"So how much do you need for the trip, Mike?" asked Luke.

"$1,200."

"We have $1,100 here, Mike, and I'll throw in the other $100 from my wife and me. There's your trip. Go for it."

The youth group at Agenskalns Baptist Church was thrilled at this answer to their prayers. They now threw themselves into prayer for visas as Mike, Stephanie, Almers, and Jekabs, the representative from the youth group who would accompany them, began the wearisome process of visa application. Time passed without any tangible results, and soon Mike and Stephanie would have to return to the United States. Eventually the double entry/exit visas for Russia arrived, but there was still nothing from the Turkmen authorities. And there was only a two-week window of time left for the trip. Finally, bolstered by the non-stop prayers of both the church and the youth group, they decided to go ahead with their plans and hope to get a visa at the border. The church sent them off, visa-less but covered in prayer, as delegates of the youth group of the Agenskalns Baptist Church of Riga.

Years of travel in Russia and its neighboring countries had made waiting at the Moscow airport a commonplace occurrence, but when there was still no announcement of the flight to Ashgabat at the scheduled departure time, Almers went to investigate. The broad-shouldered Russian woman at the counter bristled at his polite inquiry. "Shut up and sit down!" she railed. "I'll tell you when the plane's going to go!"

An hour later Almers tried again. "What did I tell you?" she said with a glare. "Sit down and shut up!"

When Almers bravely asked again three hours later, she softened a bit to his persistent politeness. "Look, it's not our airline, and it's not my business. The flight never leaves on time. The pilot flies when he feels like it, and how he feels usually depends on how much he's been drinking!"

Finally, eight hours after the scheduled departure time, they were allowed to board the plane. After all the seats were full, passengers continued to file in, Azerbaijani, Uzbek, and Turkmen, squatting in the aisles and exit wells, leaning against a bag of cabbages here and a crate of chickens there. Almers' seat collapsed four times before takeoff.

They arrived in Ashgabat at 1:30 in the morning to a deserted airport—no customs lines, no visa application forms. The man who unloaded their luggage from the plane said, "You look like decent people. Take your luggage, I'll write you a note, you come back tomorrow and you'll get your visas." The next day they were issued visas with no questions asked. And their luggage filled with Scriptures that had been unpacked the night before remained unscrutinized, thanks to a holy delay and the prayers of the Agenskalns Church back in Riga.

One of their first contacts in Ashgabat was the leader of the small group of Russian Baptist believers. He was brimming with excitement. "You say you have been trying for months to come? God must have held you back for just the right time. Just last week President Turkmenbashi invited all the religious leaders in Ashgabat to a meeting—one Orthodox priest, a room full of Muslim mullahs, and me. He said, 'We have enacted a new law declaring religious freedom in Turkmenistan. As of now, you are free to practice your religion according to your own Scriptures.' So I say, let's test this new law. I've got the *Jesus* film in Russian. Let's see if we can get permission to show it!"

His enthusiasm was contagious, and the possibility of such an opportunity was more than they could ever have imagined: perhaps the first public proclamation of the gospel of Jesus Christ in Turkmenistan since the third century! The following day they spent in prayer while he went to apply for official permission. He returned with permission to show the *Jesus* film twice in a public theater and to run one two-minute advertisement on the national television channel.

By showtime at 4:00 on Friday, the theater doors were open, the film was primed, the organizers ready, the advertisement had run—but the theater was empty. They rechecked their watches and peered into the street—nothing. Then after fifteen interminable minutes of waiting, the people began coming. And coming. Soon the theater was packed.

They showed the first half of the film, and during the intermission Mike gave his testimony, translated into Russian by Almers. After the second half of the movie, Almers preached a short message in Russian. At the end of his message he paused.

"If any of you is ready to give your life to Jesus, to ask him to come into your life and take away your sin, please come forward and someone will be able to pray with you here at the front. We have New Testaments for you and we would like to talk with anyone who wants to know more."

To his amazement, almost the whole audience came forward. And on the following night the response was the same. Conservative estimates place the number of those who came forward during those two showings at between 600 and 800.

Suddenly the number of Christian seekers and believers in Turkmenistan had swelled from fewer than twenty to several hundred. The supply of Turkmen New Testaments and other Christian literature they had brought to Ashgabat in their luggage was quickly exhausted. With the help of Swedish missionary leader Kenneth Bergqvist, who had participated in our scouting trip the summer before, the four from Riga went around to the few underground Western missionaries known to them who were living in Ashgabat to tell them of this new law guaranteeing religious freedom and of the awakening they had just experienced. And then, with their allotted time in Turkmenistan at an end, they reluctantly returned to Riga.

Three months later, as Turkmenbashi's transformation into a megalomaniac solidified, the law guaranteeing religious freedom was rescinded and the government of Turkmenistan began its gradual shift toward a more religiously repressive regime. Reports began emerging of renewed persecution of Christian groups in Turkmenistan. Bibles were confiscated; churches with fewer than 500 members were not permitted to register or meet in public (there were no churches that qualified), and groups meeting in homes were harassed and raided. No foreign Christian missionary activity was allowed.

Almers' burden for the new believers in Ashgabat and beyond, however, would not let him rest. He made repeated trips back to Turkmenistan in the following years, taking people and resources from his home church to help support and train the new underground churches that were growing there. And each time he brought back stories of how the good news of Jesus Christ was being passed along to penetrate ever more deeply into this Muslim country and its neighbors. One name that continued to surface was Salome, a young music student at the university who had found her way to the showing of the *Jesus* film on that spring day in 1994.

It was a lazy April Saturday, and the university students in Ashgabat were savoring the temporary freedom of the weekend. Salome and her classmates from the Music Academy sat together in the dormitory, talking about their plans for the evening. Suddenly another friend burst into their small room.

"I just heard about something showing at the cinema downtown. A bunch of people from Latvia have a film about Jesus in Russian. Let's go!"

Salome had encountered the name of Jesus in her musical studies and she knew he appeared in the Qur'an as a prophet, but she was not prepared for what she saw on the screen in front of her that night. This man's words seemed to pierce her soul: "I am the good shepherd; I know my sheep and my sheep know me—just as the Father knows me and I know the Father—and I lay down my life for the sheep." Could Jesus really know her—and give his life for her? For a nominal Muslim, the idea was overwhelming.

When the Latvian pastor stood up after the film was over, he spoke slowly and simply in Russian. Salome's mind raced as he assured the crowded audience that Jesus had died to pay the price for their sins, the sins of each person there that night. And the only thing that was required was to accept the gift in faith and follow him.

Suddenly, the pastor was asking anyone who wanted to follow Jesus to come forward. And Salome knew that she must respond, must find out more about this man who was God.

She was met at the front by one of the foreigners, a burly man from Sweden named Kenneth. "I am a Muslim," she blurted out. "Can I become a Christian?"

"Yes, you can," he said. "Jesus knows you and loves you, and he wants very much for you to follow him."

"Then please help me. I want to belong to him!" she cried.

As he prayed for her, Salome felt as if a fog were lifting from around her. Faces and voices emerged around her in clarity and color and, for the first time in her memory, she felt at peace.

The next day was a Sunday, so she went to the tiny Russian Baptist Church in Ashgabat. She followed along with the Russian words read from the Bible and listened in amazement as the people around her spoke to God simply and in full confidence, as if he heard and understood their praises and requests. And she could not get enough.

Salome quickly read through the Turkmen New Testament she'd been given, reading passages aloud to her roommates as they sat in their room at night. Soon they were studying the Bible together, and their enthusiasm spilled over to other classmates and friends.

Two years later, by the time she had completed her studies, a vibrant—and illegal—church of forty students and other young people at the university had formed around Salome. In the heart of the Music Academy, their services were full of instrumental music and joyful singing.

When the students graduated, they returned to their cities and villages around Turkmenistan and the neighboring Muslim countries and took their dynamic faith and experience in Christian community with them. And new underground churches sprang up wherever they went.

In 1997, Almers attended a missions conference in Uzbekistan and sat across the table from an older man from Turkmenistan. During a break, Almers leaned across the table and asked, "Tell me: how did you become a Christian?"

The man smiled. "Ah, you see, I was the mullah, the Muslim leader, of my village. I had followed the Qur'an for years, but something in me was never satisfied. Then my son went off to study music in Ashgabat, and a classmate of his introduced him to Jesus. He joined a church at the university led by a girl, another music student. And when he came back home to our village, he gave me his New Testament to read. And I finally found the truth I was looking for.

"Now that the former Muslim mullah has become a Christian, the villagers are following my example and becoming Christians. We have a growing church in our village, and I have come here to get more training. God has been very good to us."

A better living example of Acts 1:8 cannot be found.

WANTED:
BRIDGE BUILDERS

I stifled a yawn before dashing from my car to the restaurant's front door through the drizzling darkness of this early Sunday morning. The waitresses had been expecting me, and my coffee was steaming at my usual table before I could struggle out of my dripping raincoat.

"Are we ordering breakfast right away this morning, Chuck, or do you wanna wait a bit?" asked Dee, my favorite waitress.

"I think I'll stick with coffee for awhile, Dee. Thanks."

"No problem, Pastor. You just holler when you're ready."

The friendly efficiency of Lyon's Restaurant had become a Sunday morning tradition for me in my pastoral life. Here in the hours before dawn I could gather myself to pray and reflect, with my sermon notes spread on the table around me, away from the grooves, pitfalls, and distractions of my familiar church office.

And on this morning in late September of 1994 I especially needed that distance, that time set apart. It was the culmination of several weeks of intense prayer by Nancy and me. We had been meeting each Tuesday morning since the middle of summer to spend extended time in prayer about our future, about personal issues and struggles within the church, and what God wanted us to do in response. Just five days earlier, during our Tuesday prayer time, it had seemed that all our prayers began focusing on a single question: "Lord, are you loosening our roots here, or do you want us to dig our heels in deeper, pray longer, and work harder?" We had walked over to the copy of the Lausanne Covenant hanging in the entrance hall of the church with the hundreds of signatures affixed to it. It was hard to believe that it had been six years now since the first of us had signed our names to that document, pledging to obey God in taking the whole gospel to the whole world. We reread each word of the covenant, marveling again at its power to make the trite and the petty disappear. "God, make it real to each member of this congregation," I prayed. And as we continued to pray for our church and our future, Nancy and I began asking a question we had put aside for fifteen years: "Lord, are you calling us to international ministry?"

Now, in my pre-dawn restaurant retreat, I began reviewing my sermon for that morning. I had been preaching a series on Hebrews 11, the great litany of faithful men and women of God: "By faith, Abraham, when called to go to a place he would later receive as his inheritance, obeyed and went, even though he did not know where he was going. . . . By faith, Abraham, when God tested him, offered Isaac as a sacrifice. . . his one and only son. . . . By faith Moses, when he had grown up, refused to be known as the son of Pharoah's daughter. . . . By faith the people passed through Red Sea as on dry land. . . . By faith the walls of Jericho fell, after the people had marched around them for seven days." (NIV)

This morning, more clearly than ever before, the faith of these men and women astounded me. They were weak, needy people, unable to do the things God asked of them, and yet they heard his word and obeyed, trusting God to do what they couldn't do in ways they couldn't do them. As I continued to read through my notes, the phrases I had written to describe faith and obedience seemed to jump out at me: seeking God's will first and counting the cost afterward; saying 'yes' to God even if others don't understand, agree, or come along; shifting fear of circumstances, the future, and the unknown to fear of the Lord, which is the beginning of wisdom. . . .

Suddenly I sat bolt upright. There, in the middle of Lyon's Restaurant, with the muted sounds of coffee cups and the smell of maple syrup in the background, God had spoken to me. Spoken to *me*, a conservative Baptist pastor in the last decade of the twentieth century! I groped for a pen and a blank sheet of paper and began to write, and within twenty minutes I had written a vision statement for a new kind of international Christian organization, one that would focus on exposing, training, and equipping churches and other organizations in North America to minister with their counterparts in Eastern Europe for further outreach, evangelism, and leadership development. The key to really influencing Latvia and beyond would be partnerships, and my calling would be that of the bridge builder between the West and the East. Immediately I understood, without a doubt, that I needed to resign my pastorate and devote myself to this new model that God had given me.

Suffused with a joy that I could hardly contain, I jumped up from my table and raced to the payphone in the entryway. "Nancy, I have something really important to tell you. It's time for me to resign, start a new ministry, and help other churches build bridges to Latvia and beyond. And the Lord's gonna provide! I'm certain of it!"

Nancy, still dripping wet from taking Scotty on his paper route, barely hesitated. "Yes, that's it, honey. That's the answer!"

The joy continued unabated. At first, Nancy and I spoke only to her father (a pastor for thirty years) and mother, and they wholeheartedly embraced the idea, immediately offering to be our first monthly supporters.

Five days later, we got together for dinner with Mike and Stephanie Parker and Erik and Charlotte Hyatt at my favorite Chinese restaurant. As always, the food was delicious and the fellowship great, but it became obvious that they had something to talk with us about.

"Chuck and Nancy," Mike finally said, "we have been feeling more and more strongly that God wants us to work together with you in some kind of international ministry. And we feel that we need to ask you this question: when will you leave your pastorate?"

Our mouths dropped open, and the joy intensified as we recognized God's orchestrating hand. We spent the rest of the evening praying with them about the future.

Further remarkable confirmations in the following days continued to deepen our thankfulness to God for his care. During the month of October, one international ministry leader after another approached me to ask me to cooperate with or lead their ministries in Eastern Europe. Almers sent me a fax from Latvia with the news that he had been asked by the Union of Latvian Baptists to be the secretary of evangelism and missions. He ended with a plea: "Please help me in developing a missions strategy for our nation." And those respected friends whom we asked for advice were overwhelmingly positive and encouraging. One summed it by saying, "We knew this was only a matter of time."

On October 11, I presented our story to the board of the Corvallis First Baptist Church, with the news that I would be resigning as their pastor. They expressed sadness but not surprise. "The Lord has been grooming you for this," said Chuck Henderer. "We are excited for you."

As we began to talk about the details of the transition, Ezra Tice spoke up with a novel suggestion: "This is a ministry that has grown out of our church's own ministry, and we need to continue supporting it. How about keeping Chuck on at full salary for the last four months of his pastorate, but letting him take each of those Sunday mornings to speak in other churches to help raise a base of support for the ministry?" There was a knot in my throat as they overwhelmingly approved this unorthodox arrangement and set the stage for a beautiful transition from full-time pastoral ministry.

While Nancy and I continued to feel completely secure in God's guidance, I did begin to have periodic panic attacks. I would wake up in the middle of the night, drenched in sweat, with a thousand tiny hammers pinging away inside my head. *What am I doing? I have four young children and a house payment, and I'm leaving behind a secure paycheck for . . . for what? What if this fails? What will people think? They'll say it's another of Kelley's knee-jerk dreams, impulsive, ill-considered, and unwise.* But then, as my heartbeat slowed again to normal and my mind settled, another voice would find its way through. *Impulsive, ill-considered, and unwise? So was marching around Jericho. Faith means hearing God's word and acting in obedience.*

During those months that led up to the foundation of Bridge Builders International, I was also forced—yet again—to face a specter that had repeatedly haunted me since my early childhood. During my adolescence, Mr. Nuckles had given me a tool to help cope with my stuttering that had given me a new freedom of expression. But though I had learned to mask it, and many people never knew I suffered from it, I had continued to struggle with my stuttering.

At various times in my life, my stuttering has left me unable to answer the phone, order a hamburger, or even say my own name. When I sought the help of a speech coach, he said I was a hopeless case. I tried the technique of inflicting pain on myself whenever I sensed the onset of a speech block, in order to distract my subconscious mind and thereby free my tongue to speak fluently. It worked, but I soon realized that such behavior was actually a greater bondage in itself. I went to a Christian psychiatrist who flippantly prescribed an anti-depressant that fogged and numbed my mind. For eight months I went though psychotherapy, analyzing the deep feelings of anger I had harbored toward the important people of my past. That helped some, but not much.

Out of desperation I had even asked a fellow pastor to expose and expel the "demon of stuttering" so that I could be effectively used by God in ministry. Yet I still stuttered. During a preaching series on the types of love in I Corinthians 13, I stuttered repeatedly one Sunday morning as I tried to describe "contented" love. "Is it possible," I thundered at God and the congregation, fighting back the tears, "to experience true c-c-c-c-c-contentment when you preach on contentment and can't even say the word?!"

Stuttering in front of my own congregation was embarrassing and painful. Why, then, would I want to take this show on the road, exposing myself to potential humiliation in front of numerous other congregations as I tried to communicate the exciting message of God's work through international partnerships? Raising money made me nervous, and that only made the stuttering worse.

Several years before I had taken a long walk to talk this matter over with God. "Lord," I pleaded, "either take away my desire to preach or take away my stuttering. It's not fair for you to plant a passion within my heart to proclaim your truth and then for you to see to it that I verbally stumble all over my tongue in the process."

I kept walking and praying, hoping to sense some sort of answer. Nothing. More walking and praying. Still nothing. Finally, I declared to God, "Lord, if you want me to preach, I'll preach. And if you want me to stutter, I'll stutter. I don't understand, but if you can use a stammering preacher, here am I, use me. I'm willing to stutter for your glory."

I had gone on preaching. And stuttering. I had been forced to evaluate my own motivation for preaching, to make sure that it was for God's glory and not my own. God had used me as a pastor in spite of it, and now I would need to trust that he would continue to use me and my stuttering in this new endeavor.

The concrete financial strategy for this new ministry remained a crucial question, however. The house payment and the support of my young family were real issues, not just phantoms of insomnia. God's surprising answer to our need was borne out of suffering and sadness, the redemptive outgrowth of the tragedy of Willie Brown's untimely death.

Willie Brown, a member of our church council and the chairman of Christian education, was a brilliant young engineer who worked for a high-tech company in the Willamette Valley. His contribution to the development of the company's signature computer modem had insured a comfortable income for him and his wife Larita and their three young boys, and they loved generously sharing what they'd been given. One night in January of 1990, shortly after the church council had made the final decision to go ahead with the sister church relationship, Willie called me on the phone.

"Chuck, Larita and I want to get audited!" he said.

I thought I must have missed something. "Hi, Willie. You want to get what?"

"We want to get audited," he repeated, enjoying my obvious confusion. "We're excited about what's happening in Latvia, and we want to give so much beyond our normal giving that the

Willie and Larita Brown
Photo courtesy of Larita Brown

IRS is going to audit us! We're planning to give an extra $200 a month just for the sister church partnership fund, so you'll never need to worry about where the money's coming from."

That monthly $200 became the nucleus of my Latvia travel fund for the following three years and the financial foundation for many of the trips of those who accompanied me in those years. Willie and Larita were always faithful, and there was always money in the account when it was needed.

Several years later, in the gentle, low-slanted heat of an Oregon Indian summer in September of 1993, Willie and I played frisbee golf on a meadow near a forest of fir at a men's retreat. He was pale and said he felt tired, but he still plied me with questions about Latvia. A week later, Larita called me at home, her voice strained with worry.

"Chuck, Willie is feeling terrible. He's at the hospital having some tests done. The doctors think it might be something serious."

I immediately picked Larita up and we drove together to the hospital. While we were there with Willie, the doctor told him that he had an aggressive form of leukemia. Ten weeks later, Willie was dead.

During those ten weeks, however, as Willie realized that he was dying, he continued to talk about Latvia in warm terms, and when he died, Larita decided to give a tithe from his life insurance policy for ministry to Latvia. When the $400,000 policy was paid out the following April, Larita invested it. And that fall, after I had announced my resignation and begun the process of raising support for Bridge Builders, I went to talk to Larita about our new organization. While my vision for the work God was showing us had not wavered, I was struggling to stay positive about the amount of money I needed to have raised before Stephanie Parker and I began to work full-time in May.

"The work in Latvia was something Willie believed in so strongly," Larita said, "and I back his desire completely. In Willie's honor, I want to give you $40,000 from his life insurance policy to help support your work. I believe God is going to take this money and reach millions through this ministry."

I was awestruck, completely amazed at something so powerful coming from a death that had saddened us so. But Larita had more surprises in store for me.

"The only possible problem is that I can't withdraw the money without penalty until April of next year," she said.

I marveled at God's timing. When the doors of Bridge Builders were formally opened in May of 1995, Willie and Larita's gift formed the solid backbone of our first year's expenses and provided a seamless transition to our full-time ministry. And in another amazing example of God's faithfulness, two years later Willie's company presented Larita and the children with a check for $80,000 as a posthumous recognition of Willie's contribution to their success.

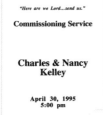

"Here are we Lord...send us."

Commissioning Service

Charles & Nancy Kelley

April 30, 1995
5:00 pm

First Baptist Church
Corvallis, Oregon

What a blessing it was for the church that I loved and served to wholeheartedly support my new direction and the establishment of BBI.

As You Serve The Lord In Missions

"...Stand firm. Let nothing move you. Always give yourselves fully to the work of the Lord, because you know that your labor in the Lord is not in vain."
I CORINTHIANS 15:58 NIV

I preached my last sermon as the senior pastor of First Baptist Church on the morning of April 30, 1995. And that same night, in the same sanctuary, the church held a commissioning service for Nancy and me to launch us into this new ministry. We were able to introduce our secretary, Stephanie Parker, and our new board of directors to the assembled congregation and friends, a strong group of men and women with outstanding skills, experience, and vision. And after the church officially commissioned us as their ambassadors, we were informally blessed by hundreds of our friends and church family as they spoke words of support and encouragement.

The next day, thanks to the financial support of many new ministry partners and by Willie and Larita's gift, Stephanie and I stepped into full-time church partnership ministry. Mike, who was working on a master's degree in intercultural studies at Western Seminary and was planning on joining us when he completed his studies, worked in the interim as a part-time project director.

The first headquarters of Bridge Builders International was a four hundred-square-foot warren of three tiny rooms tucked into a small-business incubator building in Philomath, a small town outside of Corvallis. The miniscule bathroom also served as a library, copy room, and warehouse; we made copies armed with air freshener. The smell of perms wafting over from the beauty parlor next door let us know when it was Thursday. My office, which was just big enough to jam in a desk and a few books but no filing cabinet, was a far cry from the four million-dollar church facility I had moved from. But when the board squeezed into the cramped room to sing the Doxology and commission the space for ministry, we all had a sense that significant things would emerge from these tiny beginnings.

At the end of 1994, while I was still serving my last months as senior pastor of First Baptist Church, Bridge Builders was formally incorporated in the state of Oregon. Two days later we received an unexpected phone call from Ruth York, a Latvian-American living near Seattle who had heard about our ministry. A few weeks earlier Ruth's Uncle Leon had offered to give her his farm in northern Latvia. It was in the final stages of being returned to its ancestral owners after fifty years of Soviet ownership, and Ruth wanted to know if this land might be helpful for further ministry in Latvia.

Both the Parkers and the Kelleys sensed the strong leading from the Lord to start BBI. Our first year was simply amazing!
Photo by Ake Lundberg

Charlie Fischer (far right) and Bob Long (second from right) serving as BBI's first agricultural consultants.

I was excited and perplexed. Having grown up in downtown Los Angeles, I had visited a few farms over the years—usually for lunch—and what I knew about farming could fit on a post-it note. Our new board wisely decided to form a task force of agricultural professionals to evaluate the offer. Charlie Fischer, a retired agriculture professor from our home church, and Bob Long, an executive with a large farm services company, agreed to serve on the committee, and several months later Bob and Charlie were on a plane with me to Latvia. After days of investigating and considering the complexities of farming in northern Latvia, they returned to the United States with their recommendations. Eventually the task force declined Ruth and Leon's generous offer. And we were left to question whether this first official project of our new organization had been a waste of time and money.

Our answer to this question helped to define an attitude that has directed the vision of BBI ever since: we began to ask God to surprise us—he was doing it anyway—and to look for the remarkable outcomes of those surprises. In this particular case, we did not take over the farm, but the people who joined the task force because of it caught the vision of international partnership and have been leaders in it ever since. Bob Long eventually became the chairman of the missions committee at his church and a champion of its church partnership with Golgotha Baptist Church in Riga; he also later became a chairman of the BBI board. Charlie Fischer returned with a deep commitment to promote evangelism and church planting in the most isolated areas of Latvia. He has returned to Latvia several times as a tireless advisor, combining American agricultural resources with church planting efforts in Eastern Europe. And we as a fledgling organization learned to make an organizational priority of reveling in the surprises of God.

During that first year of operation, much of the rest of my time was taken up with the nitty-gritty, sometimes tedious administrative details of starting an organization. Governmental forms needed to be filled out, policies needed to be written, letters of reference collected, and thousands of phone calls made to tell the BBI story. It was a steep learning curve for a former pastor.

Finally, in the fall of 1995, Bridge Builders co-sponsored an international missions conference in Latvia together with the Slavic-Swedish Mission. It had been Almers' dream, really, an outgrowth of the missionary vision he had caught during his year with us in Oregon that had inspired a deep desire to wake up his fellow Latvian Christians to Christ's call to missions. We invited key Latvian pastors and young people and many church leaders from Central Asia. Unfortunately, Russian and Latvian bureaucratic delays allowed only one Central Asian pastor to attend. Still, Latvian attendance was high, and an impressive group of international ministries also participated, along with Russian Baptists and Pentecostals, Jewish believers, and Latvian Baptists. In a revolutionary move for that era of post-Communist backlash, Almers and his Latvian organizers chose Russian as the conference language in an attempt to be as inclusive as possible. It was an exciting week of cooperation and community in a time in Latvia that was more characterized by friction and insularity, and many left with a new understanding of our task as Christians to spread the gospel.

Ironically, only one person had originally discouraged us from pursuing Bridge Builders. My grandfather, an international ministry veteran well acquainted with the rigors of raising money at the end of the twentieth century, had warned me against resigning my pastorate. "Don't give it up, Chuck," he said. "You have four little children. The risk is simply too great." But he himself had lived his entire life in America on the premise that such a risk for God made life worth living, and in the end his example more than his words had become our guide.

One of my first priorities after I started Bridge Builders full time was to travel to Los Angeles to try to communicate the BBI vision to Papa. At ninety years old, Papa was visibly slowing, but he was still actively and single-handedly leading the International Refugee

This was the last photo taken of me with my grandfather. It was taken on his 90th birthday.

Mission with its ministries in six countries. As I spoke with Papa about my hopes and dreams for international partnership, I could sense his growing excitement.

"Chuck," he finally said, his strong voice grown husky with age, "maybe Bridge Builders could merge with IRM, and this work can continue through you." It was an emotional moment for both of us. We had each dreamed of a succession at different times in our lives and ministries, but now, after it had seemed a dream of the past, the idea was revived. Together we drew up a preliminary agreement to merge, which I told him I would present to my board at its next meeting.

The board meeting was a long one. In the initial planning phase for BBI, I had promised myself that I would insist on having a strong board rather than a rubber-stamp committee for my pet plans, and now I began to recognize the value of this constellation. Free from the sentimental attachment I carried for Papa's mission, the board was able to objectively evaluate the costs and benefits of a merger. Finally, the members agreed to assume the assets and liabilities of Papa's life work. Papa's lifetime of frugality had allowed the IRM to save $36,000 for mission work, an amount that would help to finance our second year of operation after Willie and Larita's gift had run out. More importantly, Bridge Builders International became the next generation of the Latvian Faith Mission, the International Refugee Mission, and the life of Charles W. Singer, making us one of the oldest organizations in the Christian world to focus on the Baltic nations.

As soon as the merger had been officially announced, I began meeting with Papa's supporting churches and individuals to acquaint them with our new ministry. This was exciting territory for me as I began to meet the stuff of legend from my childhood.

I met Sam Bradley, a Texas rancher who had introduced Papa to one of his cows, named Vernon after his wife's uncle, and promised the proceeds from the sale of Vernon's offspring to Papa's mission. Each year for twelve years, when "Vernon" had her calf, Sam had sent a hefty check to the IRM.

I met Jake and Vera Diel, a prosperous, Bible-loving west Texas couple whom Papa loved like his own. Papa and Jake were like father and son, and Jake had consistently provided my grandfather with enough personal support to meet all of his needs. For the next couple of years, the Diels invested generously in BBI, just as they had with IRM.

I met Doug Oren, a former Baptist pastor from San Antonio, Texas, with whom Papa had stayed repeatedly during his Texas trips. He and his wife Bev and their six children also treated Papa like their own father and grandfather. Doug had retired early to represent the IRM in south Texas, and now he embraced the new possibilities with Bridge Builders.

I was introduced to two wonderfully faithful churches in west Texas—Frio Baptist Church near Amarillo, and Northside Baptist Church in Odessa. For more than forty years, these churches had supported IRM, and in 1996 they transferred their support to BBI. What a blessing!

Everywhere I went I was welcomed by my grandfather's strong legacy of integrity and determination. And his stories of Latvian life and the suffering of the refugees had lived on for decades in the memories of those who had heard him speak.

In May of 1996, Bridge Builders sponsored its first official "Vision Trip" to Latvia. This was our first larger scale attempt to formally link representatives of North American churches with Latvian churches in sister-church partnerships through up-close and personal, shoulder-to-shoulder ministry encounters. Mike Parker, who had just graduated from Western Seminary, co-led the team with me, and for the first time

A highlight during my son Peter's first trip to Latvia was meeting his Latvian relatives Nellija Zingere, her daughter Vija, and Vija's daughter Nellija. Peter has since returned to Latvia many times.

in my travels to Latvia, one of my children also accompanied me, my oldest son Peter. It was a great joy for me to see him "catch the vision" along with the others, and to be able to pass on this Latvian heritage that my grandparents had given to me.

For sixteen days we traveled through Latvia, matching North American church representatives with congregations in Latvia that had expressed an interest in partnering with an overseas church. The teams were housed by their prospective churches, meeting with the pastoral and lay leaders and teaching and preaching where it was appropriate. Many emerged profoundly changed from the experience.

Bill Zipp, then the pastor of North Albany Baptist Church in Albany, Oregon, wrote: "Choking back tears weeks later, I couldn't erase the images of ministry in Eastern Europe from my mind. Images of perseverance and dedication in the midst of grave economic and political uncertainty. Images of heartfelt contentment—even joy—as families lived on the equivalent of a few dollars a day, yet loved with overwhelming abundance. Images of ministry opportunities and challenges unmatched in North America."

It was an intense whirlwind of activity, of brainstorming and praying together, of preaching and teaching, and we all returned exhausted. But back in our cramped offices in Philomath, we knew that the verdict was still out on the success of the trip. The participants from both countries had seemed exhilarated, but the proof would be in the fruit of these newborn partnerships. And the results were mixed.

Bill Zipp called soon after we had returned. "Chuck, how about a humanitarian aid shipment to Latvia from the new partner churches? The government's Jeremiah Denton Program allows charitable organizations to put humanitarian aid in the bellies of planes going out on training missions. We could fill up a plane bound for Latvia with clothing and medicine for the Latvian Christians!"

Bill's enthusiasm fired this ambitious project of assembling 250 boxes of new and nearly new clothing, blankets, and school supplies valued at $60,000 for our new partner churches and schools. And the North Albany Baptist Church and the Golgotha Baptist Church in Riga continued to exchange expertise, letters, and pastoral and lay trips, working together in children's ministry, youth ministry, and small business development. In Bill's words, "This real-life, hands-on experience with a sister church on the other side of the world has energized our church in a way few things have, missions or otherwise."

Another small church on the Oregon coast, the Reedsport Church of God, sent BBI board member Jerome Kenagy as their representative on the vision trip, along with their youth pastor Matthew Klaus. They found a partner in the Russian Baptist Church of Jelgava, pastored by Dmitri Roshior. On paper, neither church looked remarkable: a small church in a remote coastal town paired with a socially ostracized Russian congregation with an unemployment rate of 80 percent among its membership. But it soon proved to be a powerful partnership, based on deep bonds of love and shared faith. Jerome's study of and lifelong passion for the Russian language bridged the initial gap, and the Russian congregation's commitment to evangelism and church planting formed a common base from which to work together with a shared purpose.

But these were the positive examples of partnership. Others were not so successful. One Washington congregation that we paired with a Russian congregation foundered on the Russian pastor's extremely conservative approach to life and ministry. Another partnership between a Latvian church and a Southern Baptist congregation in the United States fell apart because the American liaison came with a cut-in-stone agenda that didn't allow any voice for the Latvian side. Still another Latvian deacon whose church had indicated a willingness to become a partner church finally told me: "What we really want to know is how much money we're going to get out of this. If it's not enough, we're not interested."

It was a good learning experience for our new organization. We learned to carefully screen people and churches for partnerships, trying to fully inform each side of the responsibilities and expectations involved. We learned that both sides needed to understand that partnership was not primarily—or even secondarily—about financial support or gain. And we began to further hone our vision for partnerships that would mutually strengthen and encourage each party for further outreach and ministry.

Wedged into our cramped cubicles in the small-business incubator, we sometimes joked about ourselves as "the smallest mission organization in the world." But we were also continuing to learn that God's results have very little to do with what things look like on the outside.

Papa surely could have attested to the lessons we were learning from his own long experiences in God's service. But Papa's health was failing as 1996 drew to a close. His final trip to Latvia that summer had sapped most of his remaining strength. We spent Christmas with him in California, and on Christmas Day I accompanied him to the hospital for a ruptured appendix. He declined quickly after that, and finally, on March 4, 1997, at the age of ninety-two, he died.

As I set myself the nearly impossible task of writing the sermon to present at his funeral, a tribute to this man who had influenced my life more than any other, I was overcome by a swarm of competing memories. . . .

Of his insistence on punctuality, like the time he dragged me out of bed before dawn in Paris, chafing at my slowness, in order to arrive at the train platform three and a half hours early for our 11:00 am train. Of his strong hands curled around his worn Bible, hands of a blacksmith that could make anything we needed out of nothing.

Of his strong courage and convictions derived from his suffering during and after World War II. Of his vision that led him to take on new ministry challenges in Mexico and Italy when he was already in his sixties.

Of his endless devotion to his beloved Latvia. For more than forty years he had hosted a prayer meeting in his home for those suffering under the tyranny of Soviet Communism. I am convinced that my own heart and vision for Latvia were born and nourished in those deeply spiritual gatherings.

Of his stories that could hold an audience spellbound for hours and stay in their minds for decades. And of his unwavering faith that had consistently deepened during the seventy-seven years he had followed God.

After the funeral I packed up his belongings in an old trailer and began the slow drive up the coast, back home to Oregon. A week after Papa's death, Bridge Builders moved into an old church parsonage in the middle of Philomath, a lovely little white wooden building that increased our office space threefold. Into my new office we moved his old desk where I had done my homework, an old lamp and a filing cabinet that had stood in his office for years, his cherished library of books, and an old grandfather clock. And we began our third year of existence as "the smallest mission organization in the world" with Papa's tangible blessing surrounding us.

Charles William Singer
1904 – 1997

THE LONG, WINDING ROAD TO HOPE

I first heard the name Luis Palau the day I graduated from Biola University. On that June afternoon in 1977, while several hundred graduating seniors sweltered in the heat of a long commencement ceremony, the university conferred honorary doctoral degrees on a handful of noteworthy pastors, missionaries, and evangelists, including Palau. The university president described Palau's life and ministry in glowing terms, calling the native of Argentina "the Billy Graham of Latin America."

As a student in Texas a year later, I was surprised when Dr. Palau came to speak in our church and then in the seminary chapel. I was fascinated by his speaking style—a fresh blend of enthusiasm, humor, and insight—and impressed by his passion to present the gospel of Christ to as many people as possible in interesting and compelling ways.

Seven years went by before our next encounter. Our family had moved to Salem, Oregon, and I had become the senior pastor of Kingwood Bible Church. During my first week in Salem, an older pastor from one of the largest churches in town called me. "Hi, Chuck," he began. "I'm Don Bubna, pastor of the Christian Missionary Alliance Church."

I was cautious, wondering what he wanted.

Dr. Bubna continued, "I understand that you're brand new to the community and I want to welcome you to Salem. I'm so glad you're here."

After an awkward pause, I stammered, "Well, th-th-thank you, Pastor Bubna. I really appreciate that."

"You can call me Don," he continued. "I would like to take you to breakfast on Saturday morning. Then after breakfast I want to invite you to my office to introduce you to some of the people in my church. Every Saturday morning these folks join me and we pray for our church, the community, and other churches. And this Saturday, Chuck, we want to pray for you and Kingwood."

Don Bubna is one of the finest examples of Christian leadership I have ever met. Under his leadership his church had grown in size and, more importantly, in depth. It was a church characterized by countless small groups where many hundreds of people cared for one another in deeply meaningful ways. He was a highly sought-after speaker, writer, and consultant.

Over scrambled eggs and sausage, Don welcomed me with warmth and affirmation to the community of pastors in Salem. He told me about the spiritual history of Salem and how the unity between the churches was rather shallow; in fact, he described a deep sense of competition between the pastors of the four largest churches. His prayer was that someone from the outside with a compelling vision would be in a position to build the necessary bridges between the rival churches.

I couldn't get my encounter with Don Bubna from my mind, and the next week I told the leaders and staff members at Kingwood what had happened. During that prayer meeting, Gary Bauman, our gifted minister of music, informed me that Luis Palau lived just an hour away in Portland. I wondered aloud, "Do you think if we invited Palau to Salem that the big churches would get involved? Do you think he would actually come to Salem?"

Although I was only twenty-eight years old and in the first week of my first senior pastorate, somehow I wasn't afraid of the question. Deep inside I sensed that I was supposed to do something about it. The next week I set up appointments with the other pastors of the large churches and, to my surprise, I discovered that each of them was willing to move ahead toward a citywide outreach. But each felt that the others would not be willing. I began meeting with various business leaders from my church and the community to see if they would be interested in working together for the greater good of the city. Several agreed.

So I wrote a letter to Palau with spaces for the key pastors and business leaders to sign. It was a happy day when I drove around the city gathering the signatures. Within a few weeks we had put together a leadership team for Salem Festival '85 with Luis Palau. The theme was "Let All of Salem Hear the Voice of God." The chairman of the local leadership team was a car dealer, Dick Withnell; I served as vice-chairman.

Shortly before the festival began, I made my first life-changing visit to Latvia. During my visit I was invited to be the special guest at the choir practice of the Matthews

Baptist Church in Riga. When I accepted the invitation I thought that I was simply going to listen to some wonderful Latvian choral music, so I was surprised when I was welcomed with large bouquets of flowers, asked to speak, and then subjected to a lengthy time of questions and answers.

Those two hours were fascinating. Moderated by the congregation's distinguished choral master, Janis Ezerins, people asked me all sorts of questions about my life, family, and church. When one person asked if I knew Billy Graham, I said, "No, but I do know another evangelist, Luis Palau, who is known as 'the Billy Graham of Latin America.'"

"Tell us about this Luis Palau," asked Mr. Ezerins.

So I did. I described his unique giftedness and vast ministry, and I told them that we were right in the middle of making plans for Salem Festival '85. They were intrigued: they couldn't imagine engaging in public evangelism that featured breakfast meetings with government leaders, radio and television broadcasts, and large group meetings in an arena owned and operated by the military.

My first sermon in Latvia was delivered from the pulpit of Matthews Baptist Church in Riga. It was interpreted by the pastor, Arvids Vasks, my grandfather's cousin.

After a period of silence, the distinguished choral master rose to his feet. "When are these meetings with Luis Palau going to take place?"

I told him.

"We will pray . . . then and now." And then Mr. Ezerins prayed.

I was surprised and touched. Here was a suffering church in Soviet-occupied Latvia that was going to pray for our prosperous church and city! I returned to Oregon a changed man.

Finally, after one year and dozens of seemingly endless planning, prayer, and fund-raising meetings, Salem Festival '85 took place. We expected the normal rain characteristic for November, but we weren't prepared for the snow, the sleet, and the coldest temperatures on record for that time of year. Even so, over the course of

When I served on the leadership team of Salem Festival '85 I had no idea that one day I would organize and preach in numerous saturation evangelism campaigns.
Photo courtesy of the Luis Palau Evangelistic Association

the five-day event, about 15,000 people heard the gospel, with more than 700 making public professions of faith in the Lord Jesus. Several churches in Salem were significantly impacted by this effort.

After the festival I told Luis about the prayer that had been lifted for him in Riga. He was as touched and humbled as I had been by the care and faith of these Latvians he had never met. Who would have thought that fourteen years later we would work together in a free Latvia, proclaiming hope to the nation?

Fast forward to 1998. So much had changed in Latvia since our first Hope outreach in 1991. The country was free of the restrictions of Communism. It had weathered deep economic depression, from which it was only now slowly recovering. Gradually the country was regaining stability and credibility on the international stage as it began to court a seat among the nations of NATO and apply for membership in the European Union.

And the materialism and hedonism of the American and Western European system of values—or non-values—were being adopted wholesale. The resulting spiritual vacuum had spawned any number of religious cults and self-actualization gurus to prey on the religiously unsophisticated.

During the Communist years the churches were forced to turn inward for the sake of survival. Ministry outside the four walls of the church had been fiercely prohibited, including Sunday School, outreach, publishing, radio ministry, religious education, and youth work. Many churches were shut down and active church members were discriminated against. These were the years when the believers grew strong in faith, perseverance, and prayer.

When freedom came, many churches were thrilled with the new opportunities to finally publicly proclaim Christ, and they did so with great enthusiasm, taking part in Western-initiated outreaches like our Hope events. Of course, we weren't the only ones who saw the demise of the Soviet Union as a rare opportunity to preach the gospel. Numerous Christian ministries sprinted to Eastern Europe to do mass evangelism and establish their long-term ministry presence.

After the initial feverish outreach efforts, however, most churches had turned inward again by the mid-to-late '90s, refining their programs, remodeling their buildings that had been ravaged by decades of Soviet occupation, and searching for resources to make it possible. In 1998, Almers conducted a research project which revealed that the rate of church growth among Baptists had been in a state of steady decline for the past four years.

Almers was alarmed, continually urging the churches to look outside at the culture beyond their boundaries. He had taken on a new pastorate in Riga, building up a newly returned church from a few families to a dynamic fellowship. But the missionary vision he had gained from the Lausanne movement, his stay in the United States, and his numerous trips back to visit and support the growing church in Turkmenistan would not let him become complacent. "Chuck, we must have another 'Hope' event," he would tell me each time we spoke. "What would you think if we invited Luis Palau to Latvia?"

I agreed to take the next step of contacting Luis about working together again, this time on a much broader scale. And we began to dream again of engaging the country with the message of Jesus Christ in a fresh way.

We traveled to England to meet with the leaders of the Luis Palau Evangelistic Association about producing a nationwide event in Latvia that we would call Hope '99. We envisioned Luis preaching in Riga while other evangelists (mostly pastors from our sister churches) ministered simultaneously in smaller cities across the country. We outlined a saturation of all levels of society and remote rural areas through the media. We dreamed of inviting government and business leaders to special banquets. And we wanted to have dozens of Christian music groups and bands fanning out across the country to give concerts.

We presented our case enthusiastically, and Luis Palau and his staff eagerly agreed to headline and anchor a crusade if we would provide the organization and the infrastructure.

But a much greater hurdle still loomed before us. We were committed to reaching the entire country. To do so we needed to mobilize the entire Christian community of Latvia. And therein lay the problem. During the Soviet occupation, the Protestant denominations had been officially lumped together, creating an uneasy de facto unity. Since liberation, though, the denominations had rediscovered and redefined their own distinctions, creating walls of difference and distrust in the process.

Even more divisive were the walls between Latvian and Russian speakers within the Christian community. Russians made up nearly half of the Latvian population after liberation, and the deep-rooted antipathy in the society at large among Latvians toward Russian-speakers—and vice-versa—could be felt even in the churches.

We felt strongly that these obstacles within the church had to be overcome before we could effectively work together to spread God's love outside the church. So the Hope '99 executive committee issued an invitation to seventy church leaders from a wide spectrum of denominations and ministries in Latvia to a three-day prayer retreat in a coastal Latvian city. We were uncertain of what the response would be to this unusual invitation, but before long RSVPs began pouring in. Before the response deadline had passed, more than one hundred people had registered for the retreat, representing sixty different churches and ministries. These included Baptists, Lutherans, and Pentecostals — the only three major Protestant denominations in Latvia—and both Russians and Latvians, a significant and potentially volatile mixture in these divisive times.

There was a lot of curiosity about our program as the participants arrived, and there was some alarm when we emphasized that the bulk of our time was going to be spent in prayer with one another—not listening to messages or special music or other content-heavy structure. And to begin with, it was awkward. Most were unaccustomed both to the relative lack of structure and to praying with people from different denominations and ethnic heritages. But as Almers welcomed the participants, he explained why overcoming the awkwardness was worth the effort: "The unity among believers in Latvia is less today than ten years ago, but it's starting again in a different way. If we want revival, we need to have unity. If we want to have unity, we need to pray together, from different denominations and from different national backgrounds."

So we persevered, and gradually we could feel the Holy Spirit directing and inhabiting our prayers. People became more comfortable praying aloud with one another. We sang familiar worship songs together in three languages simultaneously. At the end of the first evening I asked the Russians to select their favorite Russian hymn as our closing song. For about a minute they debated among themselves about what song to select. Then they started to sing, "O Lord, my God, when I in awesome wonder. . . ."

The only Swede in the crowd, my beloved mentor Ingemar Martinson, couldn't resist laughing. After lifting the roof with our multilingual rendition of "How Great Thou Art," Ingemar asked, "Don't you know that's a Swedish song?"

"Can't be," replied one of the Russians. "It is so good it has to be Russian!"

Everyone laughed. That spirit of joy continued as we headed for the swimming pool and saunas where the next several hours were spent playing together.

The next morning, the atmosphere was much freer. We prayed for each other's ministries and families. And after Tim Robnett, Palau's crusade director, gave us an overview of Hope '99, we prayed for the upcoming event and especially for revival in Latvia. As one pastor said, "Barriers have been broken. We are starting to understand each other. There will be less competition between us. Instead of fear, there is love."

On the final evening, however, I realized that one barrier had still not been breached: the wall between Russians and Latvians. I was very nervous, but I felt strongly that it would be wrong to ignore this. So as the session began, I invited all the Russians to sit in the chairs in the center of the room. I then encouraged the Latvians to gather around them, lay hands on them, and pray prayers of blessings for their Russian brothers and sisters.

After a few awkward moments, some of the Latvians approached the center and placed their hands on the heads and shoulders of the Russians. Janis, a young Lutheran priest, quickly found a place in the center of the Russian group where he knelt and lifted his folded hands upward. Dmitri, a Russian pastor sitting in the middle, immediately dropped to his knees and began to weep.

Kristine, a young Latvian woman, moved toward the center and began praying blessings on the Russians, but as she prayed it was evident that she had harbored resentment toward Russians in general for what they had done to her country. As she confessed those feelings, she switched into tearful Russian and cried out, "Lord, when you saved me I asked you to forgive me of my hatred for Russian people. You did, and I am grateful." But then directing her voice toward those in the center she continued, "But my dear brothers and sisters, I have never asked a Russian to forgive me. Will you please forgive me?"

Literally before she could finish her prayer there was a loud response. "We forgive you, we forgive you, sister," exclaimed one Russian after another.

Some Russians asked both God and the Latvians to forgive them for their negative attitudes toward Latvians. They continued to thank God for Latvia and for the Latvian people who were their brothers and sisters in Christ.

Sadly, not all in the room were pleased with what was taking place. Several pastors actually took steps away from the center and hugged the walls. This bold step was simply too much too soon for them. One older brother asked with agitation, "Why should I bless the Russians? I have nothing against them!"

But in the center of the room, the prayers continued from both sides, deeply, fervently, and with many tears. Vladimir, a Ukrainian who pastors a Russian Baptist church in Riga, later said, "I was crying with such tears of joy that I couldn't stop. But I didn't have a handkerchief, so I used my necktie to wipe the tears from my eyes. I will never wash that necktie, for it is stained with holy tears."

The prayer retreat was a strong foundation of holy prayer and tears to build upon as we continued to plan for Hope '99, paving the way for the honorary spiritual chair to be shared equally by the Latvian Lutheran Archbishop, the Baptist Bishop, and the Pentecostal Bishop. And on this framework, for ten days in September, the country of Latvia was saturated with the message of Christianity.

PRAYER DAYS 1999

Prayer knows no denominational or ethnic barrier. Here Pastor Janis Smits, a Baptist Latvian, prays with Pastor Slava Altohov, a Ukrainian Pentecostal.

Agris Ozolinkevics, a Latvian Pentecostal pastor, looks over my shoulder as Fred Wilson, pastor of Calvary Church, Los Gatos, California, and Vladimir Andrijecs, a Ukrainian Baptist, examine the Word of God.

The international nature of Hope '99 was illustrated by Tim Robnett from Portland, Oregon, praying with Indian-born and British-educated Malcolm Firth.

Vladimir prays together with Albert Sisenis, a Latvian pastor who spent more than forty years in Siberia.

It was a marvelous day in February 1999 when Almers and I met with Lutheran Archbischop Janis Vanags, Baptist Bishop Andrejs Sterns, and Pentecostal Bishop Janis Ozolinkevics to go over the joint letter we were writing to President Ulmanis inviting him to take part in Hope '99.

"I'VE NEVER SEEN ANYTHING LIKE IT!"

CHAPTER 1 2

"I've never seen anything like it!" exclaimed Robin Edwards, lead singer of an African-American worship band from the west side of Chicago. "Those kids were racing down to the front to listen. It was electric!"

These were strong words coming from a singer whose choir is used to electrifying crowds with its high-powered, energy-filled style of music, but it was indicative of the stunning effect this music of hope was having on the country of Latvia. Robin had just stepped off the outdoor stage near the center of Riga. Throngs of young people still crowded the platform, clapping, hopping, singing, and swaying with the music.

Robin and her friends from Chicago's Crusader West Church were among twenty musical groups from eight countries that had flooded Latvia for Hope '99. From early in the afternoon until late in the night, the rickety wooden stage in Riga's Central Park vibrated to a smorgasbord of musical styles—folk, praise and worship, country, jazz, black gospel, classic rock, heavy metal, and punk. And in between songs, the musicians shared their testimonies and their hearts, inviting their listeners to hear the gospel and respond to Christ's invitation.

Hope '99 took place simultaneously in thirty-three cities in September of 1999. It was the most comprehensive evangelistic effort in the history of Latvia. Jointly organized by Bridge Builders International, the new Latvian Partners Foundation, and the Luis Palau Evangelistic Association, and supported by the newly formed alliance between the

Latvian Lutherans, Baptists, and Pentecostals, Hope '99 involved 153 Latvian, Russian, and international churches, and organizations from fourteen nations.

Opening night was magnificent. Thirty-three hundred people filled Riga's Sports Arena as *King's Kids* (YWAM), a high-spirited group of children and young people, brightened the stage with brilliant colors and artistic movement. Their energy and enthusiasm helped create an atmosphere of expectation. Special guests of the evening included President Ulmanis, who gave the opening greeting and emphasized his support for the theme of the week, "God is Relevant."

As the television cameras zoomed in on Luis Palau, he spoke on the same theme: "God is relevant. He is relevant for young and old, rich and poor, the powerful and the weak. He has never been more relevant than today. But is he relevant to you?" Palau continued to share God's plan of salvation and then gave an opportunity for people to publicly respond to an invitation.

While former beauty queen Diana Dravniece and the hard-working Hope '99 youth choir sang, several hundred people responded that first night. I remember watching with tears in my eyes as people from all walks of life walked to the front seeking spiritual guidance—students, couples, soldiers, people in wheelchairs, small children, and senior citizens . . . all speaking and praying with our corps of trained counselors.

I wasn't the only one shedding tears that evening. Several on the platform were overwhelmed at what the Lord was doing in the old Soviet-built sports complex. It was simply wonderful.

Photo by Don Ferguson

As the opening events of Hope '99 were being conducted in Riga, outreach services and concerts were being held in many cities throughout the country. While Luis shared the gospel in the nation's capital, others ministered in smaller cities and towns. Two of Palau's associates, Dan Owens and Mike Silva, held major crusades in the cities of Liepaja and Daugavpils. Mike Parker preached in Saldus, and one of our board members, Herb Anderson, ministered in the tiny village of Misa. Pastors from several of BBI's sister churches served alongside their partner churches to blanket all of Latvia.

The music groups also took to the roads, crisscrossing the country to provide appeal, inspiration, and enthusiasm for local Hope '99 efforts in town squares, public schools, restaurants, pubs, clubs, theaters, parks, and churches. It was a monumental feat of organization simply arranging the logistics of schedule, travel, lodging, food, and sound equipment for each group.

The Sons and Daughters of Levi was another wonderful hand-picked choir from Chicago that represented the Salem Baptist Church, an African-American congregation with more than 15,000 members. Their exuberant singing thrilled audiences all over the country. In some places, locals who had never seen black skin close up timidly approached choir members and asked if they could touch them.

Pastor James Meeks, who often preached when his choir sang, described the impact of their ministry through music: "The music broke down barriers and helped soften people's hearts to receive the gospel. By the time Luis came to speak, the field was plowed and the people were ready for that seed to be planted."

Gatis Lidums said later, "Based on informal conversations, I believe about a third of the people who came to Hope '99 events came to hear the music of these energetic and Christ-centered African-American choirs."

My son Peter was the drummer in the only Hope '99 punk band, *The Beldings*. After playing in the town square in the city of Kuldiga, he described the scene: "At first the crowd of about 200 was hanging back. But by the end of the concert when the gospel was presented, they were surrounding the stage. About half of them filled out cards saying they wanted to receive Christ."

HOPE '99
September 12 - 19, 1999

BRIDGE BUILDERS
INTERNATIONAL

RIGA
Luis Palau
• Evening Meetings
• Target Group Events
Presidential Banquet,
Women, Youth & Children
• National TV & Radio
• Multiple Concerts
Gospel Choir, The Beldings,
All Star United, EPPIC,
GEM Sax Fourth Avenue,
• Services for both
Latvians & Russians

Leaders Mini School
Youth Ministry • Sexuality
Business • Christian Education
Evangelism • Gospel & Media
Prayer • Pastoral Ministry
Marriage • Men's Ministry
Technology & Faith • Preaching
Drama/Mime • Women's Ministry

MAZSALACA
Bob Costa
Grace Baptist Church
Salem, OR

SIGULDA
Syd Brestel
First Baptist Church
Bend, OR

TILZA
Marc Andresen
Calvin Presbyterian
Corvallis, OR

SALDUS
Mike Parker
Bridge Builders International
Philomath, OR

MISA
Herb Anderson
Bridge Builders International
Salem, OR

MADONA
Brian Borgman
Grace Community Church
Minden, NV

JELGAVA
David New
Church of God
Reedsport, OR

SKRIVERI/OGRE

LIEPAJA
Dan Owens
Luis Palau Team
Associate Evangelist

DAUGAVPILS
Mike Silva
Luis Palau Team
Associate Evangelist

This map represents just a few of the cities, evangelists, and special events of Hope '99.

Rev. James Meeks, one of the most powerful and popular African-American pastors in the U.S., proclaimed the gospel every time the Sons and Daughters of Levi sang.

Sons and Daughters of Levi singing in Saldus.
Photo by Don Ferguson

The heavy metal band *DISCIPLE* had their work cut out for them, primarily in winning over those who were alarmed at the unconventional sound of their music. But the young men in the band loved the Lord and that was clearly evident as they sang and preached. Pastor Elmars Plavins recalled, "I was surprised to see how young people came to the Lord. When I first heard *DISCIPLE,* I thought, 'What have I done inviting this group to Skriveri?' But when I saw the response, I realized that every method we use to proclaim the gospel is important."

Not all of the music was for the young. One night a soloist from Latvia's national opera sang in the Sports Arena in Riga. In Latvia's second largest city, Daugavpils, a city near the Russian border, a singing family from Belarus performed several times to enthusiastic Russian crowds. The music for the Presidential Banquet was provided by *Sax 4th Avenue,* a multi-national jazz saxophone quartet. Jim Jenkins, the group's leader, reflected: "So much of what happened in Latvia can only be described as the powerful moving of the Holy Spirit over this land. In ten days we participated in presenting the gospel eighteen times to a total of 7,000 people. Our lip muscles got very tired, but our spirits were strong."

Music is one of the most powerful languages in the world, and it is especially important in the musically oriented land of Latvia. One of the most effective ways to connect with Latvians is through music. Maris Dravnieks, the Hope '99 music director agreed: "Our task was to speak in a language people could understand. The music of Hope '99 was deeply Christian and highly professional." And people understood.

The Beldings and DISCIPLE played many times to throngs of young listeners, many of whom expressed deep interest in spiritual matters.

❖

My fifth-floor room in Hotel Latvia served as the nerve center during the week of Hope '99. It was a place of continual planning, decision-making, problem solving . . . and little sleep. But I am convinced that my room was not the most powerful place in the hotel. Twelve floors above me, in room 1701, seven women from Oregon continually followed the promptings of the Lord as they prayed from dawn until dark. These ladies had developed the habit of meeting to pray for Hope '99 on a weekly basis for many months before they came to Latvia; when they arrived on the scene, they simply continued. They prayed deeply and passionately for people, events, places, and problems.

On the second day of Hope '99, when the hotel received an anonymous phone call announcing that a bomb had been planted in the building, the first people I turned to were the praying ladies. Thankfully the bomb scare was a hoax, yet the anxiety that such opposition produces is paralyzing. The best antidote is prayer.

When Riga's hostile print media compared our efforts to that of a circus and then later suggested that this was simply a giant scheme designed to take Latvian money to America, I turned to the ladies in 1701. They prayed and God answered. By the end of the week the attitude of some of the media had changed. The final night of Hope '99 was filmed, broadcast, and rebroadcast by Latvian National Television— free of charge.

Ingemar Martinson joined the ladies from Room 1701 as they traveled from city to city praying for various outreaches: (back row) Karen Smith, Kay Gingerich, Cathryn Passmore, Beth Arends, Barbara Pearson, (front row) Stephanie Parker, Ingemar, and Connie Dougherty.

After Hope '99 was over, we put together a chart we called "The Numbers of Hope" to communicate the scope and breadth of Hope '99 from a numerical perspective:

THE NUMBERS OF HOPE	
50,000	The approximate number of people who heard the gospel presented live at the many Hope '99 events
5,000	The approximate number of people who either raised their hand or came forward to profess their faith in Christ
3,500	The highest number of people who attended a single event
2,189	The number of people who filled out response cards indicating their spiritual decisions
215	The number of services, concerts, school assemblies, and other events where the gospel was presented
180	The number of foreigners who participated
180	The number of 60-second radio messages by Luis Palau that were translated into Russian and Latvian and broadcast nationwide
160	The number of doctors and spouses who attended the special Physicians' Luncheon
160	The number of political and cultural leaders who attended the Presidential Banquet
153	The number of churches and ministries that joined together to carry out Hope '99
150	The number of university students who crammed into a room that accommodates 100 to hear Dr. Palau speak on the subject, "Is God Relevant?"
33	The number of cities, towns, and villages where at least one Hope '99 event took place
29	The number of students who made public professions of faith in Christ at the university outreach
20	The number of special music groups that participated in Hope '99, with styles ranging from choral to folk to jazz to contemporary to rock to opera
17	The number of physicians who made public professions of faith in Christ at the Physicians' Luncheon
15	The number of cultural and political leaders who made spiritual decisions at the Presidential Banquet
14	The number of nations represented in Hope '99
13	The number of consecutive days that the Lord provided perfect weather for all the outside events . . . exactly the number needed
4	The number of new churches planted with a connection to Hope '99
1	The only ONE who should receive the glory!

It's easy for people like me to get excited about big things, large numbers, and historic events. But the most important stories from Hope '99 focus on individuals.

A veteran of the Soviet army came forward after Pastor David New preached to a Russian-speaking crowd in an open air meeting on the streets of Jelgava. "I was in Afghanistan," he said in obvious anguish. "I killed many people and live with great guilt. Can this Jesus forgive me?"

David assured him that he could be forgiven. The man repented and received Christ as his Savior and Lord, right there on the street.

After one of the mini-school sessions on the topic of the family taught by Wally Schoon, an American who lives and works in Sweden, one man said, "I have wasted twenty years of my family life. Now I want to start fresh. I want Jesus to be the center of our family. I want to be the husband and the father that God wants me to be."

Ten high school students from Sisters, Oregon, presented the gospel message in a powerful mime drama in the city of Ogre. Pastor Dennis Kizziar preached, interpreted by BBI board member Dr. Gunars Iesalnieks, and many responded—some with questions, some with tears, and some with hearts ready to give to Jesus. Two local men who had attended church occasionally came forward. Three days later, the ten-year-old son of one of the men followed in his father's footsteps and was born into the family of God.

Pastor Vladimir Andrejets, who organized our Russian-language meetings, beamed after one of the services: "Tonight is an answer to prayer. For many years my wife and I have prayed that our son would come to Christ. And tonight we celebrate because our son and his wife have repented. Hallelujah! God is great!"

Countless other stories of touched hearts and changed lives can be told. I suspect that we will never hear most of them this side of heaven.

Hope '99 was a team effort. I was amazed that so many leaders from so many churches, ministries, and countries heard about the project and offered to help. Greater Europe Mission, whose Latvian director was Forrest Hendrix, was deeply involved. Forrest shared the vision with his network and before we knew it we had talented musicians and mime specialists flying in from France, Germany, Ireland, Canada, and Peru.

Led by Almers Ludviks and Gatis Lidums, the local leadership team brought the best Latvian and Russian leaders together on a regular basis together for the better part of a year with various people taking different areas of responsibility. (See Appendix B for a complete list of the Hope '99 Latvian Leadership Team.)

The Palau organization provided one of their most experienced crusade directors, Dr. Tim Robnett, to guide the process. Tim and I traveled to Latvia many times that year to work together with the local leadership team. There were literally thousands of details to coordinate, but by September 12 our preparations were finished and Hope '99 was officially launched.

Meanwhile, back in our tiny Oregon office, our devoted staff worked tirelessly on another list of endless details. Marsha Hill helped provide strategic planning and support staff management, and she wrote fund appeal letters and emails. Naomi Strauser organized travel and hotel accommodations for countless international participants. Jennie Smith made all of the mass mailings possible through her devotion to the construction and management of the database.

Mike Parker helped coordinate the small city campaigns and prepared diligently to serve as one of the regional evangelists. And Hope '99 represented a turning point in his life. Although he had always had a burning desiring to see people come to Christ, he had never before had an opportunity like the daily Hope '99 meetings in Saldus. It is more than coincidental that Mike now continues to partner with Palau as a full-time evangelist in evangelistic projects all over the world.

Mike's experience of serving as an evangelist in Saldus and meeting Palau prepared an excellent foundation for his own future as an evangelist.

One very large surprise was the cost of the project. We never dreamed that we would have to raise approximately $300,000 for Hope '99, in addition to our own general fund budget. This was further complicated when our most generous supporter decided to no longer support BBI because of our decision to work together with Pentecostals. My wife Nancy learned as much as she could about grant writing, and we submitted proposals to as many charitable foundations as we could. Nancy also edited our newsletter, BRIDGES, which promoted Hope '99 to our ever-growing list of prayer supporters, donors, and contacts. Though Hope '99 was a major financial challenge for us, eventually all of the expenses were met and the bills were paid.

Neither numbers nor words can describe the glorious praise that was offered to God the last morning of Hope '99 in Riga's Dome Cathedral. The austere thirteenth-century brick church, with its soaring whitewashed nave, stained-glass windows, and 6,000-pipe organ, resounded with music of a sort never before heard within its hallowed walls: *The Sons and Daughters of Levi* joined their exuberant voices with a Latvian orchestra and the Hope '99 youth choir for a rendition of Händel's Hallelujah Chorus that threatened to raise the Dome's historic roof, rendering the capacity crowd more than ready to hear the message of hope.

After both James Meeks and Luis Palau preached, the invitation was offered and more people responded than we were able to count, many to give their lives to Christ and many to publicly affirm their faith. And incredibly, among those who stood were President and Mrs. Ulmanis, declaring to their entire country in a powerful and moving step of faith that they had placed their hope in God.

This photo was taken just moments after the final service of Hope '99 was completed in the Dome Cathedral.
Photo by Don Ferguson

Photos by Don Ferguson

Photo by Betty Lu Anderson

Photo by Don Ferguson

Photo by Betty Lu Anderson

A President,
a Colleague, a Friend

W e walked up the snow-lined entrance to the Presidential Palace, nervously adjusting our dark suits, the bishops straightening their clerical collars. Back on that cold February day in 1999, the five of us had been invited to meet with the president of Latvia, His Excellency Guntis Ulmanis, Latvia's first freely elected head of state since pre-Communist times and hugely popular with his people.

Granted, we had initiated the meeting by the letter we sent him introducing our plans for Hope '99, but now, as Almers and I stood with the bishops of the Lutheran, Baptist, and Pentecostal churches in the grandly decorated presidential receiving room waiting for the president's entry, we wondered what his response would be.

We shuffled our feet and waited uneasily as a television cameraman and the president's chief of staff, press secretary, photographer, and official interpreter waited with us to record the event. Then, finally, President Ulmanis came into the room, greeted us cordially, and invited us to join him for coffee.

Over coffee, it became evident that President Ulmanis had studied our letter carefully and had a surprising level of understanding of the Hope '99 plan. He listened with interest as we fleshed out the details for him.

After we'd made our presentation, President Ulmanis asked how he could be more specifically involved. This was far more than we had hoped for, but I gulped and said that we would be honored if he would publicly endorse Hope '99 to the nation, give greetings at the sports arena on the opening night, and host the banquet for government leaders. To our delight, he agreed to each of the requests without hesitation. He then went on to explain his ready acceptance. "Latvia needs more than new laws and policies," he said. "We desperately need a moral foundation."

As we stood to leave, I snapped a photo of the president with Almers and the three bishops. On the snowy walkway outside the palace, we reflected on the events of the past hour. The prayers of the Prayer Summit and decades before had truly paved the way for this momentous encounter.

Suddenly it occurred to me that we had a budget to raise for Hope '99. I lifted my camera. "Okay, gentlemen, I have here historic photos of each of you with the president of Latvia. They're yours for the bargain price of just ten *lats* each!"

Coffee with the president.

From left to right: Pastor Almers Ludviks, Bishop Janis Ozolinkevics, President Ulmanis, Archbishop Janis Vanags, Bishop Andrejs Sterns. A portrait of Latvia's first president, Janis Cakste, presides over the meeting.

Guntis Ulmanis was born on September 13, 1939, in Riga, Latvia, during the last months of his great uncle Karlis' presidency. His birth came just days after the infamous Molotov-Ribbentrop Pact between Nazi Germany and the Soviet Union which set the stage for Germany to invade Poland and the USSR to conquer the Baltic states. A few weeks later, Soviet tanks and troops occupied Latvia. Latvians remember his uncle's presidency—called a "benevolent dictatorship" by many political scientists—with great nostalgia. It was a brief flowering of Latvian independence and freedom that was both preceded and followed by brutal foreign occupation. When Guntis was less than a year old, his uncle was arrested by the Communists and deported to Soviet Turkmenistan where he died in prison and was buried in an unmarked grave. Soon after his uncle's arrest, Guntis' family was deported to Krasnoyarsk in Siberia, where they struggled to eke out a living in their hostile surroundings. When he was seven years old, the family was permitted to return to Latvia. A few short years later the Ulmanis family was deported to Siberia a second time, only returning to Latvia after Stalin died in 1953.

Growing up as an Ulmanis in the Communist era in Latvia was difficult. Soviet propagandists referred with outrage to the "fascist" dictatorship of Ulmanis, and the stigma haunted the family. Still he was allowed to pursue higher education, and in 1963 he graduated from the State University of Latvia with a degree in economics. After his two years of compulsory service in the Soviet army, during which time he joined the Communist Party, he began working as an economist in the building industry and on the Riga Public Transport Board. He was promoted to the position of deputy chairman of the Planning Board of the Riga Municipal Council, but again the stigma of the Ulmanis name caught up to him and he was dismissed after just a few months.

During his studies he had married a fellow student, Aina Stelce, and together they had two children. Eventually he became the manager of the Riga Municipal Communal Services, and a lecturer on construction economics at Riga Polytechnical Institute and on economic planning at the Latvian State University.

Along with most Latvians, Guntis welcomed the independence movement of the late 1980s, and he took the first opportunity to leave his Communist Party affiliation behind him. After Latvia's declaration of independence, he was elected to the board of the central Bank of Latvia and joined his uncle's former party, the Farmers' Union of Latvia. He was elected to the Latvian parliament, the Saeima, in Latvia's first parliamentary elections since independence, and then was elected by the Saeima to become the first president of Latvia since his uncle Karlis held that office in the 1930s.

Dear Chuck Kelley
and BBT
With best wishes
Guntis Ulmanis

02.00

His Excellency Guntis Ulmanis
Photo courtesy of President Guntis Ulmanis

By European standards, the presidency in Latvia is an influential position. As president, Ulmanis now had the authority to nominate the prime minister, ratify international treaties, approve and receive diplomats, initiate laws, and send laws back to the Saeima for review. During the turbulent 1990s, while the popularity of the legislature plummeted among Latvians in general amid reports of scandal, corruption, and inefficiency, President Ulmanis managed to actually gain in popularity; a poll published in the mid-'90s gave him the highest rating of all three Baltic nations' presidents as ranked by their own people, with a 75 percent approval rate. This personal popularity remained constant despite some of his more unpopular decisions related to citizenship for minorities and the Latvian foreign legion.

In 1995, at a highly symbolic ceremony on a former Soviet military base in Skrunda, Ulmanis and the nation rejoiced when the huge anti-NATO Soviet radar detection tower was destroyed, thus completing the full withdrawal of Soviet troops without the shedding of blood. Latvia's final bloodless liberation from occupational forces was to become the most important legacy of the Ulmanis presidency.

In June 1996, Ulmanis was elected for a second term. This term was marked by great advances toward Latvia's membership in both NATO and the European Union. Viewing the death penalty as inhumane and uncivilized, Ulmanis declared a moratorium on the death penalty and called on Latvia to eliminate it altogether.

When we spoke with him in February of 1999, he was nearing the mandatory end of his tenure as president and still riding high on this wave of popularity.

President Ulmanis was faithful to his promise that day, serving as the patron of Hope '99 and using his influence to open doors and smooth the way for the highly successful week. When he and Mrs. Ulmanis stood to publicly affirm their faith in Christ at the final service in the cathedral, it was a monumental step for Latvia as a nation and for them personally, at a pivotal time in his career.

Ulmanis' second term as the first president of post-Soviet independent Latvia ended in the summer of 1999, and he was in the process of evaluating his continuing role in the region and the world. His involvement in Hope '99 and his very public declaration of faith led to a Luis Palau-initiated invitation to the National Prayer Breakfast in

President Ulmanis addressed the nation on national television during the opening night of Hope '99.

Photo by Don Ferguson

Washington, D.C. in February of 2000. He asked Bridge Builders to plan an American goodwill tour for him at the same time.

This was an exciting opportunity to set up meetings with Christian legislators, academics, and business professionals from across the United States, both to raise the visibility of Latvia in their minds and to expose President Ulmanis to evangelical Christians in the public arena, until now an unknown entity in Latvian life. Almers and I traveled with the president, his wife, and his secretary-interpreter Eva as they met with Latvian expatriates in Philadelphia and the president spoke in his first church service in a Latvian Baptist Church. Two days later in Washington, D.C. the president launched into a whirlwind of meetings with congressmen and senators, ambassadors and heads of think tanks.

The meetings were intense and productive, and a realization was emerging that without the heavy burden of protocol attached to an acting president, Ulmanis now actually had more access and open communication to power brokers than he had had while in office.

Before the Prayer Breakfast on February 2, President Clinton invited President Ulmanis and four other acting heads of state to a private meeting. Clinton greeted Ulmanis by his first name, telling the others, "This is the man who negotiated with Boris Yeltsin for the withdrawal of Russian troops from the Baltics." It was deeply moving for Ulmanis when they all prayed together before joining the larger and more formal Prayer Breakfast.

The Prayer Breakfast has its roots in a Methodist ministry from the 1930s, but it gained stature in 1953 when President Dwight Eisenhower hosted the first Presidential Prayer Breakfast. Now called the annual National Prayer Breakfast, it is based on core groups of senators and congressmen who meet weekly for prayer throughout the year, committing to uncommon candor and confidentiality in their dealings with one another. I hope and pray that one day such a tradition will be established in Latvia as well.

For President Ulmanis, the Prayer Breakfast was an entirely new experience, a place where international leaders from vastly different backgrounds came together for the expressed intent of lifting Jesus high. It was thought-provoking and stimulating, and

Ulmanis met with the U.S. Congressman from Illinois, John Shimkus, who co-chairs the Baltic Caucus and has been a strong advocate for the development and security of the Baltic nations. He is the only Lithuanian-American in Congress.

from back-session meetings and brainstorming we emerged with intriguing new ideas on how he could use his influence among other heads of state and high-level leaders from around the Baltic and Nordic region. I am optimistic that God will shape those ideas into future bridges with other leaders in Europe.

Those days were also a remarkable personal experience for me. I accompanied Mr. Ulmanis to his various appointments with senators and congressmen. One afternoon while we were sitting in the back seat of the Latvian embassy Suburban, driving between appointments, I called my mother on my cell phone.

"Hi, Chuckie, where are you today?" Mom inquired.

"Well, you won't believe it. I'm in Washington, D.C. I just finished a meeting with Senator Durbin and we're in the car on our way to see Congressman Kucinic."

"Really? Why are you meeting with them?"

I grinned, put my hand over the phone, and spontaneously asked Mr. Ulmanis to say a few words to my mom. I was delighted to hear him say in Latvian, "Hello, my name is Guntis Ulmanis."

And then, through the tiny speaker on the cell phone, I could hear Mom shriek. Ulmanis smiled and continued to talk with my mother for about five minutes, telling her all about our trip through America and the national leaders we'd met. He even told her some good things about me. When he hung up the phone he commented on how well she spoke Latvian, and he playfully asked when I would be able to speak so fluently.

Mike West presents
Mr. Ulmanis with a
lithographic canvas of
Thomas Kinkade's "Sunrise."
This painting now hangs in
the Ulmanis home in Riga.

Mom was delighted. She had been a little girl when the first President Ulmanis served Latvia. And now she was able to converse with the second one. It was a moment she'll never forget, and neither will I.

The rest of our trip was equally full of events and meetings, both official and informal. There were in-depth meetings in California and Oregon with Christian executives from Intel, Hewlett-Packard, and other industry leaders, where President Ulmanis was introduced to the idea of "Christian businesspeople," long perceived to be an oxymoron in Latvia. At one meeting in the corporate boardroom of Thomas Kinkade's company, Ulmanis was presented with a large canvas lithograph of Kinkade's painting of the cross, "Sunrise." There were meetings on both coasts with clergy, politicians, and faculty of universities and seminaries. We had meetings at the elite Hoover Institution at Stanford with Reagan's secretary of state, George P. Schultz, and George W. Bush's future secretary of state, Condoleezza Rice. There were speeches before Latvian cultural centers in San Francisco, Portland, and Seattle. These meetings were set up with the wonderful assistance of Walt Wilson, Chris Zarins, Uldis Seja, Ruth York, and Roland Strolis.

But all work with no play is exhausting. We made sure to include some fun in the schedule: an NHL hockey game, two NBA basketball games, a pantomime performance by Marcel Marceau at Washington's famous Ford's Theatre, and a tour of the splendid Oregon coast.

And, most meaningful for me, we brought him "home" to the BBI headquarters,

Our luncheon at the Hoover Institution featured a most interesting conversation between President Ulmanis and George Schultz, standing on Ulmanis' left.

After a Portland Trailblazer basketball game we met with Arvydas Sabonis, the 7'5" center from Lithuania. Since hockey is Latvia's national sport, we attended an NHL game in Washington, DC, where we met with the Latvian superstar Arturs Irbe.

our little white house in Oregon's Willamette Valley, and home to our own house to meet Nancy and our children. Before the visit, Nancy was quite nervous. We have a nice and comfortable home, but we don't normally host international VIPs. But Mr. and Mrs. Ulmanis were graciousness itself. He greeted Nancy with a cosmopolitan kiss on the cheek and gave her a lovely amber necklace. We retreated to the family room for coffee and tea while Scotty, our seventeen-year-old budding illusionist, did a few of his simple magic tricks that left us all howling with glee. A few days later, Mr. Ulmanis told me that the highlight of his trip was to visit our home and see the office and staff of Bridge Builders because of the impact it had had on the country of Latvia.

The next day, as Almers and Nancy and I stood with Mr. and Mrs. Ulmanis at an overlook on the spectacular Oregon coast, watching a breathtaking sunset, that nervous February day in the snow outside the Presidential Palace seemed like a lifetime ago. Here standing next to me was a former president, now a friend and brother in Christ, who was eager to continue the rebuilding of his country on the basis of Christian principles.

And he welcomes our partnership.

The meeting with Senator Mark Hatfield was surprisingly warm and deep. The senator shared his spiritual journey with the president.

Drawing on a map of Russia, President Ulmanis traced the final journey of his great uncle President Karlis Ulmanis for Mike Parker and me.

I was very pleased that Mr. Ulmanis spoke at a public forum at my home church in Corvallis. Dr. Gunars Iesalnieks, one of BBI's longest serving board members, interprets.

Photo by Don Ferguson

I enjoyed it when Mr. Ulmanis sat at my desk to sign some papers. For many years that desk was used by my beloved grandfather.

"Pick a card, any card," implored 'Scott the Good.'

I was delighted that the president and his wife could visit us in our Oregon home and meet our kids (from left to right) Phillip, Scotty, Karen, and Peter.

The Birth of the National Movement

W hat's a bridge? Most people imagine a structure that carries a road between two high points. But sea captains also issue their orders from command centers called bridges. The thin piece of wood on a violin that the strings stretch over is a bridge. And when a composer connects two movements, he writes a bridge. Still, the most important aspect of any bridge is what it does. Connects. Supports. Brings together. Spans the gap.

When we first set up Bridge Builders, we pictured ourselves as the classical networking, bridge-building ministry—introducing people, building partnerships, and then getting out of the way. For some partnerships, this is still the way it works. But we had been increasingly realizing the need for more long-term, on-site shepherding of the partnerships that had been established than we could consistently provide from our

These men and women were the first members and legal organizers of BBI's Latvian affiliate, 'Partners Foundation': (left to right) Almers Ludviks, Mike Parker, Gunvaldis Vesmins, Bill Shultz, Edgars Mazis, Forrest Hendrix, Rinta Bruzevica, Signe Kurga, Gatis Lidums, and myself.

headquarters in Oregon. Further, we were convinced that God wanted us to build more, stronger, and more diverse bridges between churches and leaders in Latvia itself so that together they could accomplish what would be impossible for them to do alone.

At the same time, Almers was looking for new frontiers. Having taken an infant church and grown it into a vibrant fellowship, he was eager to move on to new challenges, especially in evangelism and missions. And as we began planning in earnest for Hope '99, our need for an affiliate office in Latvia, staffed with Latvians, became acute. So, after Almers had left his pastorate in early 1999, he became the director of a new ministry, *Fonds Partneri*, or "Partners Foundation," as the Latvian Bridge Builders affiliate would be called.

From a cramped 10' x 13' room with a couple of rickety desks and a sporadically functioning phone system, Almers and his new staff at Partners successfully juggled the myriad details of Hope '99. They were the backbone of the project, with virtually all members of the staff and the ten-member board serving in leadership positions on the Hope '99 executive committee. And central to the new organization and especially to the success of the Hope outreach was a talented young man named Gatis Lidums.

Born in Riga in 1965, Gatis was descended from a long line of intellectuals, broad-minded and highly educated men and women who laid a family foundation of curiosity, mental acumen, and social responsibility that Gatis thrived on. His parents, "runaway" Lutherans who had met at a Baptist church, sent him to the underground Sunday school of the Matthews Baptist Church, where he soaked up the teachings of the Bible. Still, he felt ill at ease with most of the people his age he met in the church; to him they seemed gloomy and otherworldly, unaware of and uninterested in the world outside the church walls. Even before Gatis became a Christian, the picture of Jesus that emerged from his reading of the Bible was a socially active one, challenging the establishment rather than ignoring or bowing to it, and he was determined to follow suit.

While he was working toward his engineer's license in thermodynamics, however, his world caved in: he received notice that he was being drafted into the Soviet army. For Gatis, this seemed like a death sentence. Thousands of young men from the Baltics were being sent to die in Afghanistan during those years, and suddenly Gatis was confronted with his own mortality. He made a cognitive decision that if he was going to face death, he needed some assurance of salvation, and the day before he was sent to serve in the Soviet military, he was baptized. He had previously identified himself with the idea of God, but not with his people; this formal commitment now pushed him over the edge into necessary community with the church. As it turned out, Gatis ended up spending his entire two years of military service not in Afghanistan but in Kaliningrad, serving as the personal secretary to the garrison's second-in-command.

When he resumed his studies as a civilian again, he defined himself as a Christian, but he still hadn't really understood the basic message of the gospel. He hooked up with some "rebel" Christian friends, young people who defied the churchgoing stereotype and were deeply into the underground Christian music scene. They invited him to go with them to a church in Tallinn, Estonia, where Christian rock singer Scott Wesley Brown was performing. Gatis still found the combination of rock music and church unfathomable, and his curiosity impelled him to go.

During a break in the music, Scott Wesley Brown told a story that would change Gatis' life forever: A man had taken his young son with him to his job at the railroad, flipping the switches that changed the tracks as the trains came through the station. As a long passenger train full of people approached the station, the man realized that his son had crawled onto the track that the train had to travel. He was faced with an instantaneous and horrible choice: switch the track and kill his son, or do nothing and leave the hundreds of passengers to their certain death. He made the awful choice to switch the track, crushing his young son beneath the train's tons of steel.

Scott Wesley Brown concluded by saying: "That's exactly what God did for you. You were on the train and his son was on the tracks, and he crushed his son so you

When Gatis and Charlotte were studying in Oregon they visited our home frequently.
Photo by Charlotte Liduma   Photo by Mark Johnston

might live." With a rush of unexpected emotion, Gatis suddenly understood his role in God's world, and the final piece clicked into place for his faith, completing that cognitive decision he had made several years earlier.

Back in Riga, Gatis began freelancing as a journalist as a way of engaging the culture while he completed his studies. In 1989, before he could speak any English, he interviewed me through an interpreter for a Lutheran newspaper called "Sunday Morning." By the time I returned to Latvia for Hope '91, he had graduated, mastered English, and was strongly feeling the call to pursue ministry. In partnership with Greater Europe Mission, we arranged for him and three other promising Latvian students to receive one-year scholarships to the Nordic Bible Institute in Sweden.

Gatis came back eager for more training, and during Hope '92 Dr. Jim Sweeney, academic dean of Western Seminary, offered him a four-year tuition-and-books Presidential Scholarship to Western Seminary in Portland, Oregon. This was a step of faith for Gatis and his new wife Charlotte, for we only had sufficient funds to support them for one semester. However, they decided to follow where they felt God was leading them, and for four years the money was always there, never overflowing but always just enough, even down to a donated air ticket from SAS for Charlotte to accompany Gatis home during Hope '94.

Gatis excelled in the seminary environment, studying pastoral counseling and graduating as a master of divinity with honors. When he returned to Latvia, his theology background, remarkable fluency in English, and keen organizational abilities made him a natural to serve as the administrator for Hope '99. Interestingly, in one of God's beautifully designed full circles, Charlotte had become a Christian during Luis Palau's ministry in Latvia in 1989. Now her husband's vision and energy were giving Luis a platform to reach thousands more.

After the dust of Hope '99 had settled, Rinta Bruzevica, Partners' director of public relations, ended the year by producing a five-week national television series that profiled the work of four outstanding Latvian Christian ministries. Latvia's new President Vike-Freiberga also participated in the project, and it resulted in a surprisingly positive response from Latvian viewers. Through it all, this new organization emerged as a seasoned team, with unprecedented contacts through President Ulmanis to high-ranking government officials, economic leaders, and ambassadors, the power brokers of their country.

Equally or more important for Partners, however, were the bonds forged with other Christian leaders across denominations and cultures during the prayer summit and the preparation and fulfillment of Hope '99. For the first time in the history of Latvia, Russian and Latvian Baptists, Pentecostals, and Lutherans were meeting regularly for prayer and eager to work together to reach their country for Christ.

In the spring of 2000, a local Christian businessman who had attended Hope '99 offered Partners a beautiful, airy 1,300-square-foot office for one-third the going rate for rent. Friends of the ministry supplied furnishings for the office, and in no time the new Partners office had become the hub for cooperative Christian effort in Latvia, a brainstorming and activity center for articulating strategies to impact the nation. American Ambassador to Latvia James Holmes, who had attended one of the major events sponsored by Partners that summer, said that he had seen "no finer example of grassroots partnership and networking."

News of Hope '99 and its success spread quickly through the other Baltic nations, and the leaders of the Estonian Evangelical Alliance came to Latvia in 2000 to look into what Partners was doing. They introduced Almers to the concept of a formal, affiliated alliance of evangelicals, and in the fall of 2000 Almers traveled to Hamburg, Germany, to attend the General Assembly of the European Evangelical Alliance.

The European Evangelical Alliance has existed as a regional group since the 1950s, but it traces its roots to the 1846 conference at which the World Evangelical Alliance was established. It serves as a meeting place, a platform for common action, and as a voice for Europe's evangelicals, uniting the national evangelical alliances of Europe with a large number of pan-European mission agencies.

Almers returned impressed with the possibilities of forming an Evangelical Alliance in Latvia. And apparently the respect was mutual. When Derek Copley, the former general secretary of the European Evangelical Alliance, traveled to Latvia several times the following year to explain what the alliance is all about, he made it clear that what Partners had built through its cooperative efforts and prayer summits already amounted to a very mature Latvian organization that was representative of the very best that Europe had to offer.

In 2002, in partnership with the Alliance for Saturation Church Planting, we organized an opportunity for twelve leading Latvian pastors to travel to Budapest for Hope 21, a conference sponsored by the European Evangelical Alliance and Hope for

Derek Copley visited Latvia several times to help us establish the Latvian Evangelical Alliance.

Europe. This was a tremendously encouraging time for them, not only because of the opportunity to network with Christian leaders from across Europe, but also as a coming-of-age benchmark for them as Latvian evangelicals. For so long Latvia had been an obscure and forgotten country, dominated by a long succession of foreign powers. Now, however, they were receiving confirmation from leaders from all parts of Europe that what they had built in Latvia was of singular value for the entire European community. The leaders spoke approvingly of "the Latvian model" for evangelism, networking, and mobilizing young people for missions.

After an enlightening field trip to Slovakia and Romania to meet with leading Central European church planters, Almers and the pastors returned to Latvia with a reaffirmation of their efforts toward unity and cooperation and a confirmed belief that Latvia should formalize the foundation that had already been laid. And on September 20, 2002, the establishment of the Latvian Evangelical Alliance was proclaimed in a special dedication worship service in the Dome Cathedral of Riga.

The benefit of establishing an organization like the Latvian Evangelical Alliance was that it represented a more permanent glue than Hope '99, a central point that could attract a variety of people and organizations in many different ways. The Alliance's new motto of "Unity, Initiative, and Voice," together with its philosophy of being "as broad as Christ and as narrow as Christ," dispenses with the need for denominational permissions and conflicts and paves the way for cooperation on future evangelistic projects. As a result, many groups that hadn't been formally included in major interdenominational initiatives would now have a home, including the Salvation Army, the Reformed churches, the Methodists, free churches, and others.

The LEA does its work through working groups that each focus on different ministry tracks. Some of the working groups are directly led by Partners staff: Peteris Eisans leads the Mission Mobilization group; Maris Dupurs heads the group that encourages and equips Latvian and Russian pioneers to plant new churches throughout Latvia; Signe Kurge is an integral part of "Proforma," the working group that brings

Christian business professionals together for fellowship, encouragement, and outreach; Almers gives leadership to the informal network of Christian politicians as they endeavor to use their platforms to instill Christian values in society and encourage prayer with and for Christians in the government; Rinta and our office manager Vineta Zale provide administrative and public relations support for all the groups; and our webmaster Andris Sprogis works with Rinta to provide one of the finest Evangelical Alliance websites in all of Europe.

Happily, more and more working groups are led by those who are not directly linked to Partners or supported by our budget. Gunta Irbe, a gifted and godly Lutheran pastor's wife, gives careful and wise leadership to the Prayer Mobilization team which is increasingly responsible for the national pastors' prayer summits, national prayer chains, intercessory prayer training, and regional prayer events.

Raimonds Locs, who went to Turkmenistan with us back in 1993, is Latvia's national director for Prison Fellowship International. He is ideally suited to encourage and equip those dedicated chaplains who serve in prisons, military bases, hospitals, and overseas.

Our youth ministry department provided leadership to the "Protein" youth ministry leadership network for several years. Now the network has matured significantly and the leadership is shared by several key Latvian and American youth specialists.

Despite our organizational and spiritual priority of asking God to surprise us, I continue to be amazed at how Almers' heartfelt desire—"I want to work for BBI!"— has evolved into such a quality national organization of Latvians, led by Latvians for Latvians. It is far bigger than me or my original dream, and now people are being brought into the Latvian Evangelical Alliance to work together for the country of Latvia quite independently of me. It is humbling and very affirming that we are on the right track in doing God's work.

Partners has continued to flourish and expand, both as BBI's Latvian affiliate and as a facilitating organization for the Latvian Evangelical Alliance. Working groups of the LEA are actively planning major evangelistic events that will reach outside Latvia to include the entire Baltic region. Exciting plans are underway for new church plants in rural areas of Latvia. And a dynamic Latvian missionary venture into the Republic of Bashkortostan is changing the lives of both the Latvians who go and the Bashkirs whom they encounter.

❖

From left to right: Derek Copley, Rinta Bruzevica, Guntis Ulmanis, Dainis Smits, Almers Ludviks, and Mike Parker.

Peteris Eisans was selected to be the first General Secretary of the LEA.

Pastor Ainars Bastiks, who is also a Member of Parliament and government minister, is on the LEA Executive Committee.

THE LATVIAN EVANGELICAL ALLIANCE IS BORN

Photos by Talivaldis Talbergs

While Mike (upper left) taught this small group of Tilza students about the unreached people of the former Soviet Union, a vision for Bashkortostan was born.
Photo courtesy of Mike Parker

It was March of 1999 and Mike Parker had spent the last two weeks teaching the history and theology of missions at the Tilza Evangelistic Training Center in eastern Latvia. His students were young people from various regions of Latvia, each of whom had committed to an intensive period of study at the training center followed by a two-year mission of church planting in a rural area of Latvia. They were dedicated students with a clear sense of God's call in their lives and a passion for learning more about him and how to spread his message.

As each class session began, Mike unveiled the needs of a different ethnic group in the former Soviet Union that had not been penetrated by the Christian message. The students then joined him in prayer for the Turkmen, the Kazakhs, the Uzbeks, and others. As Mike taught day after day, the class began to understand a world-changing concept: just as Christianity was originally spread using the roads of the Roman Empire, so it can be propelled today throughout the former Soviet Union using a language common to all adult citizens of the former Soviet republics—Russian.

On the day of Mike's last teaching session, he had reached the end of the list of groups he had actually visited and researched first-hand. He asked God to tell him which of the remaining ethnic groups to present to the class. As he thumbed through one of his resource books, his eyes fell on the page that described the people of Bashkortostan, and he whispered, "Lord, is this who you want me to talk about?" God's answer was a quiet, clear "yes."

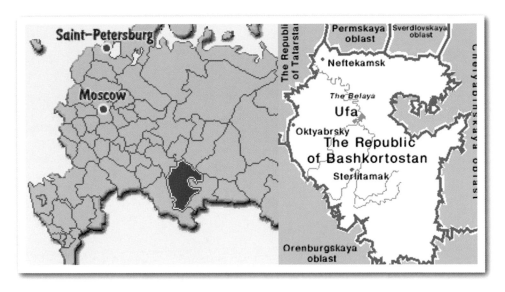

Later in class, the students listened intently as Mike told them about an ethnic group in a republic of the Russian Federation located in the South Ural Mountains, next to Tatarstan and about 800 miles east of Moscow. The Islamic headquarters of Russia, Bashkortostan has a handful of often persecuted Christian churches to reach out to its four and a half million inhabitants, only two books of the Bible in Bashkir, and very little missionary presence. As on previous days, Mike and the students began praying, this time for the people of Bashkortostan. But they didn't know that this prayer session would stand apart from the others as a launch into a powerful missionary vision.

Mike recalls, "As we prayed, I began crying for the Bashkirs. It was like a light bulb turned on. Everything we had been discussing about Central Asia crystallized in my mind."

Of the regions they had studied together, Bashkortostan is the closest to Latvia. Its transportation lines and border control make it the most accessible. Only a three-day train ride from Latvia, it is the most inexpensive location for Latvians to send missionaries. Along with these thoughts came a strong, distinct urging in Mike's heart to take a few pastors from Latvia on an exploratory trip to Bashkortostan.

In May 2001, Mike put together a Bridge Builders trip to Bashkortostan. One of the Latvians who took part in the journey was twenty-eight-year-old Peteris Eisans. The son of a Baptist pastor who had also served as the bishop of the Latvian Baptist Union, Peteris was a member of the first graduating class of the Latvian Baptist Seminary in Riga in 1994. Peteris received hands-on missions training on a trip to Kenya in 1997 during his three-year internship with churches in Minnesota and Alabama. And when he returned to his hometown of Jelgava in 1997, he began serving as a pastor.

However, Peteris has not always been convinced that missions was for him. In fact, the notion of Latvians ministering in Russia made him cringe. Peteris explains, "In 1991, just a couple of months before Latvia broke free from the Soviet Union, I heard a sermon in my church on Acts 1:8 by a visiting Swedish pastor, Ingemar Martinson. He was preaching about how we Latvians have to preach in Jerusalem (the city where we live), Judea (our country and our kind of people), Samaria (people of different ethnic origins or people we dislike), and the whole world. When he said that we need to preach in Samaria, which for us would be to preach and do missions in Russia, I was very upset. I thought he was being very insensitive to our history.

"At the time there was no way that we could know that God would give me a passion for mobilizing Latvian churches to do mission work in the Russian Muslim Republic of Bashkortostan. But time and God changed my mind."

Joining Mike and Peteris were Vladimir Andrijecs, a Ukrainian pastor ministering in Riga; Dan Roth, a Russian-speaking Oregonian from Tilza, Latvia; a student at Tilza, Armands Avotins; and Katrin Bjuhr, the director of the Solåsen Training Center in Sweden. Katrin had made several earlier trips to Bashkortostan, and her contacts paved the way for the delegation to meet with members of the local Baptist and Pentecostal Unions.

The team spent seven days getting to know the church leaders, meeting with three church planters, and traveling through the countryside, becoming familiar with the

Even before joining the Partners team in 2000, Peteris Eisans had been extensively involved in many aspects of our ministry. He brings a unique perspective to the mix, having been raised in the home of one of Latvia's most respected pastors, Bishop Janis Eisans. He and his wife, Baiba, have one daughter, Ruta.

colorful mixture of peoples that makes up the ethnic fabric of Bashkortostan. Of the 112 people groups represented in the republic, 39 percent are Russians, 28 percent are Tatars, and 22 percent are Bashkirs. The predominant lingua franca of Russian made it easy for the Latvian pastors to minister, and they were accepted as fellow insiders because of their common language and status as co-members of the former Soviet Union.

On information that there were still pockets of Latvians living in Bashkortostan, the group arranged to travel to a village that had formerly been settled by Latvians lured to the fertile farmland of Bashkortostan in the 1800s by a program implemented by Catherine the Great. Their guide was a Latvian septuagenarian believer who spoke fluent Latvian though he had been born and raised in Bashkortostan. As he knocked on one farmhouse door, it was opened by a Latvian woman.

"Michael!" called the woman in surprise at seeing Mike standing on her doorstep.

"Katrin?" asked Mike as she ran out to shake his hands. "Katrin?! What are you doing here?"

"Come in, Michael, come in everyone, please," she said, leading them into the small house. "Michael and I met when he preached in my hometown of Saldus for Hope '99," she explained to the others. "I helped organize his talk at the high school where I am a teacher. I never forgot what he said one night during his sermon—that God is relevant not only for those of us who believe, but for our families, our neighbors, our co-workers, and all of the people of all nations of our world. Michael, you challenged us to look at the opportunities God had given us to tell his story in the East. So when I was contacted to ask if I would be interested in teaching Latvian to the grandchildren and

Mike Parker and Dan Roth (far left), Armands Avotins (lower center) and Katrin Bjuhr met with leaders at the main mosque in Ufa, which serves as the headquarters of Islam in Russia and the "seminary" where thousands of "mosque-planters" have been trained and commissioned.
Photos by Peteris Eisans

great grandchildren of former Latvian immigrants in Bashkortostan, I jumped at the chance. And here we are!"

She introduced her teammate Sarmite Fishere, one of a handful of female Latvian Lutheran pastors. Katrin and Sarmite had come to the village for a year to teach the children Latvian using the Latvian Bible and other resources and to help with a fledgling Latvian language congregation. The Bashkir and Tatar children of the village were so eager to learn that they too were coming to the Latvian lessons and learning about Jesus in the process.

Mike and the Latvians were dumbfounded at the bedrock obedience and faith of these women. The team eagerly distributed New Testaments to the local children, and they passed on the offerings that their churches had gathered for church planting in Bashkortostan to local leaders. The team members returned to Latvia convicted and excited about the potential for ministry in Bashkortostan, and eager to communicate this vision to their home churches. Peteris said to Mike: "I see now that we may not confine our work to our own congregation's needs and boundaries. God has given us the opportunity and the obligation to share what he has given us."

For Mike, this trip and his experience of preaching in Saldus during Hope '99 combined to confirm a call he had been hearing from God to go "to the ends of the earth" to preach the gospel. This would eventually lead him to leave Bridge Builders at the end of 2002 and found his own ministry, All Nations Ministries, which is committed to reaching out to the people in the world who have not yet encountered the gospel.

Since that first trip, several groups of pastors and lay ministers have returned to Bashkortostan under Peteris' leadership. As tensions rose in other parts of the world between Americans and Muslims, it became more and more clear that Latvians had a definite advantage in their ability to minister to the Bashkirs. In 2002, a Muslim leader

One of the most important ways to begin to minister to a nation is children's ministry, even in Muslim countries. Because so many Latvians also speak Russian they can be wonderful missionaries.
Photos by Peter Eisans

in the Bashkiri capital of Ufa declared *jihad* against all Americans, and one Bashkiri Christian leader specifically requested: "Don't send us any Americans."

Where Americans have been excluded, however, the Latvians have been faithful. Peteris, who has also served on our Partners staff as the director of church partnerships, has become the major champion of Latvian outreach to the East, so much so that he has even asked the Latvian Evangelical Alliance to shift his focus from that of general secretary to the director of mission mobilization.

In August of 2003, Peteris led a team of Latvians representing four denominations, nine congregations, and six Latvian cities to Bashkortostan to support a recently established ten-member congregation in the city of Beloreck. They conducted an outdoor Vacation Bible School for 130 children, built bridges to the people of the city, and offered events for adults in the evenings. Along the way they encountered harassment from drunken policemen and official threats of imprisonment, but many children indicated an interest in following Jesus, and more than seventy people attended the church service at the end of the week. Since then, more groups from Latvia have followed with an ever-increasing spectrum of ministries and hands-on service projects.

Even more important, the people of Bashkortostan have captured the hearts of those who have gone to minister. And the Latvians have gained a deeper understanding of what

has motivated so many Americans to minister in their homeland. Girts Asnevics, pastor of Vilandes Baptist Church in Riga, wrote this about their 2003 trip: "We cried as we said goodbye. God put them in our hearts. And now we really understand why those from our sister church, First Baptist Church of Richardson, Texas, love us so much."

❖

The bridges continue to grow. When they begin, we don't always know what shape they will take or where they will end. But they all have this in common—they connect, bring together, support, and span the gap. And we know that the true bridge builder is none other than God himself.

Peteris' vision is clear: "Our desire is for Latvians to once again become a missionary-sending nation, and we are seeing the first steps in that direction."
Photo courtesy of Peteris Eisans

HOPE FOR A NEW GENERATION

A Saturday night in May 1999 . . . unable to sleep, I wandered the downtown streets of Old Riga. As I walked, I saw throngs of young people, roaming aimlessly. The largest group was near a church—sitting on a short wall, smoking cheap cigarettes, and drinking beer.

Outside the church, not in it, I thought. *They think all the church can offer them is this wall.* At that moment, my heart was overwhelmed by the desperate need for youth ministry in Latvia.

Later that same year we launched Hope '99 with all its different components—preaching, mini-schools, outreaches to varied segments of society—and music. It was a time of surprise and excitement all across the board. But what particularly amazed me was the reaction to the Christian rock bands. Kids literally ran to the concerts. They stood throughout, singing along. Each night, teenagers by the hundreds responded to the gospel.

After Hope '99, many of these young Christians sought out churches as they'd been encouraged to do, but what they found in most churches was a traditional and rigid structure that had nothing of the cutting-edge vitality they'd responded to during the concerts of Hope. Furthermore, congregations were uneasy with the influx of worldly-looking young people searching for contemporary worship and teaching, and the youth were perplexed at the old-fashioned structures they encountered. This conflict raised difficult but important issues within the Christian community in Latvia: Is it ethical to draw kids in using one set of forms and then attempt to squeeze them into a church with an entirely different set of forms?

It became clear to Almers and me that one of Partners' emphases must be placed on youth ministry, to reach out both to the hundreds of new Christian youth and to those perched on the church wall at night with no idea of what the inside of a church building has to offer. The burning question, however, remained how to begin. The few Christian youth programs that did exist in churches were organized by dedicated volunteers or part-time leaders. To recruit from this group could mean the end of a thriving outreach in a local church. What were our alternatives?

Lienite Bemere was an energetic twenty-two-year-old with short dark hair, a bright smile, and a heart to tell other young people about Jesus. Interested in all things fashionable, she blended seamlessly into the youth culture of the new Latvia. But she had much more on her mind than the latest trends from Milan and Paris—and much more to bring to it.

Lienite had coordinated all of Hope '99's major musical outreaches for youth with spectacular success, and now she had also seen the incredible potential of mobilizing Latvian youth for Christ. So when she came to me after Hope '99 and said, "I want to do youth ministry," we were thrilled to provide her with training and guide her on her way.

Lienite had a bachelor's degree in theology from the Latvian Christian Academy and was working on an MA in cultural management at the Latvian Academy of Culture. She was driven by the potential she saw in appropriating Latvian culture and cultural events to communicate the message of Jesus Christ. She had a widespread network of

Lienite Bemere

contacts in the Academies of Art and Music—composers, musicians, poets, graphic artists, and classical artists—who were searching for ways to express their Christian faith through their art. And as Partners' first coordinator of youth ministry and special events, she drew on them widely to begin providing an answer for the thousands of youth in Riga and its surrounding cities who were searching for one.

Latvians have a long tradition of excellence in and appreciation of the fine arts, and Lienite was uniquely situated to tap into that mine. She mobilized this network of friends to organize the more than two hundred Christian concerts in thirty-three cities for Hope '99, mastering the myriad details of multiple bands, vans, managers, and sound equipment fanning across the country, and in the process exposing thousands of people to the gospel. When the musicians gave testimonies about God's work in their lives, many audience members from all over Latvia made public professions of faith in Christ.

Inspired by the success of the concert program and its resonance among Latvian youth, Lienite committed her energy to developing a cohesive youth program throughout the country. Several facts galvanized her sense of urgency: There were no full-time youth pastors in the nation of Latvia. The number of Latvian youth addicted to drugs was greater at that moment than at any other time in Latvian history. In Riga alone, thousands of youth roamed the streets at night in search of something to do. The average age of the average evangelical church member in Latvia was increasing every year, standing at its highest point in the post-Communist era. Even more disturbing, one study revealed that half of the evangelical churches in the nation had no more than three teenagers. Lienite made her case clearly: the youth of Latvia were in need, and they were not being reached with the message of hope.

To meet this need, Lienite recruited volunteer youth leaders and several young Latvian pastors to join together in the Latvian Youth Network, an organization designed to help encourage and equip Latvian youth leaders for dynamic, modern youth ministry.

One exciting outgrowth of Lienite's vision was the annual New Year's Eve party at Barbins Christian

School that was first held on December 31, 1999. Lienite's network of painters, designers, and photographers descended on the school in preparation for the party, transforming the school with their artwork and creativity. And then the bands came, professional musicians donating their time as well as amateurs eager for a venue, to play for a marathon ten hours into the new year. More than three hundred young people came from all over Latvia to be part of the scene, and they went home inspired by the fellowship and Christian excellence they had found.

The Latvian Youth Network soon turned its sights to practical training for youth workers around the country, organizing two training seminars each year so that volunteer Latvian youth leaders could meet successful American and European youth ministers and expert guest speakers from leading youth organizations. At these "Protein Training Conferences" they were exposed to sessions on basic ministry principles, discipleship, the spiritual life of the youth worker, working with youth in a post-modern culture, youth ministry in churches with old-fashioned pastors, and integrating youth into the local church.

They chose the term "Protein" because of its connotation of health and nourishment. Also, since so many Latvian young people speak English, the sound of the word reinforces the need to be "pro-teen."

For several years these semi-annual training sessions were reinforced by a weekly radio program produced by the Youth Network team with music and call-in sessions to provide spiritual nourishment for the young people of Latvia.

The training conferences also represented another way for some American sister churches to bring their expertise to bear in Latvia. Several successful youth pastors from churches in Washington, California, Oregon, and Texas have been guest speakers at the Protein conferences.

The Protein events have become highlights of the year, both for the Youth Network team and for the hundreds of youth who attend each time. Because youth ministry is seen as something to do until a "real" job or ministry comes along, many of the leaders who attend are youth themselves. But as they interact with leaders from around the world, singing with hundreds of other kids enthused about following Jesus, studying principles of spiritual leadership, worship, and youth work, sleeping on floors and hanging out

BBI and Partners
have organized
several nationwide
"Protein" conferences
that provide
fellowship, training,
and heartfelt worship
for young youth
workers.

together, they catch a vision for what they can build in their hometowns and churches. And they become bolder in sharing their faith and bringing in their friends to share in the excitement.

I look forward to each of the Protein conferences, to preparing talks for these eager young people and rubbing shoulders with them between programs. For me, this represents an interesting and very fulfilling circle in my life of ministry. I left full-time youth ministry at the age of twenty-eight because I felt I was having more and more difficulty relating to youth. But now, two decades later, I am thriving in ministry to youth as never before.

One reason for this is the bridge our own four energetic children have built to draw us into their world.

❖

In 1997, our oldest son Peter's passion was drumming with his band, *The W's*. We had converted our garage into a semi-sound-proof practice studio, and when they weren't playing in local pizza parlors, he and his music buddies would jam in the garage for hours on end, producing a unique combination of jazz, swing, and ska.

Finally, in the fall of 1997, their big break came, opening for *Five Iron Frenzy* at their album release party. They made a big splash, quickly selling out their supply of homemade demo tapes, and eventually they were signed by a record label. The night before they were to begin recording their first CD in San Francisco, Peter was goofing off on his skateboard in our driveway with some friends. When Nancy pulled out of the driveway in our family car and accelerated down the street and around the corner, she had no idea that Peter was holding on to the back of the Suburban. The resulting spill he took left him with a broken arm and a premature end to his career as a recording artist.

The W's went on to cut their CD the next day with a borrowed drummer. Their debut album, "Fourth from the Last," reached #4 on Billboard's Heatseekers chart and became the highest-selling debut in the history of EMI Christian Music Group. Within a year, *The W's*—and their now-permanent replacement drummer—would be opening for *dc Talk's* sixty-five-city tour, playing before crowds of more than 400,000, and earning two Dove Awards.

Though Peter's arm had healed well, he was still on the outside looking in at *The W's* success, eighteen years old and wondering what God wanted him to do with his life.

At the same time, the pastor of the church next door to our BBI office invited Peter to work with the small handful of youth in his church. Though it was a new idea for Pete, he plunged into the challenge. With a start-up core group of four kids, he began reaching out to the youth of the community, drawing on his musical background to organize deep worship and using his own experiences and Bible knowledge to provide in-depth and relevant teaching. His younger brothers and sister were ignited by the excitement of "the HUB" and began bringing their friends, and soon the group had grown to more than a hundred.

In 2003, the HUB developed a youth ministry–to–youth ministry partnership with Matthews Baptist Church in Riga. HUB teams have traveled to Latvia to help minister with music, children's work, a sports outreach, orphanages, and a summer camp, but mostly to spend time singing, praying, and playing with the Latvian youth.

As for Peter's musical aspirations, in 1999 I invited Peter and his new band, *The Beldings*, to come to Latvia where they played before packed houses at Hope '99. The

Latvian kids screamed for more and bought up all the recordings they had brought with them. Later, in April of 2002, Peter stood before a Protein Youth Conference in Riga to tell his story, couched in his topic of "Starting a Youth Ministry from Zero." And after his session, he was again surrounded by Latvian youth who told him how listening to the music and the testimony of *The Beldings* three years before had changed their lives.

This was powerful confirmation for both Peter and me of God's guiding hand, to see how he brilliantly orchestrates life-changing impact. God is continually building bridges, and how he uses us in the future is always related to how he used us in the past.

Peter, translated by Kristine Namavire, who also served as our youth ministry administrator, told his story to more than 200 eager young youth leaders.

During the summer of 2004, the Protein Youth Network took a giant step forward in the process of equipping young people and church youth groups to impact

their world. Motivated by the Protein conference teaching of Sam Williams and Eric Swanson, consultants with CitiReach International and Leadership Network, on the importance of blessing and impacting cities through service, more than one hundred Latvian young people, with a handful of eager Americans, invested ten days in ministries of public service and outreach in Riga. The idea, according to Sam, was to "change the conversation between the church and the city."

A year earlier Sam and Eric had invited three key Latvians, including Almers, to England to observe more than 5,000 youth from the whole of Europe serving the city of Manchester for the week, culminating with a weekend evangelistic festival with Luis Palau. The young people completed more than 300 practical service projects, resulting in numerous long-lasting benefits for the city. In fact, the media, community leaders, and police reported that six months later there was a 40 percent reduction in crime and a 60 percent increase in property value where many of the projects took place. When the gospel was proclaimed in the park after the projects were finished, locals attended by the tens of thousands.

The Latvians returned home enthusiastic about the Manchester model, and we decided that the best group of people to carry out the "city reaching" model of ministry in Latvia would be the Protein Youth Network.

Kristaps Talbergs, our youth ministry director in 2004, was equally enthusiastic about this challenge, so he eagerly recruited an exceptionally bright and capable colleague, Liena Krumina, to help him lead and manage the project. Together they built bridges to the Riga city council and other community leaders, offering them the labor of more than one hundred young people wherever it would have the greatest impact on community livability.

Sam Williams, left, and Eric Swanson have influenced us to add the dimension of community service to our bridge-building strategy.

They called the project "teRiga," which means "Here in Riga." Nothing like this had ever happened before in Riga so the city officials were not sure how to respond, but eventually nine service projects were identified. Kristaps and Liene traveled to churches around Latvia inviting and challenging the students to come and serve the city. Brochures were designed and ads were run over Latvian Christian Radio announcing the opportunity.

Kristaps said, "The goal of the project is to motivate Christian young people to demonstrate their faith in a practical way, serving the city by cleaning it up externally and lifting it up spiritually, and then to provide evening events that will help people become aware of the role that God could play in their lives."

Young leaders (from left to right) Jeremy, Liena, and Kristaps worked with all their hearts on the myriad complexities of teRiga.

Meanwhile, back in the U.S., our office, spearheaded by our ministry intern, Jeremy Andresen, recruited Americans to also take part. I was thrilled to learn that several people from my home church in Corvallis had decided to participate and that the church had given this effort its strongest endorsement and support.

So for ten muggy days in July 2004, more than one hundred young people lived in a local elementary school in Riga, sleeping on the floors, eating cafeteria food, and showering in the gym facilities. Each morning began with worship, followed by a message from the Scriptures. My long-time friend and colleague Jeff Harris, the director of Campus Ambassadors at Oregon State University, was the Bible teacher in the mornings and a work horse in the afternoons.

The city gave the teams free public transportation passes to get to the work sites. At the end of each workday, the students returned to the school, got cleaned up and had dinner and free time until 9:00 pm, and then came together again for a time of more worship and sharing.

One particularly challenging work site was a marketplace that had burned down two years before. Since the end of the Soviet occupation, the city council had done a nice job of making sure that the city was clean. But this horrible half-acre site was an exception, situated on a major thoroughfare and abutted against several Soviet block house complexes. It was littered with tons of trash—broken roof tiles, shards of glass, burned fiberboard and plywood—and overgrown with weeds.

As people walked by the cleanup site, many stopped to stare at the hard-working youth. The kids interacted joyfully with passersby, and when asked why they were cleaning the city, they answered that it was their way of showing Christ's love to the people of Riga. One pastor who stopped by the site said, "What these young people are doing to share the love of Jesus with the city is tremendous. Next year there will be even

before   after

Photos by Eric Swanson

more people." After spending a whole day filling twelve giant construction dumpsters with debris, the group sang a worship song and prayed.

On the last day of teRiga, the youth assembled at the Ethnographic Museum outside of Riga for a work project, followed by a picnic and a special ceremony where city council officials expressed their thanks on national television for the work that was done. As Eric Swanson said: "The Christian youth of Latvia were letting their light shine in a way that got the attention of the city."

That evening, teRiga featured a full concert on the steps of City Hall, right across the square from the House of the Blackheads, where at that very hour Thomas Kinkade was exhibiting his five new paintings of Latvia at a BBI-sponsored VIP reception. Kristaps and his band and several other bands played and shared testimonies for several hundred enthusiastic youth and passersby.

Nearly every day there were stories and pictures of teRiga in the newspapers of Latvia. An article in Latvia's largest newspaper, *Diena*, was entitled, "Christian Youth Declare Their Faith Through Their Good Works." The headline story on the front page of the *Rigas Balss* was "Christians in the Dirt," followed with a huge picture and impressive story. The largest television station in Latvia filmed the various project sites and broadcast a special half-hour documentary on

Kristaps was one of several musicians who sang at teRiga outreach concerts.

teRiga. As young person after young person was interviewed, each had the opportunity to share the message of Christ's love with the people of Latvia.

Again, Eric Swanson summed it all up: "The good news came over the bridge of good deeds to the city."

Reaching out to youth continues to be a core value of Partners and Bridge Builders. We hope that what we pour into the Latvian youth and their leaders will translate into a large contingent of Latvian youth on fire for God and out sharing his good news, building bridges and potentially transforming a nation in the process.

Living Partnerships: Church to Church

Bridge builders are partner makers. The backbone of our vision has always been to create, strengthen, and mobilize international partnerships. My original dream was to be used by God to build a thousand living bridges, each with its own distinctiveness, emphasis, and potential. Today our bridges connect schools, publishing houses, social ministries, and businesses, but church partnerships remain the nucleus of what we do. And through them, remarkable ministry takes place.

The Philharmonic Hall was filled to capacity for an unprecedented second time that hot July week in the 800-year-old city of Riga. Local musicians were stunned: even at the height of their concert season in this music-crazed city of Riga, the hall is seldom more than one-third full. But on the stage again before a sell-out crowd were musicians from the First Baptist Church of Richardson, Texas, accompanied by members of the Latvian orchestra *Crescendo*. The result of their combined efforts was a superb blend of skill and hearts, woven together by the international language of music.

The ninety-voice choir from the mega-church in Richardson, under the direction of Don Blackley, had prepared for months to present the story of Christ through "Savior," a powerful new oratorio in its European premier tour. But the choir members had also been working hard all week on ministry projects with Vilandes Baptist, their sister church since 1997. Women who had been teaching lessons and playing games with

Vacation Bible School children just a few hours earlier now stood on the sweltering stage in their black dresses and red capes. Men who had been covered with sweat and sawdust from the construction project at their sister church were now pressed and polished in their tuxedo attire. The percussionist who had positioned a young boy's fingers on a baseball bat at sports camp that afternoon, now carefully laid out his mallets, brushes, and cymbals. Those who had taught English classes would soon be singing two songs in Latvian, much to the delight and surprise of their audience.

Other members of the choir had been singing all day at various locations around the city. Small ensembles had sung for hours at the train station, the Dome Cathedral Square, and outside McDonald's, handing out thousands of invitations for the evening concerts. Some in the audience had received a flyer while munching on a Latvian Big Mac, some had participated in seminars designed for women, deacons, music directors, and pastors, and still others had heard about the concert after attending one of the business forums held by business executives from the Richardson church. And now the hall was full of a clear cross-section of Riga society.

Those who had come were not disappointed. From the first note, the audience could tell that the musical quality was of the highest caliber. The program provided a powerful musical story of the life, death, and resurrection of Christ followed by a clear presentation of the gospel by Dr. Brian Harbour, pastor of Richardson First Baptist Church. And conversations following the concert made it clear that audience members understood the connection between the story told on stage and the practical outreach that the choir had performed throughout the week.

The soloists from Richardson with their traditional Latvian bouquets: (from left to right) Greg Luttrell, James Westbrooks, Kelle Henson, Scott Cameron, Denise May, Brent Ballweg, and Gerald Ware.

At the end of the concert the Texans gave bandanas to members of the audience. Surprisingly, the Latvian man on the right was already wearing a cowboy hat and shirt when he greeted Bill and Dotty Morrison.

From early morning until late night Tommy managed every detail, adjusting the team's plan to meet countless unexpected needs and opportunities.

During that single hot week in July of 2000, a group of 139 Christians from the heart of Texas used their musical, ministry, manual, and professional skills to enthusiastically bring the message of Christ to the hearts of many in Latvia.

Coordinated by Tommy Weathersbee, a senior executive with Texas Utilities and one of the warmest, friendliest, and hardest-working people I know, Dallas-Riga 2000 was our most ambitious cross-cultural exchange to date. They say that everything that comes out of Texas has to be big, and as this project began to emerge from the drawing boards down south, its scope and complexity had American and Latvian staff members alarmed. We worked with the Richardson group for more than a year to provide strategic consultation, cross-cultural training, and logistical support. When it came time to carry out the project, Tommy and his hard-working team worked hand-in-hand with our staff and managed it all with skillful assurance. It was a huge success, both for the folks from Dallas and for those they ministered to in Riga.

In the years that followed, this partnership has continued to grow. Large teams returned to Riga in 2002 and 2004 to offer programs for youth, a children's VBS, construction projects, English language instruction, and business development consulting. A construction team led by Dave Harless returned to build a playground for their sister church with materials donated from hardware stores in Dallas. These men were touched by how a simple playground was able to reach out to an entire neighborhood, and they decided to make this an annual event, moving out to other churches as ambassadors of their sister church to build playgrounds and revitalize neighborhoods, sending ripples of love from Dallas into Riga and beyond.

Little did Dave Harless realize when he built this playground that it would begin an ongoing playground construction program embraced by other American and Latvian churches.

For BBI itself, the Richardson church has been much more than a

Pastor Harbour's love for children was evident at the Bible School held at Barbins School.

congregation with an effective Latvian partnership. Tommy and his friends have tirelessly and generously begun a partnership with our entire ministry. They have organized annual BBI banquets in Dallas, resulting in many members of their congregation who now support BBI on a regular basis. Three men from Dallas—Tommy, Roger Dalton, and Clark Red—fly to Oregon twice a year to serve on our board of directors. And they are spreading the news about Latvia and BBI to other churches and folks across the heart of Texas.

Dmitri Roshior was born in the Soviet Socialist Republic of Moldavia to Bulgarian parents, learned Russian in school, and went to Latvia in 1971 at the age of twenty-two to work in the forests after a devastating storm uprooted thousands of trees. His father gave him permission to go to Latvia for three months; now, more than thirty years later, he is still here "temporarily."

When asked how he defines himself, he pauses, then replies, "Russian!" Dmitri is a Bulgarian Moldovan living in Latvia, but in Latvia his Russian language defines his identity—at least officially.

When questioned, Dmitri will speak of the heartache it has meant to be a "Russian" in independent Latvia. Though Russian-speakers make up 40 percent of the population of Latvia, there has been much anger and blame toward them for the years of brutal occupation. Dmitri understands the reasons for the hostility, but he feels that it is slowly ebbing as the old hurts heal and the new Latvia finds its identity.

And far more important for Dmitri than his Russian-ness is his true identity: "Maybe it is good that we are not true Latvians," he says. "We understand what it means to be aliens and strangers in a strange land. We understand what it means to long for heaven."

Dmitri is the pastor of a 170-member Russian Baptist Church in Jelgava, about thirty miles south of Riga. His journey to Christian faith began in his small village in Moldavia, on the heels of World War II. When he was fourteen his father sent him to a neighbor's house to borrow a famous mouse-catching cat, and there he saw his first Bible. It was illustrated with pictures painted by a famous artist, and Dmitri was enthralled; he stayed for hours studying this amazing book, and the cat—and mice—were forgotten.

The neighbors were known in the village as evangelical Christians. Soviet propaganda taught that they sacrificed children to their gruesome god, but Dmitri was surprised at the tender way the husband spoke to his wife and the love that was a part of their family. He asked if he could study the Bible with their children, and for two years he visited the informal gatherings of the local Christians.

In 1965 Dmitri finished school and began for the first time to think seriously about his future. He was a good student and wanted to go on to college, but he knew that if he were a believer he would not be allowed to enroll. The former Soviet Premier Nikita Khrushchev had boasted often of his plan to show the last surviving Christian on television, and it was a time of extreme persecution for Christians. The village mayor, a decorated hero of the Soviet Union and one of Dmitri's relatives, reproached his father with the shame that Dmitri would bring upon the family if he became a believer.

Dmitri struggled with God for two weeks, and finally, on May 1, the international socialist holiday, he decided against Christianity. Why should he throw his life away? Why should he join those who were suffering? He wanted to be normal! To his old friends' surprise, he agreed to join them in the village at the big demonstration commemorating the holiday. But halfway up the steps to the Communist Cultural Palace, he was overcome by a powerful foreboding. He suddenly knew without a doubt that if he climbed one more step, if he continued in this way he had chosen, something terrible would happen to him. He turned around, ran back down, and has followed God with no turning back for the past forty years.

Along the way he met his wife, Tamara, with whom he has three children. He was arrested on his first trip outside the Soviet Union as he tried to return from Poland in 1979 with suitcases full of more than 150 Bibles and Christian books. He was interrogated by the KGB, the literature was confiscated and destroyed, and he was told that he would never again be allowed to leave the borders of the USSR.

John Carty (left) and I first met Dmitri in 1990 while he was ministering in a Soviet women's prison in Riga. Now he and Pastor David New have formed deep bonds of pastoral ministry. Photo by Jerome Kenagy

He was disappointed, but his undiminished love for God's word prompted him to later become the chaplain of Latvian Christian Mission, the first interdenominational mission in the Soviet Union, in 1988. With the feeling that this window of opportunity opened by *perestroika* might be only temporary, he worked feverishly with Gideons International to channel Bibles throughout the vast territory of the USSR. He visited schools and hospitals in every part of Latvia, telling the gospel story and handing out Bibles to students, teachers, patients, and doctors. And amazingly, people were hungry for news of God from these Christians who had once been ostracized and feared.

In 1990 Dmitri reluctantly accepted a position as interim pastor of the Russian Baptist Church in Jelgava. He did not think he was properly suited to be a pastor—he feels he is more gifted in helping people with more tangible needs—but more than a decade later he is still the "interim" pastor, and well loved by the church members. With his practical gifts this humble man has led his largely unemployed congregations to acts of great sacrifice and service to the community around them, planting churches, supporting orphanages, and spreading the love of Christ through their own selfless love.

In February 1999 Dmitri attended the first prayer summit hosted by Bridge Builders in preparation for Hope '99. During the retreat he took part in groundbreaking prayer and reconciliation between Russians and Latvians, asking forgiveness from one another and from God for the barriers that had stood between them. Dmitri wept as he told of how they had blessed one another and prayed for each other: "We were formally in the Baptist Union together, but we were not united. Now BBI has made a bridge between Russians and Latvians, and we are united again in Christ."

The sister church relationship between the Jelgava Russian Baptist Church and the Church of God in Reedsport, Oregon, has been fruitful and important for both the congregations and their pastors. There have been numerous visits by members of the Reedsport congregation to the church in Jelgava, and Reedsport's former pastor David New has stayed in the Roshior home many times. Dmitri has especially appreciated the solid theological teaching that David's doctorate in theology and long experience as a pastor have enabled him to offer to the congregation in Jelgava. And the two pastors have formed a deep friendship. As David says, "Dmitri Roshior exemplifies the true Christlikeness of the servant's heart. In this, he has been my teacher. Both of our ministries have been enriched through our association as sister-church pastors."

The bond goes so deep, in fact, that after his retirement in 2003, David moved to Latvia for the academic year to become an instructor at the Riga Bible Institute, teaching classes in theology, pastoral counseling, and biblical exposition. A veteran of international ministry, David says, "No people have touched my hearts like these Russian and Latvian sisters and brothers."

In April of 2000 Dmitri approached the American Embassy in Riga with documents requesting visas for his entire family to go to the United States for the wedding of his older son, Viktor, and a visit with their sister church in Oregon. Knowing full well the U.S. government's reluctance to issue visas to entire families, the words of the KGB agent echoed in his ears as he handed over his papers: "You will never leave the country again!" When the papers were handed back, each of the family members had received visas, four of them for ten years with unlimited entries!

"We are such timid children," Dmitri says. "We ask God for so little, but he wants to give us so much!"

My own home church, the First Baptist Church in Corvallis, Oregon, holds the distinction of being the founding church of our sister church partnership movement. Predating even the birth of Bridge Builders, this first partnership was the outgrowth of my first encounter with Almers and the stories I told my church of the needs in Latvia.

Carole Wille's love for children, and their love for her, is remarkable.
Photo provided by Carole Wille

Shortly after the foundation of the partnership between our church and Agenskalns Baptist Church in Riga, the church brought Almers and his family to Corvallis for a year of fellowship and seminary education. This cemented the relationship that continued for many years between our churches, including repeated trips in both directions and many ministry outgrowths.

Over the many years of partnership, one woman became synonymous with the continuity and enthusiasm that formed the glue of this relationship: our longtime friend, Carole Wille. Carole was a teacher in the public schools, in Sunday school, and with Child Evangelism Fellowship. Our kids had attended her Good News Clubs for years. She and her husband Jerry had traveled with the church youth to Mexico, but Carole had some reservations about going to Latvia.

Carole's first response when asked to help teach a class in Latvia in 1994 was adamant: "No . . . I could never do that." Significantly, however, it wasn't her final response.

A few weeks later, Viesturs Kalnins, a Latvian pastor visiting the United States, spoke at our church. "The greatest need in Latvia today," Pastor Kalnins said, "is for people to train our teachers. We have all of these children coming to our church, but we really don't know how to reach them. No one has ever trained our teachers."

Those simple words touched Carole's heart. "The verse that kept coming to mind was 'To whom much is given, much shall be required,'" Carole recalls. "God had given me so much—a degree in education, years of experience with child evangelism, and a deep love for children. He now wanted me to use it."

A definite "no" became a tentative "yes," and soon Carole was off to Eastern Europe. She teamed up with veteran missionary Karen Neuman from Western Seminary, and together they taught one of the most popular courses presented by visitors from the West—Creative Bible Teaching.

"We wanted our class to be very, very practical, not just theory," Carole says. "We took all kinds of materials with us—flannelgraphs, pictures, colored paper, and other visuals. Students took these materials home at night and prepared a lesson for the next day. Their creativity and diligence was amazing."

After teaching their first Creative Bible Teaching class to over fifty students, word got out. A leading Latvian pastor asked the pair to present their material at the Baptist Seminary in Riga.

Again Carole was skeptical. "I thought, 'Yeah, right. Me teach in a seminary? I could never do that.'" But she did, the next year. And did again, two years later—returning to Latvia for her third ministry trip.

Over the years, Carole's obedient spirit was the fuel for

The "Latvia Committee" held the vision of the church partnership high to the church for thirteen years. (from left to right) Clayton Wenger, Carole Wille, Pastor Bill Knopp, Doris Andrews, Bob Sweany, and Kay Gingerich (not pictured: Shirley Henderer and Mike Parker).

the entire group of incredibly faithful people who made up the Corvallis First Baptist Church's Latvia Committee. They raised money repeatedly to send humanitarian aid to the churches in Latvia. They brought the pastors of Agenskalns Baptist Church to Corvallis for conferences, training, and friendship-building. They went to Riga themselves—Carole alone went five times—to lead Vacation Bible Schools, coordinate evangelistic events, work on construction projects, do youth ministry, and serve wherever they were needed. And they prayed faithfully.

I watched with sadness then when after thirteen years both churches finally decided to end their formal partnership relationship. It was time for a new focus, and new avenues of ministry were opening up for both congregations. Still, I have been incredibly encouraged by the continuing faithfulness of the Corvallis First Baptist congregation. Individuals from this congregation still make up a significant percentage of Bridge Builders' financial support base. They still pray diligently. And members of the congregation—like Carole—are always ready to serve in any of our ongoing Bridge Builders programs in Latvia.

In fact, in 2004 the church decided again to make ministry in Latvia a priority, sending more than a dozen men, women, and young people to minister side-by-side with Latvians in the youth service project teRiga and a unique art camp at Barbins Christian School involving the well-known painter Thomas Kinkade and his family.

Photo taken by Karen Kelley

2001
VACATION
BIBLE SCHOOL
AT AGENSKALNS
CHURCH

I was delighted that my daughter, Karen (upper right), was part of this ministry team.

As Carole says, "Everyone has something to give. Just share the love of Jesus through the skills he has given you, and you'll be surprised at how much he can use you."

Christmas Valley, Oregon, is high desert country far east of the Cascade Mountains, a remote and vast expanse of sagebrush and dry flat land. The ranchers and farmers who live there are tied to their cattle and this inhospitable land by years of hard work and sacrifice. Once a month they drive the hour and a half to the nearest grocery stores to stock up on food and supplies. The small Christmas Valley Community Church of less than a hundred members is an important social and spiritual hub for these isolated desert dwellers, but one would hardly expect it to be aware of the world outside its own dusty boundaries. That assumption, however, would be a grave mistake.

Several years ago, their young pastor preached a series of sermons on missions, challenging the small church repeatedly with this statement: "You have a responsibility as a church to be a part of world missions." They agreed with him, certainly, and they did budget monthly amounts to help support several missionaries, but what more could they do from Christmas Valley?

Still, their pastor was unrelenting: "You as a church have a responsibility to be a part of world missions." The words reverberated in their hearts. Finally, they became inescapable, and these ranchers and farmers took decisive action.

Now, every fall in Christmas Valley the church holds a community-wide auction. Members of the church donate items to be sold—a few cows, a ton or two of hay, farm implements, or their own considerable elbow grease and expertise. Each of the donations is auctioned off to the highest bidder in town. In an average year, the auction raises more than $25,000 for the exclusive use of world missions.

In 1996, a church member donated a section of land to the church. Together the congregation shares the responsibilities of working the field from seed to market, a missions field for the mission field. This cooperative effort yields $45,000 annually for world missions.

The auction, the field, and contributions from Christmas Valley Community Church's general fund have resulted in an annual missions budget of $90,000, an amount of money that rivals the budgets of congregations five times their size.

The ranchers from Christmas Valley were ideally suited for renovating the Baptist church in Tilza.
Photos by Mike Parker

But the giving doesn't stop there. In 2000, twenty-five Christmas Valley members went on short-term ministry trips to destinations as diverse as Latvia, Mexico, and the Russian Far East. These trips have been as short as a few weeks and as long as a few years.

Through Bridge Builders International, the Christmas Valley congregation organized, financed, and built the new student housing, parsonage, chapel, and education center at the Tilza Evangelistic Training Center in eastern Latvia. As the first construction teams we sent into Latvia, they pioneered our building team ministry by braving the foreign building styles and expectations they encountered in Latvia. With a chainsaw as their primary tool, these practical farmers and ranchers were the ideal builders for the developing world, able to creatively make anything out of anything to get the job done, and in the process opening up the possibilities of missions construction all over the country.

Dan and Katie Roth and their little ones, Jonathan and Anna.
Photo by Aigars Jecis

Dan Roth, a Christmas Valley rancher who spent several years planting churches in the Russian Far East, has become a tireless worker in Latvia. His Russian-language fluency and cultural sensitivity have allowed him to participate in scouting trips into other Russian-speaking regions and oversee loan programs for Christian cottage entrepreneurs. He and his British wife Katie have started a vibrant youth ministry in Tilza and are involved with a myriad of ministry outreaches in the country, and in 2004 we invited them to become part of our staff team.

Dan sums up the Christmas Valley commitment like this: "It's not how large or how wealthy the congregation is, it's just how prepared they are to do what they hear God telling them to do."

Space and time do not permit me to highlight all of our living partnership examples. I am thoroughly surprised at the way the Lord has called and used churches from Oregon, California, Texas, and Georgia to connect and minister with churches from the four corners of Latvia. (See Appendix D for a full list of BBI-facilitated partnerships.)

Over the years, we have seen many congregations establish church-to-church partnerships involving thousands of people on the front lines of international ministry. Many partnerships have been successful, deeply loving, long-term relationships; some have been for a season; others have floundered; and a few have failed. But we have learned one amazing thing that inhabits them all: God is the ultimate partner. He always does what he says he is going to do. And astonishingly, he has chosen to partner with his children to reach out to a needy world. This ultimate partnership imbues all others with passion and purpose, and makes the partnerships as multi-faceted as God himself.

Friendship forged through shared ministry is apparent between these folks from the Sisters Community Church in Sisters, Oregon, and the Baptist Church in Ogre, Latvia.

Bulletin boards like this one at Calvin Presbyterian Church in Corvallis, Oregon, keep the partnerships visible to their congregations.

Tara Eichinger from Calvary Church in Los Gatos, California, joined with other congregation members in ministering to children with their sister church, Riga's Salvation Temple.

This mime team from Foothills Community Church in Santa Rosa, California, powerfully communicated the gospel to Russian speakers in Daugavpils, Latvia's second largest city.

This pastor-to-pastor relationship grew closer when Bill Zipp of North Albany Baptist Church in Albany, Oregon, hosted Pastor Andrejs Sterns of Riga's Golgotha Baptist Church at the Oregon coast.

Barbara Spottswood, a watercolorist from Richardson Baptist Church in Richardson, Texas, presents one of her original paintings to their new sister church, then pastored by Almers Ludviks.

MORE PARTNERSHIP EXAMPLES

Lake Tapps Community Church in Sumner, Washington, invited their sister church pastor, his wife, and a deacon to take part in their world missions conference.

The beginnings of a very fruitful friendship between the First Baptist Church in Houston, Texas, and Jelgava Baptist Church in Jelgava, Latvia: (left to right) Jerry Ford, Jerry Ivy, and Doug Oren (second from right) meet Pastor Peteris Eisans (center) and his father Janis Eisans.

Photo provided by Jerry Ford

223

CREATIVE EXPRESSIONS: SIDE BY SIDE

God's creativity has no limits. We continue to be amazed at the variety and breadth of individual ministry expressions that have blessed many in Latvia and the U.S. This is one of the most exciting aspects of "bridge building." When we link churches with churches, we can predict that they will be engaged in children's and youth ministry, construction, humanitarian aid, and outreach. What we can't predict is what happens when people from these churches—and people in Latvia—bring their unique sets of gifts, talents, and interests to the mix.

"I am the good shepherd; I know my sheep and my sheep know me . . . and I lay down my life for the sheep."
John 10:14,15 (NIV)

Charlie Fischer, a stocky white-haired man with jolly eyes and a colorful story for every occasion, is professor emeritus of agricultural sciences at Oregon State University. He first visited Latvia in 1995 as part of a BBI agricultural scouting team deciding whether to take on ownership of a farm in Latvia. While he was there, he was impressed by the hospitality and determination of the rural Latvians he met. But he also saw them struggling to keep their families fed and clothed with their limited resources and opportunities.

The sudden withdrawal of the Communists had made conditions in the countryside difficult, returning the land from the collective farms to individual farmers without capital, farm equipment, or training for the new generation of farm families. Productive soil lay barren and overgrown with brush and weeds while the average farm family tried to make ends meet on a monthly salary that was less than half what their urban counterparts earned. Latvian-born missionary Kristine Peterson, who lives and ministers in rural Latvia, told Charlie, "Most families have one cow and a small garden. Parents can't afford to provide protein. The farm children in Latvia are surviving on milk and potatoes."

Charlie Fischer is a colorful man with the heart of a shepherd.
Photo courtesy of Charlie Fischer

Although he was already in his mid-seventies, Charlie realized that God had given him good health and a background that uniquely equipped him to help the people of rural Latvia with agricultural development. So he began praying, researching, assembling a team of specialists, and developing a plan.

Charlie formed a group of agricultural specialists, and soon a plan emerged for a project called "Hope for Farm Families." It involved sheep . . . lots of sheep . . . to provide meat and a sustainable livelihood for Latvian farmers. The team of specialists included Dr. Genovefa Norvele, a Latvian graduate of Moscow University who had worked for twenty-five years as a sheep researcher on a collective farm in eastern Latvia.

In 1999, however, Charlie's plan was suddenly interrupted by open-heart surgery. The doctor told him later that as Charlie lay on the operating table, the team of surgeons saw his last heart artery close. "If you had been anywhere other than on that table at that moment," the doctor said, "you would now be dead."

It was a clarifying experience for Charlie. But instead of slowing him down, it renewed his vision and drive. God had dramatically saved his life for a purpose, and he saw that purpose clearly in his Latvian agricultural work.

In August of 2000, Charlie and the rest of the team brought Dr. Norvele to the United States to expose her to sheep production technology and farm management in a free-market economy. In December, Dr. Norvele and veterinarian and sheep breeder Dr. Fred Frederiks went to Poland and Germany to shop for high-quality breeding stock to import to Latvia. On a return trip to eastern Latvia in the fall of 2001, Dr. Frederiks confirmed Charlie's earlier analysis: "The thing that struck me most was how little of the tillable land was being used for raising crops or livestock. There's definitely a lot of potential for livestock production."

Now, after years of preparation and research, "Hope for Farm Families" has become reality. Recently a young pastor and his wife trained at the Tilza

Dr. Norvele (left) has provided care for hundreds of sheep in the Hope for Farm Families program. Steve Hauser (right), from my church in Corvallis, has served on the team for several years. Other team members include Fred Frederiks, Dan Roth, Bill Riddell, James Nichols, and Marsha Hill.
Photo courtesy of Steve Hauser

Evangelical Training Center received the first flock of ten Latvian Blackface ewes and two rams. Their forty acres of gently sloping pasture land is ideally suited for the small flock, and they should be able to handle several times that number in the future. And another flock of prize Romney breeding sheep donated by Dr. Frederiks arrived at another farm in Latvia in early 2002. Now the new sheep farmer Talis Kopels is being overrun by lambs, and others are standing in line to set up their own sheep farms. Dr. Norvele is giving sheep-breeding seminars to as many as will come, and Talis will soon pass on a starter flock to another farmer.

Charlie is thrilled to see his hopes converging with the hopes of his friends in Latvia. Nothing can compare to his satisfaction at seeing Latvian farmers who are trained and able to provide for the needs of their families. And in the process, they can readily be told about a Good Shepherd who gave his life for his sheep.

He was a true hippie of the 1970s, a long-haired Christian rebel with perfect pitch in the gray tuneless years of the Soviet Brezhnev era. A piano tuner and brilliant musician, Talis Talbergs traveled from his home in Latvia throughout the Soviet Union, giving illegal "underground" concerts of cutting-edge contemporary Christian music.

Out of necessity he became adept at repairing and improving the second-rate sound equipment they were forced to use, creatively rewiring and reconfiguring to produce optimal sound and quality.

When we went to Latvia in 1989, Talis and his wife Ingrida provided the music at our first open-air evangelism in the park in Riga, and he was a natural as the chief sound technician for the citywide Hope '91. Later that same year, as Black Berets threatened violence and Soviet troops mustered ominously during the Latvians' demonstrations for freedom, Talis set up his equipment on the makeshift barricades of buses and trucks and tractors at the national television center in Riga, fearlessly proclaiming God's message of hope in a musical medium that the uneasy throngs of demonstrators could understand and claim as their own. Toward the end of one evening, with the terrible noise of Soviet tanks in the background, Talis said to the crowd, "Tonight we can either bend our knees before the Soviet army or before the Lord God. It is our choice. For me, I will kneel before God." At that moment, to Talis' amazement, multitudes of Latvians fell to their knees in a spirit of humility and prayer before God.

In 1992, when the Communists pulled out of Latvia, Talis learned that the Latvian government was selling the newly vacant FM radio frequencies for next to nothing. With his characteristic gift for recognizing opportunities for ministry, praying for guidance, and then fearlessly forging ahead, Talis pooled his money and purchased an FM frequency for the city of Riga, valid for broadcasting twenty-four hours a day, seven days a week. With the financial help of Ilgvars Vermelis, a Latvian-American friend from Oklahoma, and his church, Talis began the daunting task of building Latvia's first-ever Christian radio station with $700 in start-up funds.

He rented the sixth floor of the Latvian Baptist Union building, an unfinished attic carpeted in dust and mouse droppings. Slowly, room by room, the dilapidated space was converted into a working radio station for the fledgling Latvian Christian Radio—a broadcast studio, a technical/sound studio, a restroom, an office, a meeting room. Talis assembled a small

Talis Talbergs is a man of faith, vision, and steadfastness.

team of dedicated men and women to join him, and they worked tirelessly to create all of the programming, borrowing from their personal music collections and recruiting area pastors for daily broadcast devotions. On Sunday evenings Talis invited families of prison inmates to broadcast messages of encouragement to their family members in prison.

Latvian Christian Radio survived financially in those early years through the help of foreign donations and Talis' ingenuity and willingness to barter advertising for services. When a seafood cannery wanted advertising time, Talis collected their payment of canned fish in a truck and sold fish for awhile. To furnish his radio station, he made similar arrangements with furniture stores, electronics suppliers, and wallpaper and paint merchants. And slowly the listenership grew.

Meanwhile, half a world away, the CEO of a widespread group of Christian radio stations was listening to a call from God to downsize and refocus. After attending a Family Life Marriage conference, Bruce Erickson and his wife decided to buy one of his family-owned radio stations in Montana outright and move up to the edge of Glacier

Bruce and Ann Erickson

Park to be able to devote more time to their family and ministry.

And God soon provided the opportunities for ministry. At the National Association of Broadcasters convention that year, his friend Jerome Kenagy, a BBI board member, asked him if he had any interest in missionary radio. "Of course," Bruce replied. After all, he had relatives involved in missions work and he'd spent time overseas in short-term missions himself. "I know of a radio station in Riga, Latvia, that could use some expertise," said Jerome. "Here are some phone numbers to call for more information."

Bruce pocketed the phone numbers, but he couldn't seem to forget Jerome's question: Do you have an interest in missionary radio? An interest, yes, he had that, but did his passion and pocketbook really prove it? That was not so lightly answered.

Eventually, after much prayer, soul-searching, and phone calls with Talis' friend Ilgvars in Oklahoma, Bruce purchased a round-trip plane ticket to Riga. He thought of it as a Joshua and Caleb trip, to "spy out" the land and see what God had in mind. But a week before his departure date, he was hospitalized with severe chest pains. His doctor strongly advised him to stay for further tests, but Bruce felt compelled to go. "I have to go," he told his friend and doctor. "I can't do any more tests. If I die over there, I'll die. But I'm absolutely sure God wants me to go to Latvia." I Corinthians 9:16 (NASB) seemed to sum it up for Bruce: "If I preach the gospel I have nothing to boast of for I am under compulsion." It was this compulsion that propelled Bruce forward.

In Riga, Talis was initially skeptical. With his characteristic bluntness, unusual for a Latvian of his age, he looked across his desk at Bruce and asked, "Why are you here?" Bruce understood the implication: Do you have something to sell? Some ulterior motive? What's the real reason behind your presence here? "I'm here to help," Bruce said simply.

And so began a partnership that has influenced both men and their ministries. Talis opened up his business and his books completely, and Bruce rolled up his shirtsleeves and went to work. During that first visit Bruce was able to advise Talis on developing a philosophy and approach to musical programming. This was an extremely important step in the evolution of the radio ministry which permanently changed how the radio station would select and broadcast music.

Bruce returned repeatedly, bringing along his wife or son or a collection of friends and colleagues who had specialties to share and could help to carry and set up the various pieces of equipment they donated. Each time, Bruce claims that he—and those who accompanied him—learned far more than they imparted from Talis' natural entrepreneurship and his clear focus on what God has called him to do.

Talis' broadcast ministry has grown to cover more than 70 percent of Latvia with repeated and translated signals. And his programming has grown to fill his market with a solid Christian message, including translated sermons from overseas and international programming.

Since that first Joshua and Caleb trip, Bruce has sold his last radio station and is devoting himself to other consulting partnerships around the world. He continues a long-distance relationship with Talis, but now he travels to many developing areas to share his expertise with Christians involved in broadcasting. As the opportunities for ministry have multiplied, he has modified the now-famous prayer of Jabez—"enlarge my territory"—to the prayer of Psalm 119:32 (NASB): "I shall run the way of your commandments, for you will enlarge my heart." And God is answering his prayer for an enlarged heart to see and respond to a world in need.

❖

Although Latvian Christian Radio has grown in scope, quality, and stability, a significant need remains: roughly 95 percent of the Christian music played over the airways is in the English language. This isn't because of any shortage of Latvian musicians and original music. Latvia has a highly developed musical heritage, and some of Europe's finest musicians and composers are Latvians. What has been lacking, however, is a place where Latvian musicians can record their original music in a ministry-oriented environment. Talis recognized this need many years ago, and he set aside two good-sized rooms at the radio station for a future recording studio. He faithfully used occasional special gifts to begin constructing the studio, but he knew that apart from fresh interest and assistance from donors and experts from abroad, the recording studio dream would have to remain on hold.

Enter another piano tuner and musician, Joe Tom McDonald, who accompanied the Richardson church ministry team to Riga in the summer of 2002. Several young Latvian musicians spent every afternoon with the soft-spoken Joe Tom studying both the

Nehemiah Project team members: (top row) Talis Talbergs, Tommy Weathersbee, Joe Tom McDonald, JR Torres; (bottom row) Joycelyn Torres, Valdis Indrisonoks; (not pictured) Kim Akers, Bill Lee, Marilyn Hanson, and Shelly Pierce. Brian Lindsay, the recording studio specialist, is inset.

biblical and technical aspects of the heart and art of leading people in worship. One of these musicians was Talis' son Kristaps, a uniquely talented worship leader at Matthews Church. When Kristaps spoke about the need for a place for Latvian artists to record their own music in their own language, Joe Tom's heart was touched in an unusually deep way.

He returned to Richardson as a man on a mission. Wherever he went he told people about the burning burden in his heart to help Talis and his friends build a Christian recording studio. Before long he had put together a colorful assemblage of musicians, bankers, and marketers from Texas. The team named this endeavor "The Nehemiah Project" in reference to the way God blessed the building efforts of the Old Testament leader. The mission of The Nehemiah Project team covers everything from technical and business consultation to fund development.

When I told my Oregon staff about this project, my bookkeeper and daughter-in-law Crystal seemed to catch fire: her brother, Brian Lindsay, was a recording studio design specialist in between jobs. Soon Joe Tom, Brian, and another musician, J.R. Torres, were in Riga working with Talis and his partners on a master plan. Brian has returned to Riga for extended periods of time, living at the radio station and devoting his full time to studio design construction. As this book goes to press, Brian is still in Riga and the team back in Texas continues to serve as behind-the-scene champions. Even now, the airwaves of Latvian Christian Radio are increasingly filled with psalms, hymns, and spiritual songs written, performed, and recorded by Latvian musicians in Latvian and for Latvians.

On that rainy Sunday morning in September of 1994 when I made the decision to step out in faith and start BBI, I wrote out a list of high-quality ministries that I wanted to introduce to Latvia. Near the top of the list was a publishing house with a stellar reputation for quality, both in content and production.

In 1998, Sisters Community Church in the beautiful town of Sisters, Oregon, established a partnership with Trinity Baptist Church in Ogre, Latvia. As it turns out, quite a few people from the renowned Christian publishing house Multnomah Publishers attend that church: owner Don Jacobson is an elder; Don's daughter took part in the team sent by his church for Hope '99; and during the summer of 2001, Jeri Weber, the wife of Multnomah's vice president Eric, worked with children and young people in Ogre.

During the 2001 ministry trip, Jeri asked me about Christian book publishing in Latvia. I told her that there was a significant need to establish a new interdenominational publishing house. I also told her about the relatively new Christian magazine *Tiksanas* ("Meeting") that was produced by Latvian Christian Radio. At the time it had a monthly distribution of more than 4,000, a very good circulation considering Latvia's tiny evangelical population. More importantly, the magazine reflected Talis' strong commitment to quality in content and style.

I love it when people think creatively and strategically about how they can use their talents, positions, and connections to really make a positive difference in international ministry. Jeri returned home and recruited her husband to approach Don with a proposal for Multnomah Publishers to help start a publishing house in Latvia. The timing couldn't have been better: the year before, God had blessed Multnomah's international bestseller *The Prayer of Jabez* by Bruce Wilkinson beyond anyone's wildest dreams. It had already sold some nine million copies. Don and his team decided to invest a portion of the profits from the book in the Lord's work around the world.

Publishing specialist Peter Cunliffe (right) has provided invaluable mentoring to Talis and his daughter, Simona, who directs Atklasme, twice a year since 2001.

When the agreement between Multnomah, BBI, and Latvian Christian Radio to start the new publishing house was written, we bathed it in prayer.

Their faithfulness has now financed a Christian Latvian publishing house. They provided enough capital to get it started and then, equally important, they have supplied ongoing mentoring to the staff. Peter Cunliffe of Christian World Publishers, a veteran international publishing consultant with extensive experience in Europe and South America, was invited to join the mix, and he lent his ongoing expertise to Talis and his team in all areas critical to running a successful and self-sustaining publishing house.

In March of 2002, Atklasme (Discovery) Publishing House was officially launched with a gala celebration in Riga. More than 150 Christian leaders from Latvia assembled to rejoice with Talis and friends as they dedicated Atklasme's first release, a Latvian edition of *The Prayer of Jabez*, to the Lord. It is Atklasme's mission to publish great Christian books in Latvian, including classics like my all-time favorite, *The Knowledge of the Holy* by A. W. Tozer, every few months.

It could be that the partnership built between Multnomah Publishers and Atklasme Publishers will prove to be the most significant and long-lasting bridge we will ever build. It thrills me no end to realize that books that are produced today can continue to speak and minister to countless people for countless years to come.

Since Jerome Kenagy had first begun traveling to Latvia from Oregon to meet with his sister church in Jelgava, he had been wondering how he could put his years of experience in business ownership to work to help this Russian congregation. Jerome and his partners had built an internationally successful broadcast software company in the sleepy coastal town of Reedsport, and he knew from firsthand experience the value of well-placed start-up capital in the hands of people prepared to work hard. But the needs of this Russian Baptist congregation seemed overwhelming.

The post-Communist backlash in Latvia against all things Russian and the stringent Latvian language requirements for anyone holding a professional position had dealt a crippling blow to the Russian population in Latvia, many of whom had lived in Latvia all their lives and had no association with the Communists. Former medical doctors were doing custodial work to try to support their families because they could not pass the Latvian language test; former teachers took in sewing work. Unemployment among the Russian-speaking congregations in Latvia was hovering at 80 percent when Jerome made his first visit in 1996.

Jerome continued to visit Jelgava periodically, giving his money and time when he could, building his friendship with Pastor Dmitri Roshior, and being encouraged again and again by the faith of this Russian congregation and their persistent efforts to reach outside their own struggles and ostracism to the hurting world around them.

Finally, in 2000, Jerome retired. With time now to devote to answering that question that had been nagging at him for years, he began researching. A college friend pointed him toward the Business Professional Network, a Christian organization that sets up structures for loan programs geared toward small and medium-sized businesses in the less developed countries of the world. And Jerome's dreams began to grow more specific.

Under the direction of Pastor Dmitri, several families were invited to submit business plans for consideration for a small loan. It was made clear from the beginning that these loans would be made available for the express purpose of helping church members become self-sufficient, creating jobs for other church members, and enabling them to better financially support their pastor and the work of their church. The loans would be repaid into a fund that would then issue more loans for other church families.

One of the first business plans that was submitted came from the Savchenko family. For years they had worked on a collective farm several miles outside Jelgava, Aleksandr as a skilled metal worker and his wife Irina as a cook. But when the collective was disbanded after the Communists lost power, Aleksandr and Irina were left unemployed, with an allotment of two and a half hectares of the farm's rich and fertile land. Aleksandr was offered metal-working jobs farther from home, but he did not want to leave Irina and their two daughters, and he was committed to helping their new church and volunteer pastor in the neighboring village of Oglaine, a church planted by the Jelgava congregation.

They had no money to buy seeds for their land, so they collected seed potatoes and planted them. The first year they had a bumper crop, but when the second year's crop became infested with aphids, there was no extra money to buy pesticide, and they watched as one plant after another shriveled up and died. By harvest time there was not a single potato to dig. Irina got a job as a cook in the cafeteria of a local school to help keep the family from starving.

Meanwhile, the small church in Oglaine struggled to remain afloat. The pastor and the rest of the Russian-speaking congregation had their own financial woes, and it was difficult to focus on ministry and outreach when the ministers themselves were straining to put food on the table.

Aleksandr and Irina puzzled over their business plan at their small kitchen table. How could they wisely use what they already had, invest what God had given them to effectively and productively serve him? Slowly a plan began to emerge. When they finally sat down with Pastor Dmitri and Jerome, their painstakingly prepared business plan requested a loan in the amount of one thousand U.S. dollars to buy ten piglets with feed, and fertilizer and seed for planting potatoes, tomatoes, and cucumbers. Their teenage daughters would help them raise the piglets through the nine-month cycle to maturity, at which time they would repay the first half of the loan and use the remaining proceeds to buy ten more piglets.

John and Kay Antos, a couple from Jerome's home church who had visited the mission in Oglaine in 1999, immediately embraced the "Pigs for the Pastor" project and donated $1,000 to the loan fund, making Aleksandr and Irina the proud owners of ten tiny piglets.

And the business plans have continued to flow in. One man, a chaplain in two prisons around Jelgava, received $4,000 to expand his chicken farm. Another member of the Jelgava Russian Baptist Church who works one week out of every month for a Christian mission in Finland, was given a loan for $12,000 to buy damaged cars in Finland, bring them to Latvia for cost-effective body repair, and drive them back to Finland for resale. And yet another part-time pastor of a mission church and foreman of a construction crew is working on a plan to start his own construction company.

The logistics of banking and loaning money in Latvia are sometimes complicated. And for Latvian and Russian Christians, many of whom have never formally borrowed money in their lives, the concept is a new and strange one. But it is slowly making a significant difference in the lives of individual families and, inevitably, in their churches as well. And that makes Jerome—for whom retirement has meant anything but leisure— very happy.

We sat on a park bench in Riga in 1985, watching his four-year-old soar on the swings, her braids flying out behind her. Viljams Shultz was talking about life as a Christian in the repressive Communist regime of Latvia in the mid-eighties, stories of heartache and glory and pain. But each time he spoke of these personal things, this straightforward man lowered his head, staring at the dust beneath our feet as he formulated his eloquent words.

"Viljams, why do you keep looking at the ground while we talk?" I asked.

"Do you see that hotel across the street from the park?" he asked in response, still not looking up. "There are KGB agents there with telescopes, trying to read our lips as we speak."

Viljams Shultz is not a paranoid man, but he has always been able to assess situations around him and act accordingly. And I took his warning

I met Viljams ("Bill") during my first trip to Latvia in 1985. He was my first interpreter and my first Latvian friend.

seriously. He was my Latvian interpreter while I was in Latvia, a slender, athletic man who spoke many languages fluently. When I asked him how he had managed to learn English in Communist Latvia, he nodded toward his four-year-old on the swings and replied, "From my daughter."

"What?" I asked incredulously.

"From my daughter. When she was born I decided I would only speak English to her. That's how I learned."

His wife was Lithuanian, he spoke only French to his two-year-old son, and he naturally learned Latvian and Russian growing up in the dual-language society. German, Swedish, and Spanish were other projects for his free time. But growing up in a Christian home and active in the growing underground opposition movement, this brilliant young man was denied any higher education or even a driver's license, and was relegated to working in a job at Riga's central heating utility. A sympathizer of Latvia's Popular Front opposition movement, he and his wife Dana would later be featured in a 1989 BBC television documentary about family life in Soviet Latvia.

Viljams and I met again in Manila in 1989 when travel restrictions had eased and he was allowed out of the country. At that time he asked me to start calling him "Bill." During the Lausanne II meetings, Bill urged Almers and me to plan an evangelistic outreach in Riga that summer to help the Latvian Christians look outside their church walls to tell the gospel story.

This little girl is only one of the thousands of children that Mission Pakapieni has helped over the years. *Photo by Bill Shultz*

After the Communist withdrawal, Bill was finally released from his dead-end job and allowed to blossom. He became a youth leader and launched a magazine he called *Pakapieni* or "Stair Steps," a vehicle he hoped would help people move upward and closer to God. He grappled honestly and bravely with relevant social issues in his magazine, including a scathing exposé on abortion in Latvia. During his research he was horrified to find that abortion rates in Latvia were seven times higher than in the West. And he felt intensely convicted to do something about it.

Bill never does anything halfway, so he worked day and night to establish a socially practical Christian ministry on the shore of the Baltic Sea, in the city of Jurmala. Mission Pakapieni, a complex of homes, a warehouse, playground, and guesthouse directly on the beach, is a direct outgrowth of Bill's research on abortion and the state of the family in Latvia. Since 1992 it has been a beacon of hope for literally thousands of Latvian children and their parents.

For many years, Mission Pakapieni's Children's Village was home to twenty-five orphans who lived with four married couples and their own biological children in houses in the Pakapieni complex. These children who would otherwise have grown up in one of Latvia's many orphanages thrived on the opportunity to live in the atmosphere of loving Christian families.

About two hours away from Riga is the Pakapieni Life Center, a maternity home for single pregnant girls and women who choose not to abort their babies. They can stay in the Life Center for six months before their baby is born and up to six months after, surrounded by supportive staff and medical caregivers.

The Pakapieni warehouse serves as a humanitarian aid clearing-house for nearly one hundred orphanages and social organizations that represent 10,000 institutionalized children. Shipments from the United States and Western Europe regularly arrive at

The new Latvian Buckner board of directors is a wonderful mixture of Latvian and American specialists: (from left to right) Almers; Amy Norton, Buckner's International Program Director; myself; Ainars Bastiks, Member of Parliament and Minister of Children and Family Affairs; Dace Rence, Director of Buckner Latvia; Olafs Bruvers, Latvia's Director of Human Rights; and Bill Shultz. Not pictured: Inese Slesere, Member of Parliament; and Mike Douris, Vice President of Buckner Orphan Care International.
Photo courtesy of Bill Shultz

Pakapieni for further distribution to Latvia's orphans and other needy children: half a shipping container of brand new shoes donated from a Wal-Mart in east Texas; new and nearly new infant car seats and clothing from churches in Oregon; games and toys from a Sunday school program in Seattle; and much, much more.

Bill's wife Dana and the staff at Pakapieni also keep detailed files on more than 300 impoverished families in Latvia, with the names, ages, and clothing sizes of each member of these families. Four times a year each family, many of which have only one parent, receives an aid package from the warehouse at Pakapieni with toys, clothes, shoes, and sometimes food. The Pakapieni staff personally delivers as many packages as they can, making sure to sit down and spend time with the people, sharing tea, cookies, laughter, and hope.

Over the past three years, a new overseas partnership has given Bill's ministry exciting new opportunities. Buckner Orphan Care International, based in Dallas, Texas, and part of one of the largest social services ministries in the United States, has become an enthusiastic partner in reaching out to the orphans and families at risk in Latvia. With their long track record in Romania and Russia, Buckner quickly saw the opportunities for ministry when we approached them in late 2001. By October of 2003 they had already established an office in the country and were beginning to work in three orphanages in Latvia, with the potential of reaching many more as they expand with their loving and practical emphasis on foster care and adoption rather than institutionalization.

As one of the first board members of Buckner's Latvian organization, Bill has helped pave the way through the Latvian bureaucracy. And Buckner's long-standing "Shoes for Orphans' Souls" program is donating 10,000 pairs of new shoes every fall to Mission Pakapieni to be ably and gratefully distributed to Bill's network of needy families and orphanages.

Confronted with the ugly evil of abortion, Bill was compelled to action. But he resisted the tunnel vision that so often surrounds this issue, choosing instead to promote and support life in all its stages— before, during, and after birth. Mission Pakapieni, in its loving dedication to unmarried mothers, unwanted children, and families struggling to survive, is a powerful force for the promise of life and God's love in Latvia today.

MORE CREATIVE EXPRESSIONS

MISSION FEST 1998

In 1998 the choir from Santiam Christian School in Corvallis, Oregon, visited their sister school in Riga. They also sang in churches, squares, parks, and even the Latvian National Song Festival. My son Scotty (the blond kid in the black tux) and I both enjoyed singing in the 15,000-voice mass choir.

BASKETBALL

Another excellent potential bridge is sports. In 2000 BBI organized Latvia Hoops 2000 and brought a boys' and girls' team to Latvia. They conducted basketball clinics in the mornings for children and in the afternoons and evenings they played Latvian teams, including Latvia's pre-Olympic champions. My son Phillip (with the "P" cap) took an elbow to the forehead and found himself in the emergency room. Nevertheless, he loved ministering to the Latvian kids.

SPECIALIZED TRAINING

For several years the Evangelical Development Ministry of Dallas, Texas, provided strategic and ongoing training for Latvian leaders in the areas of leadership and fund development.
In 1997 EDM and BBI brought nine key leaders to Orlando, Florida, for their annual training institute.
A trip to Disneyworld was a fun way to end the training.

DENTISTRY

For several years Dr. Dan White (at left, shown here with his wife Sandra) and his lovely assistant Sam Bradley (right) have devoted two weeks every summer providing basic dental care to poor families. They use the portable dental clinic that was donated to BBI.

DOME CATHEDRAL TOWER CLOCK

Before and after
Photos courtesy of Ed Beacham

Ed Beacham is one of the world's finest clockmasters. In 2001 he and his wife Kathi reconstructed the 15th-century turret clock of the Dome Cathedral. It is one of the finest examples of medieval tower clocks in Europe.

PAINTING THE LIGHT IN LATVIA

CHAPTER 18

I first saw a painting by Thomas Kinkade when Nancy and I visited her parents in Sacramento in 1994. After lunch we strolled into a tiny art gallery where I was astonished by the sense of serenity that radiated from the canvas lithographs . . . scenes of the English countryside, California mountains, and Victorian mansions at Christmas. Intrigued, I leaned over to Mom and Dad and said, "I don't know who this artist is, but he's got to be a Christian. He communicates hope." Then I thought of my vision to connect the very best specialists in America with Latvian life and culture. "Someday I would love to bring a high quality artist like this to Latvia to minister in a way that no one else can."

Latvians are lovers of all things artistic. This is expressed in magnificent architecture, spectacular musical events, and a deep admiration for artists and musicians. In fact, some would say that in Latvia it is the artists and musicians who are the most influential elements in society. They not only reflect modern culture, they set the tone.

As we began planning for Hope '99, I wrote a letter to Thomas Kinkade describing BBI and the Hope '99 project. I was hoping that he would come to Latvia to paint and take part in specific special events designed to appeal to the world of art. Though I was disappointed when he graciously declined, I felt that I wasn't supposed to forget about it. So a couple of years later I wrote to Kinkade again, this time without a reply.

But God's timing is infinitely better than mine. I had no idea that the Kinkade family would begin to attend Calvary Church in Los Gatos, California, in 2003, or that Thom and his wife Nanette would be in an adult Sunday school class when I shared an update about our ministry. After class Thom approached me and told me he was interested in taking his family to Latvia to combine painting with Christian service. I was

242

delighted and immediately began to design a program that would merge the worlds of art, children's ministry, and outreach.

Thom is a uniquely talented artist who is able to paint in multiple styles: an interesting blend of classical realism, early impressionism, and romantic expressionism. He chooses motifs that he embellishes with his imagination, resulting in surreal paintings that bring out warmth, color, and light.

He's also an avid student of art history. Thom's home studio contains thousands of art books, including volumes that depict the work of the great nineteenth- and early twentieth-century painters of the Baltic Sea region. He believes that the Russians Ivan Shiskin and Isaak Levitan are among the greatest landscape artists of all times. When I told him that Latvia's best early painters studied in St. Petersburg at the feet of these Russian masters, he was more than intrigued. As Thom perused Latvian masterpieces by Purvitis, Rozentals, and Libberts, he couldn't wait to get to Latvia to paint in the same forests, perhaps even the same motifs.

Part of what motivates Thom to paint and market his paintings so creatively is his strong desire to make a difference in this world. Over the years his art has been used to raise more than twenty million dollars for numerous charitable and Christian causes such as World Vision, the Salvation Army, and the National Park Foundation. That he was adding Bridge Builders to his list was very encouraging to me.

Thom's combined passions of painting and influencing people prompted us to develop two schedules for him: we set aside large blocks of time for Thom to select locations, paint, and then wind down, and we surrounded those times with life-on-life interaction—in churches, schools, galleries, museums, restaurants, and homes.

This unique week required unique preparations. On the Latvian side we brought our former Youth Network leader Lienite back into our team to help organize local arrangements and to serve as Thom's personal interpreter. Almers cleared his schedule, rented a large new minibus, and put his Soviet army training as a chauffeur to good use. He not only served behind the wheel, but was able to spend many hours conversing with Thom about life and ministry in Latvia.

On the American side I recruited Kim Akers from Richardson, Texas, to serve as my right hand for the project. A former marketing executive with JC Penney, she was able to skillfully interact with Thom and the president of his foundation, Bob Davis, about the best way for BBI to work with the Kinkade Company to utilize the art that was going to be created.

Saturday, July 10

We met the Kinkades at the airport with a customary large bouquet of flowers. The party included Thom, Nanette, two of their four daughters—Merritt and Chandler—and Bob Davis. Thom's brother Pat, a writer and academic from Ft. Worth, Texas, had arrived five hours earlier. He had come to research the off-the-beaten-path places and people of Latvia. The final product would be a book enhanced by Thom's paintings and sketches from Latvia.

A warm airport greeting: (top row) Almers, Vija, and their daughter Renalda; Naomi Strauser; myself; Thomas Kinkade; (bottom row) Lienite Bemere; Kim Akers; and Nanette, Chandler, and Merritt Kinkade.

Sunday, July 11

We began the day with a walking tour in Riga's Old Town and then arrived at Salvation Temple, Calvary Church's sister church, where we were warmly welcomed by Pastors Janis Smits and Petr Samoylich. During the morning service Thom greeted the congregation and shared a brief testimony. He spoke about how he had learned to use his talent for God's glory and encouraged the church members to use whatever talents they have in service to the Lord. Then, in the name of his church, he gave a fine lithographic canvas of his painting of the cross looking over eternity, "Sunrise." This is the same

During my sermon I emphasized that we may not have equal talents, but we do have equal responsibility to use our talents for the Lord.
Photo by Don Ferguson

After Thom presented a copy of his painting to the church, Pastors Smits and Samoylich presented him with a welcome gift.
Photo by Shelly Pierce

painting he had given to Presidents Clinton, Bush, and Ulmanis and Pope John Paul II. It is also the same lithograph that hangs on our living room wall in Oregon. Pastor Smits reciprocated and gave Thom a lovely framed piece commemorating the church's seventy-fifth anniversary.

It was then my turn to preach. I'd had no idea that Thom would speak about talents when I prepared my message on the Parable of the Talents, emphasizing the importance of each of us using our gifts to the best of our abilities.

In the afternoon our party headed for the country home of former President Guntis Ulmanis. His picturesque ten-acre estate features a new log cabin-style home and a splendid sauna house close to a small lake. While the rest of us relaxed and enjoyed the Ulmanis family's magnificent hospitality, Thom put on his game face to search for the motif to be painted. It's fascinating to look at one's surroundings through the eyes of an artist as he factors in subject composition, color, and light . . . where it is now and where it will be in three or four hours. Thom decided to set up his easel on the president's small boat dock and paint a western view of the lake as the sun met the horizon. It was a motif that Levitan or Purvitis would have relished.

Photo by Bob Davis

I was amazed to learn how little time Thom requires to create a painting. Though some paintings require many hours in his studio, most of his *plein air* pieces, which are painted on location in the open air, take between three and five hours.

Art can be more than simply art—it can be a wonderful tool in the Master's hand to touch hearts and build bridges. So, after helping Thom set up, several of us gathered in a circle to pray for the painting. We did this every day. It is remarkable that Thom's practice of praying before each painting surprised me. For years I have prayed over my sermons both before writing them and delivering them. Why shouldn't an artist do the same when engaging his God-given talent and calling?

Thom began painting on the dock in peace, but elsewhere less artistic plans were afoot. Pat and Bob had expressed enough curiosity in the Latvian sauna custom that Raimonds, Ulmanis' son-in-law, agreed to fire it up. When the sauna was sufficiently hot—about 190 degrees Fahrenheit—Pat, Bob, Raimonds, and I started the ninety-minute ritual. Wearing only our smiles and pointy felt sauna hats to prevent our scalps from burning, we sat on the wooden benches, slowly pouring water over the hot rocks. The sizzle of the water vaporizing as it touched the hot rocks meant that it would be only a few seconds until an intense wave of heat would descend like a blanket. Conversation was soon replaced with a chorus of *oohs, ughs,* and *whoas.*

The sauna is one of the places left in the civilized world where men compare sheer toughness: the first one out simply isn't as tough as the others. I'm afraid I succumbed first, exiting to the cold shower and a small table set up with fruit and beverages. Steam rose from my shoulders like a cloud. Soon the others joined me at the table, Pat and Bob howling with glee. They had never experienced anything quite so rustic.

Round two was the same as the first except that we made it hotter and sat there longer. This time Bob fled first. More fruit, more fluids, and more laughter-filled stories.

As a veteran of many Latvian sauna experiences, I knew what to expect during round three. After stoking the wood and dousing the rocks, we took turns beating each other with dried and bound birch tree branches. This procedure, barbaric to most Americans, is actually quite healthy. It stimulates the skin, opens pores, and releases a medicinal extract from the leaves that makes you feel simply wonderful.

Finally, wrapped in towels, we walked down to the boat dock where Thom was rendering the details of his landscape—the trees, forest, clouds, water, and reflection. He broke out laughing as he watched the four of us dive into the frigid lake. We could bear the cold water for only a few minutes so we climbed back onto the dock, regirded ourselves in the towels, and walked toward the painter and the painting.

Suddenly we heard a creak in the dock and felt one of the boards split. Time stood still as I waited for the whole dock to collapse, spilling the precious cargo into the lake: my heart skipped a beat as I grabbed Thom's paint box to

Whenever Kinkade begins a new painting he dedicates it to the Lord's honor and glory. The answered prayer took the form of a stunning painting. Photos by Bob Davis

As Thom was drawing the lighthouse he invited this little artist to help him fill in the grass.
Photo by Bob Davis

Almers' daughter Renalda was a fantastic art tutor for many children.
Photo by Don Ferguson

Each little artist was immensely proud of his work.
Photo by Bob Davis

keep it from falling; Thom held on to the easel and the painting; Pat, Bob, and Raimonds held on to their towels. As the dock slowly stabilized, we dissolved into laughter again.

Back at the house, we awaited the finished masterpiece. Soon Thom came hurrying across the meadow, balancing the fresh painting on his fingertips. President Ulmanis was thrilled with Thom's rendition of the sunset over the lake. Thankfully Thom hadn't included the four sauna guys in his first painting of Latvia. It wouldn't have been a pretty sight. But one thing I know for sure: whenever I see this peaceful painting I will . . . smile.

Monday, July 12

While Thom's main assignment in Latvia was to paint, Nanette and the girls worked at the art camp at the Barbins Christian School. Each day about seventy children, including thirty-five from a local orphanage, came to the school to develop their artistic skill and learn about the greatest artist of all, the Lord God who created the beauty of the world. It was a great week for the children. They drew, painted, worked with crafts, and even sculpted; they sang, played, and went on excursions.

It was also a great week for the nearly twenty volunteers who came from all over the United States to help. There were teachers, artists, teenagers, and ladies who simply loved to love children. Diana Long, the wife of BBI's long-time board member Bob, organized the educational portion of the week, developing a teaching plan via phone and email with several people she hadn't yet met. The art camp was an enormous administrative undertaking, but Naomi Strauser, BBI's office manager and detail queen, was up to the task.

On Monday afternoon, Thom gave the kids a drawing lesson. I saw it as a good opportunity to learn something new, so I grabbed a sketch pad and sat on the floor with the children. Each child copied Thom's work mark by mark. All the while he talked to the kids about how to draw clouds, birds, buildings, and water. Some of their sketches were remarkable. Toward the end of the session Thom told his own story and shared the gospel.

After the art lesson, Vija Ludvika of Barbins Christian School hosted Thom and Nanette for coffee and goodies. She told them a bit of the history and vision of the school. Ainars Bastiks, who is currently a Member of Parliament and the Minister of Children and Family Affairs, also spoke about the profound needs of the ten thousand children growing up in Latvian institutions. We discussed various other ways that proceeds from the prints of Thom's paintings of Latvia can be applied to make a significant difference. It is my prayer that thousands upon thousands of people will want copies of the Latvian paintings, enabling thousands upon thousands of children's lives to be changed forever.

Tuesday, July 13

The Kinkades stayed on the ninth floor of the Radisson Hotel with a splendid view of the skyline of Riga. Laboring for hours on the hotel balcony, Thom painted the panorama at dusk. The painting that emerged is breathtaking in terms of composition, light, and detail. When Thom showed this painting to the art camp children the

"Sunset Over Riga, Latvia"
Lithographs are available to the public. See www.bridgebuildersint.com for details.

Two passionate artists, one accomplished and the other just learning, thoroughly enjoyed painting the palace.

next day, he told them to squint their eyes and look at the man in the foreground walking his dog. "This is Chuck Kelley," he said, "walking over the bridge." Sure enough, I am tiny and barely recognizable in the painting, but the thought behind the image is perfect: I not only love building bridges to Latvia, I thoroughly enjoy taking others—this time a painter and his family—to the land that I love.

Wednesday, July 14

Birinu Palace is a relatively new manor built for a German baron in 1860. It was used as a health rehabilitation center during the Soviet years and neglected terribly. When freedom came to Latvia, descendants of the legal owners of the palace were given the opportunity to reclaim it and renovate it to its previous luster. Today it is a popular place for weddings, parties, and conferences.

While the art camp children toured the palace and grounds, Thom set up on the bank of the small lake on the other side of the palace. Again we prayed for the process and painting, and then I sat guard for the next couple of hours. All over the grounds children and teachers drew, colored, and painted their renditions of the palace. One by one, two by two, and then in small groups, students and teachers drew closer to watch Thom work his craft. When we brought all the children together around Thom, he told them about his rendering and answered their questions. It was truly beautiful.

Thursday, July 15

Latvia's famous landscape painter Vilhelms Purvitis founded the Latvian Academy of Art around the turn of the century. Today the art of *plein air* painting is kept alive by the vice-rector, Dr. Aleksejs Naumovs, one of Latvia's better-known artists. Several months earlier, Lienite and I had visited Dr. Naumovs for the first time in an attempt to build a bridge to the artistic community. We discussed art, artists, and Kinkade's proposed visit. The professor was intrigued, and when he suggested that it would be interesting to paint side by side with Kinkade, I loved the idea. So did Thom.

As a subject for the side-by-side painting by the masters, Thom decided to paint the Dome Cathedral. Though a very difficult motif, it is the most prominent spiritual symbol of Latvia. I applauded the choice, for the cathedral has had a special spot in my heart since my first visit to Latvia, when the KGB tour guide told me with a straight face that the people had asked the government to take the building away from the five congregations who worshipped there. Years later, I took part in a serious prayer meeting at the Dome focused on national repentance. When I learned that Ed Beacham, a master clockmaker from Oregon, wanted to use his talent in Latvia, I helped make it possible for Ed and his wife Kathi to rebuild the ancient clock in the tower of the Dome. And it was during the final services of Hope '99 in the Dome that President and Mrs. Ulmanis stood to declare their faith to the nation.

Late Wednesday night Thom, Bob, and I walked around the Dome, examining it from every angle, especially thinking about where the light would be in the late morning and early afternoon. Thom selected the vantage, we called the professor, and first thing in the morning both masters set up their canvases side by side. When Thom travels, he usually paints on 12" x 16" canvas covered panels, smaller than

most people would imagine. But the professor wasn't on the road, so he brought a 3' x 4' canvas. He was going to take advantage of the opportunity to paint a major work.

The tiny street adjacent to the Dome Square was buzzing with activity. There were deliverymen, Japanese tourists, and an official motorcade of a Scandinavian president. Two television camera crews and a newspaper reporter showed up to cover the story. I decided to add a bit more atmosphere, so I ran down to the Swedish Gate, the last existing city gate in Riga, and recruited three splendid street musicians who played classical music for the next forty-five minutes. It was unbelievable, almost like a fairy tale.

After about an hour it was clear that two great paintings would emerge. Thom's would be a brilliant impressionist piece with muted colors that suggested the majesty of the cathedral. It is destined to be a classic. Naumovs' painting would be a bit looser and brighter, more reminiscent of post-impressionist fauvists like Raoul Dufy. The professor took more liberties with composition, and the results were splendid.

Five hours later we all sat down to a light lunch. One of Aleksejs' protégés, who had been taking pictures all day, joined us. We discussed the day and the world of art, and then the conversation changed to deeper topics, topics of eternal significance. The protégé told us that he had been studying for Christian ministry many years ago when the KGB began to question and intimidate him. To his own shame he broke and denied his faith, and to this day he felt that he couldn't be forgiven for denying God. Thom and I assured him that there is hope and grace for someone like him, and the next evening, at the reception in the historic Blackhead House, Thom and Nanette prayed with the artist as he recommitted his life to the Lord.

That evening, the sanctuary of Matthews Church was packed with more than six hundred people, including many artists. Thom told some of his life story, of growing up in a broken and impoverished home in California where he and his brother were latch-key kids. At an early age he resolved that when he grew up, his family would be different. Thom also knew from an early age that he was uniquely gifted as an artist, and he determined to accomplish great things with his art. He then spoke about the important difference that Christ has made in his life's journey.

Friday, July 16

Just outside the city limits of Riga, on a beautiful lake in a pristine forest, is the Ethnographic Museum. Here Latvians have reconstructed the old wooden buildings of Latvia from the previous 300 years. There are about 200 edifices . . . cottages, farmhouses, barns, warehouses, churches, windmills, and artisan buildings. For years Thom has enjoyed painting old cottages from the Cotswolds region of England. This would be his chance to paint something similar in Latvia.

Again, after searching for just the right motif, Thom set up his easel in front of a tiny sauna house. Perhaps he couldn't keep the sauna images from Sunday night out of his mind. Or maybe he simply wanted to paint something that truly caused one to think of simpler times. Minutes after he began he was interrupted by a grumpy groundskeeper who wanted Thom to paint someplace else, but Lienite came to the rescue and convinced the man to back off.

As Thom painted the tiny building, something exciting was going on in other sections of the park. About one hundred enthusiastic Latvian youth, with a few Americans sprinkled in, were working on the grounds,

One of the reasons Thom chose this motif was the dramatic way that his subject reflected in the tiny pond.
Both photos by Don Ferguson

cleaning debris, picking up trash and clearing undergrowth. They were part of teRiga, another BBI project, and this was their final day of serving the city.

After their special closing ceremony, several teRiga kids gathered around Thom just as he was finishing his painting. He asked the small assembly if any of them were artists. When one girl raised her hand, he put his paintbrush in her hand and brought her to his painting where she added several brilliant blue flowers. She was beaming!

The End of a Perfect Week

Friday night was truly memorable. We finished the week with a VIP reception at the House of the Blackheads, a restored fourteenth-century merchants' palace in Old Town. Rinta had worked for weeks on every detail of this evening, including the invitation list. We had invited government leaders, artists, pastors, ministry leaders, and those who had come to work at the art camp and teRiga. Almost one hundred came. Up until the last minute things were hectic in the main ballroom. While the strings played their prelude, Thom scurried to set all five of his still-wet original oil paintings in frames, while several beautiful ladies scrambled to make sure that the easels were properly

Photo by Talivaldis Talbergs

placed and lighted. I can still see Kim Akers, Shelly Pierce, Rebecca Lee, and Signe Kurga in evening gowns, applying duct tape on their hands and knees. But finally everything was in place. Thom's paintings were each displayed, as was Naumovs'. Also on display was Kinkade's "Sunrise."

Several guests of honor were present. Ambassador Ojars Kalnins, the director of the Latvian Institute, welcomed Thom to Latvia: "In Latvia we believe in a great deal of

Moments after Thom set his paintings in the frames, scores of enthusiastic art lovers, including Jeff and Teresa Harris and Eric Swanson, examined each painting.
Photo by Don Ferguson

While Kim helped Thom set up, Talis saw an ideal time for a unique portrait.
Photo by Talivaldis Talbergs

energy. Both the land and people carry energy. We know that when we bring two very powerful forms of energy together, they create new energy. This last week, one of the most prolific, popular, and creative artists in the world visited one of the most beautiful countries in the world: the result, as we can see, is wonderful. On behalf of the Latvian Institute, I want to thank you for helping us to do our job better. Our job is to promote Latvia around the world. These paintings will be carrying Latvia much farther than we ever could with our small budget."

Ambassador Kalnins was happy that his office was depicted on the upper left side of Thom's Dome painting.
Photo by Talivaldis Talbergs

Kalnins smiled as he continued, "But I also want to thank you for one more small thing. In your paint-off with Professor Naumovs, you depicted the Dome Cathedral. What pleased me is that the building just to the left of the Dome is the building that houses the Latvian Institute. So, thank you for immortalizing us as well."

After Thom had described his week in Latvia and what it was like to compose each painting, he presented copies of "Sunrise" to both the Latvian government and the American embassy. As Ainars Bastiks accepted the painting on behalf of the Ministry of Children and Family Affairs, he remarked powerfully: "During this week we have seen great talent and great light, but especially we have been pointed to the light of the world, and that is truly what Latvia needs."

Saturday, July 17

The next morning when I bid farewell to the Kinkades at the Riga airport, we all stopped and prayed again, thanking the Father for such a wonderful week. All of our hopes had materialized, from good weather and positive media coverage to interesting motifs and splendid paintings, new friendships, spiritual impact, and visions of future possibilities.

As Thom was getting his passport stamped, I said, "You know what, Thom? This week is an answer to a ten-year prayer. No wonder it went so well."

His answer summed up the week: "Unbelievable!"

Photo by Aleksejs Naumovs

Another Surprise

A few days after the Kinkades left Latvia, I called Professor Naumovs and asked him to dinner. We had a delightful time for several hours. During the course of the conversation I took a risk and shared a private dream that I have had for more than twenty-five years. "I too would like to learn how to paint. I'm a pretty good musician and photographer," I said, "but I have terrible handwriting and don't know how to draw. Do you think there is any hope for someone like me to learn to paint?"

"Why not...if you have the right master," Aleksejs replied. "Last year I taught the prime minister to paint. Maybe this year I can teach you."

I was elated.

Two months later, when I returned to Latvia, the professor invited me to his home studio where he had already set up a still life arrangement. The next few hours flew by as he taught me more about painting than I had gleaned in my entire life. The process was exhilarating.

And the results? I'll have to let you decide for yourself.

A KNIGHT TO REMEMBER

C H A P T E R   1 9

It was Independence Day in Latvia, November 18, 2003. Eighty-five years earlier, for the first time in recorded history, this tiny republic on the Baltic Sea had declared its independence from Imperial Russia. Now Nancy and I stood and watched the customary Independence Day parade, complete with bands, speeches, and the firing of cannons, as it made its way past the Presidential Palace. The celebration would continue at the Monument of Freedom that evening, climaxing with a huge fireworks display over the river.

Latvians love their freedom. And they appreciate those who have worked hard to establish and preserve it. Another custom that began in 1924, just a few years after Latvia first gained independence, was the conferring of the Award of the Order of the Three Stars by the country's president. The award is presented to visiting royalty, heads of state, government officials, scientists, educators, musicians, and artists—men and women who have demonstrated outstanding achievements for the benefit of the nation. Only a small handful of religious leaders have been honored in this way.

That afternoon, as Nancy and I watched the parade, I felt my Latvian blood surging more strongly through my veins. Just the night before, President Vaira

Photo by Talivaldis Talbergs

257

Vike-Freiberga had hosted a special ceremony in Riga to bestow the Award of the Order of the Three Stars to several dozen people . . . including me. It was a beautiful evening.

I had been notified just a few weeks earlier that the Presidential Council of the Order of the Three Stars had decided to grant me this award. Mr. Ulmanis had submitted my name to the council for consideration. He had also solicited letters of recommendation from numerous influential leaders, including ministers of the government, Members of Parliament, pastors, leaders of charities, bishops, and archbishops. I was stunned.

According to the office of the Latvian president, "The Order is awarded for merits in serving the country, . . . for continuous excellent work as well as separate outstanding achievements during the restoration of the independence of Latvia [and the] further strengthening and formation of the country."

As I scrambled to research the award, I learned that the conferring of such awards has been a common practice among many European nations since the Middle Ages. In England it's called knighthood. When Lord Baden-Powell, founder of the Boy Scouts, visited Latvia in 1935, his award was translated "Knight of the Grand Cross of the Order of the Three Stars." The American equivalent is the Medal of Freedom.

The three stars represent the three historical regions of Latvia that are depicted atop Latvia's splendid Monument of Freedom. When the Soviets removed Latvia's freedom in 1940, the practice was discontinued. It was reinstituted in 1994 during the tenure of President Ulmanis.

The formal award ceremony took place in the spectacular Latvian Society House and featured a video presentation on the history of the Order of the Three Stars award, wonderful music by Latvia's best choir, dancing children in national costumes, and a warm address by the president. Each recipient received a large certificate, a beautiful long-stemmed rose, and a medal. I was thrilled that Nancy was able to attend, as well as Almers and Vija.

The ceremony was followed by a special reception where we each met with the president. I chatted with President Vike-Freiberga several times throughout the evening, and I had the strong feeling that God would use this event to build more surprising bridges in the future.

Photo by Talivaldis Talbergs

President Vaira Vike-Freiberga addresses the distinguished guests.

I was one of several dozen recipients of the award.

President Vike-Freiberga is warm, engaging, and most impressive.

I was delighted that Nancy, Almers, and Vija could enjoy this special evening with me.

Photos by Talivaldis Talbergs

I had heard that the recipients sometimes give two-minute speeches after receiving the award, but on this evening we were told that time constraints would make individual speeches impossible. With a sense of relief I accepted my award with a careful bow to the president, a bow to the dancing children, and a bow to the audience as we had been instructed.

Later in the evening, however, a journalist from Latvian National Radio approached me for an interview. When I told her I needed an interpreter, she insisted that I do the interview in Latvian. So, with trepidation, I did. Even after years of working in Latvia, my stuttering continues to obstruct my speaking of the language, but I was able to understand her questions and give simple answers. In my basic Latvian I said, "I am honored and pleased to receive the award. I love Latvia and pray every day that God will bless Latvia, not only now as it celebrates independence, but in the future as well."

All through the next day, Latvian National Radio featured short statements by award recipients on national radio, and my statements were included. I had been praying that I would be a grateful recipient and a transparent reflector of the grace and mercy of the Lord Jesus Christ, the only one who deserves true honor. I thought I would have a chance to give honor to the Lord in front of a few hundred people, but through this radio interview I wound up speaking to the nation. Only God could come up with this idea.

As I reflected on the evening, I knew that it would have been absolutely impossible for me to receive this award were it not for the hard work and loyalty of so many friends, colleagues, and supporters. A few days after the ceremony I hosted a simple banquet in Riga attended by about seventy people, all of whom have played an important role in my life and ministry in Latvia. Many brought flowers, kind words, and warm embraces. During that evening I dedicated the award to the loving memory of Granny and Papa. I wish they could have been there. And I told my friends gathered there that the award truly belonged to us all because of our partnership with one another on so many projects and programs in and for Latvia.

Receiving the Order of the Three Stars medal was an affirmation that our partnership model of ministry works. The award also serves as a confirmation to all of our supporters that their investment of money, time, and energy is producing something of recognizable value in the nation of Latvia as well as eternal fruit in the Kingdom of God.

To Him be all glory.

EPILOGUE

Surprised by the Father's Plan is the story of one man called back by God to minister to the small country of his ancestors halfway around the world. It tells my whole particular story in detail not to suggest that my life is of special significance—or to nudge everyone into specific action in Latvia—but to show that God can also use you in surprising ways, in your community and throughout the world.

Like the loving father he is, God takes pleasure in surprising his children with his amazing goodness and grace. But we must open our eyes and our hands to welcome these surprises.

God wants to use you to minister to this world that he loves. I encourage you to reach out today with hands and eyes open for the surprises of the Father.

Chuck Kelley
Riga, Latvia
March 2005

IN GRATEFUL
APPRECIATION

This book is about surprises—the kind that only God can orchestrate. One of the surprises is that there is a book that tells the story. I never would have predicted it. But *Surprised by the Father's Plan* is possible because many people have caught the vision that tremendous things happen when you build a bridge and use that bridge to bring people together in the name of Christ.

I will never cease to be amazed at how the Lord has prompted so many wonderful people to come alongside in so many ways—as employees, volunteers, donors, and prayer supporters. One always runs the risk of offending someone by not including a person in a

As of December 2004, the BBI staff consisted of (top row) Matt Strauser, Jeremy Andresen, myself, Nancy Kelley, Marsha Hill, (bottom row) Larita Brown, Jennie Smith, Crystal Kelley, Naomi Strauser, and (not pictured) Dan and Katie Roth.

list, but I will take that risk…it is part of my nature…for the sake of saying "thank you" to those who have given of themselves faithfully as partners in ministry through the years. Some served for a season, some have just begun their service, and others have been involved from the beginning. All have done so much.

Thanks to those who have served on the staff of Bridge Builders International: Nancy Kelley, Mike and Stephanie Parker, Carey Penner, Jennie Smith, Marsha Hill, Naomi and Matt Strauser, Pam Arthur, Mike Gentle, Crystal Kelley, Craig Hosterman, Jeremy Andresen, Larita Brown, and Dan and Katie Roth.

Thanks to those who have served on the board of directors of Bridge Builders International: Terry Bell, Karon Bell, Bob Long, Jerome Kenagy, Dr. Gunars Iesalnieks, Adrian Nikitins, Bob Sweeney, Herb Anderson, Bob Riggs, George Fisher, Mark Hubbell, Virgil Freed, Gordon Baugh, Garth Rouse, Carole Wille, Larita Brown, Eric Skinner, Paula Hewitt, Paula Gamble, Tommy Weathersbee, Leo Parchman, Clark Red, Roger Dalton, Syd Brestel, and Bill Zipp.

As of December 2004, the BBI board consisted of (top row) Paula Hewitt, Herb Anderson, (third row) Bob Long, Clark Red, (second row) Roger Dalton, myself, Dr. Gunars Iesalnieks, (front row) Jerome Kenagy, Bill Zipp, Tommy Weathersbee, and Syd Brestel.

Thanks to those who have served on the staff of Partners Association (BBI's Latvian affiliate): Almers Ludviks, Gatis Lidums, Rinta Bruzevica, Vineta Zale, Peteris Eisans, Signe Kurga, Lienite Bemere, Kristine Namavire, Maris Dupurs, Andris Sprogis, Kristaps Talbergs, Liena Krumina, Dr. Genovefa Norvele, Mairita Vindedze, Zane Leja, Dace Supule, Mareks Ignats, Anita Saule, Zigmars Atvars, and Lolita Ozolina.

As of May 2005, the Partners staff consisted of Maris Dupers, Lienite Bemere, Peteris Eisans, Vineta Zale, Zigmars Atvars, and (not pictured) Anita Saule, and Dr. Genofeja Norvele. This photo was taken during Prayer Days 2005 at Birinu Palace.

Thanks to those who have served on the board of directors of Partners Association: Bill Shultz, Gunvaldis Vesmins, Signe Kurga, Rinta Bruzevica, Peteris Eisans, Ingemar Martinson, Mike Parker, Edgars Mazis, Robert Hendrix, Olafs Bruvers, and Ralf Augstroze.

As of January 2005, the Partners board consisted of (left to right) Olafs Bruvers, Bill Shultz, Signe Kurga myself, Almers Ludviks (director), and Gunvaldis Vesmins.

Thanks to the charitable foundations that have supported our ministry: The Maclellan Foundation, The M. J. Murdock Charitable Trust, Stewardship Foundation, Mustard Seed Foundation, Interstate Battery Systems of America, Inc., Huston Foundation, M. E. Foundation, The Crowell Trust, Allied Christian Foundation, Meland Outreach, Miller Charitable Trust, and several others that have requested anonymity.

Special thanks

Apart from the encouragement, sacrifice, and professional expertise of Jerome and Donna Kenagy and their gifted daughter, Kristen Zetzsche, the co-author and editor of this book, this story would never have been written. I shall always be grateful to the Lord for their confidence in my ministry, their patience with my schedule, and their flexibility to adapt and adapt again to this ever-changing story.

Thanks are also in order to the following people who helped proof this manuscript: Jerome Kenagy, Jennie Smith, Bill Lee, Robin Jones Gunn, Bob Rasmussen, Maiga Veilande, Marsha Hill, Dr. Gunars Iesalnieks, Simona Talberga, Paula Hewitt, and Nancy Kelley.

My deepest thanks

Few people know how difficult it is for me to leave home time after time after time in order to carry out my ministry. At the time of this writing I have just completed my 134th trans-Atlantic flight. I have been keeping track for more than thirty years. But I can't count the times that I have restrained the tears as I have hurried out the door to catch yet another flight.

As of September 2004, our family had grown to include two wonderful daughters-in-law: (left to right) myself, Karen, Nancy, Jenn, Peter, Phillip, Crystal, and Scotty.

266

Our children are now grown. Peter is twenty-four and married to Jennifer; Scotty is twenty-two and married to Crystal; Phillip is twenty-one; and Karen is nineteen. They have had the reputation all their lives of having the most unusual father in town, a dad who preaches from city to city, travels to strange countries, meets with a plethora of fascinating people, and comes home trying his best to fit into the hustle and bustle of an active family in a small Oregon timber town. And yet they have turned out great.

Peter, Scotty, Phillip, and Karen, thank you for putting up with my travel schedule as you were growing up. I love you each more than you will ever know.

Nancy and I have now been married for twenty-seven years. Apart from her love, understanding, supportiveness, selflessness, and phenomenal skill as a devoted wife and mom, Bridge Builders International never would have happened.

Nancy, I love you so much. You are amazing. Thank you.

Thanks to my Lord and Savior Jesus Christ

I can do no better than repeat the famous benediction first written by the Apostle Paul, "Now to him who is able to do exceedingly abundantly beyond all that we ask or think, according to the power that works within us, to Him be the glory in the church and in Christ Jesus to all generations forever and ever. Amen."

Ephesians 3:20, 21 (NIV)

HOPE '99
LEADERSHIP TEAM

THE HOPE '99 LATVIAN LEADERSHIP TEAM			
RESPONSIBILITY	PERSON	CHURCH OR MINISTRY	CITY
Prayer	Erberts Bikse	Jesus Lutheran Church	Riga
Logistics	Petr Samoylich	Grace Community Church	Riga
Follow-Up and Counselor Training	Edgars Mazis	Agenskalns Baptist Church	Riga
Special Events	Peteris Sprogis	Matthews Baptist Church	Riga
Mini-School of Christian Leadership	Peteris Eisans	Jelgava Baptist Church	Jelgava
The Presidential Banquet	Elaine Lloyd and Kristine Zonne	Agape Latvia/ Campus Crusade for Christ	Riga
Public Relations	Rinta Bruzevica	Partners Foundation	Riga
Local Music	Maris Dravnieks	Latvian Christian Radio	Riga

Latvian Orchestra	Guntars Pranis	Crescendo/Agape Latvia	Riga
Sound	Davids Lagzdins	Matthews Baptist Church	Riga
Concert Management	Lienite Bemere	Partners Foundation	Riga
Book Publishing	Janis Pauliks	St. Anna Lutheran Church	Liepaja
International Relations	Forrest Hendrix	Greater Europe Mission	Riga
Radio	Talis Talbergs	Latvian Christian Radio	Riga
Fund Development	Dainis Butraks	Riga Pentecostal Church	Riga
Women's Outreach	Diana Dravniece	Matthews Baptist Church	Riga
Russian Outreach	Vladimir Andrijecs	Bethany Russian Baptist Church	Riga
Small Town Campaigns	Dustin Peterson	Greater Europe Mission	Tilza
Children's Music and Dance	Guntis Mamis	Kings Kids/Youth With a Mission	Several Cities
Children's Outreach	Jane Howett	Scripture Union	Riga
Liepaja Campaign	Gunvaldis Vesmins	Pavila Baptist Church	Liepaja
Daugavpils Campaign	Slava Istrajti	Daugavpils Russian Baptist Church	Daugavpils

CHURCH PARTNERSHIP EXAMPLES

Writing a book about a life and a ministry is a bit like orbiting at warp speed in a spy satellite with the shutter flashing—certain blips in time become magnified while others are ignored, certain stories are featured and others, equally or more compelling, are omitted.

There are so many other stories that make up the Bridge Builders experience, just some of which are expressed in the following brief descriptions of the formal church partnerships that lie at the foundation of our mission.

Calvary Church in Los Gatos, California, and Salvation Temple in Riga

After years of exile, Pastor Janis Smits left a successful pastorate in Canada and moved his family back to Latvia. His new church, Salvation Temple—important as a 1920s center of evangelism and pastor training—was a broken and abused building, serving the very poor.

In May of 1998, a leadership team from the large, missions-minded Calvary Church of Los Gatos, California, visited Salvation Temple. They connected deeply with Pastor Janis and the church. Though Calvary Church was in the middle of an ambitious building program, the congregation responded enthusiastically to the idea of a partnership and, in a remarkable outpouring of love, earmarked half of the missions offering raised during their capital campaign to meet Salvation Temple's pressing needs. As a result, Salvation Temple now has a much-needed new foyer, restrooms, and heating system.

Calvary Chapel business leaders hosted important meetings between Christian senior executives and President Ulmanis on his goodwill tour through Silicon Valley. In 1999, Calvary's "Bridging the Gap" brought more than fifty high school students and pastoral staff to Latvia for ten days of music outreach, sports ministry, and children's ministry. And this paved the way for repeated visits in both directions for teams from both congregations, deepening the relationships and working together to reach out to the needy community in Salvation Temple's neighborhood of "Little Moscow" and beyond.

First Baptist Church in Houston, Texas, and Jelgava Latvian Baptist Church in Jelgava

Papa's faithful Houston friends Doug and Bev Oren introduced their 20,000-member Houston First Baptist Church to the BBI vision, and in 1997 they joined in partnership with Jelgava Baptist Church. Since then more than one hundred people have traveled on fifteen occasions in both directions to participate in powerful and concentrated ministry: VBS, soccer camps, baseball camps, evangelism, church planting, senior citizen outreach, construction, music ministry, and counseling. Several Jelgava Baptist church members have traveled to Houston to participate in a missions trip to San Marcos, Texas. One recent American participant echoed the thoughts of many in this partnership when he said, "This truly changed my life. Part of my heart is still in Latvia."

Calvin Presbyterian Church in Corvallis, Oregon, and Tilza Baptist Church in Tilza

Calvin Presbyterian Church and Tilza Baptist Church have forged a strong cross-cultural and interdenominational bond that has weathered the inevitable storms of partnership with grace and deep love. Together they have sponsored an annual English language camp that reaches out to more than fifty kids between the ages of ten and seventeen each year. The children receive English instruction from an American teacher in the beautiful rural setting of the Tilza campus, and they also hear the message of the gospel.

Calvin has paid the Tilza pastor's salary for years so he can devote himself to the ministry without having to pursue outside employment. Paula Hewitt, BBI's chairman of the board and Calvin's director of community life, spent several months in Tilza to immerse herself in the culture and assist in the local ministry. And Pastor Marc Andresen has provided pastoral counseling and leadership at key points in the relationship between the churches. Both churches continue to pray about new directions of combined ministry that may open up for further cooperation.

Living Faith Community Church in Philomath, Oregon, and Kandava Baptist Church in Kandava

"We will share what the Kandava Church has taught us," said Aaron Rutledge, youth pastor of Living Faith Community Church in Philomath, Oregon, after a recent ministry outreach with his sister church in Kandava, Latvia. "Pray faithfully, be content in all situations, work hard, sacrifice, and love without condition."

These are powerful lessons, and they are indicative of the strong relationship being built between these two churches in villages across the globe from one another. Under the leadership of Pastor Oskars Jegermanis of Kandava Baptist and Pastor Jim Hall of Living Faith, this new partnership has included a multi-generational summer camp and several trips of church members in both directions. As the Living Faith pastors have said, "The thought of two churches, around the world, working closely together on specific ministries, is a thought that we believe pleases God."

Sisters Community Church in Sisters, Oregon, and Ogre Baptist Church in Ogre

Pastor Elmars Plavins of the Ogre Baptist Church is not your typical Latvian pastor. Formerly a judo champion, he's a young, energetic church planter, a military chaplain who has served several stints in Iraq, and a pastor to his 130 members. When he took the first delegation from Sisters Community Church to minister at the base, they were shocked to watch him take part in a parachute drill with the soldiers. But that kind of hands-on devotion to ministry has forged a strong bond for these two churches in their joint ministry endeavors.

Cooperation between the two churches has included Bible camps and basketball camps, youth and orphanage outreaches, and sponsorship of Kristine Namavire, a Latvian student, at Multnomah Bible College. Kristine, an orphan who had translated for the Sisters group while they were in Latvia, was sponsored by Ed and Kathi Beacham, a childless couple in the Sisters Community Church. They immediately fell in love with her and informally adopted her; she now speaks of them as her parents, and they talk of finally meeting their "daughter."

Jeri Weber, whose husband is an executive vice president of Multnomah Publishers, traveled to Ogre as the team mom for the sports outreach, and her enthusiasm and creativity also sparked a new partnership: Multnomah Publishers, fresh from its *Prayer of Jabez* success, wanted to invest a tithe of its profits into ministry. The result is Atklasme Publishing House in Latvia, which has been producing translated editions of Christian classics for the Latvian market.

Pastor Elmars summed up the last cooperative outreach by saying, "These people are friends. . . . They are part of my heart."

First Baptist Church in Bend, Oregon, and Sigulda Baptist Church in Sigulda

In Sigulda, Latvia, a tired old Volkswagen bus carried people from surrounding farms to church services and other events at the Baptist church. With the help of their sister church in Oregon, Bend First Baptist, the Sigulda church was able to purchase a new van. That's just one of the ways that the folks in Bend have responded to the needs of their fellow Latvian believers in Sigulda and in Sigulda's three daughter churches in nearby communities.

The Oregon church has also assisted financially in the support of Latvian Pastor Agris Mikelsons and in the renovation of an apartment in Nurmizi, the poorest of the villages, for use as a Sunday school. Pastor Syd Brestel and three different teams have gone to Latvia to assist with summer camp, Hope '99, and leadership training. The future emphasis of this partnership will be on training leaders and equipping the churches to reach men and youth for Christ.

According to Reverend Brystel, "The greatest benefit for us from the bridge to Latvia has been the difference it has made in our own congregation's commitment to missions."

Lake Tapps Community Church in Sumner, Washington, and Mersraga Baptist Church in Mersrags

The Mersraga Baptist Church has built a reputation that "no one helps like the Christians help," and the congregation of Lake Tapps Community Church in Sumner, Washington, is working with Mersraga Baptist to deepen and broaden that reputation. With an emphasis on the power of relationships, these congregations have created a dynamic partnership that is reaching far into the community.

Hundreds of Christmas boxes have been shipped and distributed to Sunday school children and students at the Upesgrive Special Needs School. Teams of construction volunteers have built playground equipment for the church and neighboring schools and done youth outreach. And during a recent Lake Tapps missions conference, the audience was moved to tears when the keynote speaker, their sister church pastor Janis Pallo, knelt to pray in the middle of the conference. As Lake Tapps members have said, "The blessings of this outreach are many for the American church, too."

First Baptist Church in Canton, Texas, and Grace Community Church in Riga

Pastor Tim Watson described the first encounter between the team from First Baptist Church in Canton, Texas, and the new Grace Community Church in Riga like this: "Quite honestly, we immediately fell in love." After praying together, they decided to launch a partnership in 2002.

Pastor Petr Samoylich, a visionary leader from Ukraine, articulates a mission for introducing the underprivileged to Christ that has inspired both congregations. When the Texans returned in the summer of 2003, they built five cabins on a camp facility associated with the Riga church. They were followed by a team that helped with a summer camp for children, many of whom were orphans sponsored by funds from the Canton congregation. The churches continue their cooperation and investment in the long-term ministry of the Riga congregation and in the lives of members on both continents.

Abundant Life Center in Jefferson, Oregon, and Jelgava Pentecostal Church in Jelgava

My friendship with Pastor Bill Graybill of the Abundant Life Center in Jefferson, Oregon, goes back many years, to when we were fellow pastors in the local prayer movement in the Willamette Valley. It's not always easy for Pentecostal pastors to offer a Baptist the pulpit, but Bill took our friendship into account and let me speak to his congregation about the ministry opportunities in Latvia.

They embraced the possibilities and opened up our first Pentecostal partnership in Latvia with the Jelgava Pentecostal Church. Pastor Agris Ozolinkevics of the Jelgava church came to Jefferson with his wife and preached to the congregation with a passion and zeal that energized the church. Later Bill spent several weeks teaching well-received courses at the Riga Bible Institute on reconciliation in all facets of life.

After a recent trip to Jelgava, one of the Americans said, "Before we left Latvia, we prayed with members of our sister church—we in English, they in Latvian. Although I couldn't understand them, I felt we were touching God together."

The Lord has raised up more partnerships than are possible to describe in this context. We've been thrilled to introduce more churches from California (Santa Rosa and Highlands), Colorado (Denver), Texas (Longview), and Oregon (Gresham, Salem, and North Albany) to churches in Daugavpils, Riga, Talsi, Liepaja, Ventspils, and Mazsalaca— the length and breadth of Latvia being impacted by the power of partnerships.

BBI MASTER PARTNERSHIP LIST

APPENDIX D

SISTER CHURCH PARTNERSHIPS				
Began	**American Partner**	**Latvian Partner**	**Ended**	**Emphasis and Projects**
1989	First Baptist Church, Corvallis, Oregon	Agenskalns Baptist Church, Riga	2002	Hope '91, '92, '94, '99, evangelism, leadership development, humanitarian aid, mission mobilization, construction, children's ministry, youth ministry, education abroad, financial assistance, agricultural development, mutual visits, economic development
1990	First Baptist Church, Corvallis, Oregon	Matthews Baptist Church, Riga	1997	Hope '91, '92, '94, evangelism, education abroad, mutual visits
1996	Grace Baptist Church, Salem, Oregon	Baptist Church Mazsalaca	Still active	Hope '99, Bible teaching
1996	North Albany Community Church, Albany, Oregon	Golgotha Baptist Church, Riga	2002	Hope '99, evangelism, humanitarian aid, construction, financial assistance, mutual visits
1996	Reedsport Church of God, Reedsport, Oregon	Russian Baptist Church, Jelgava	Still active	Hope '99, evangelism, Bible teaching, financial assistance, summer camps, education abroad, mutual visits, economic development, construction, church planting assistance
1996	Harvest Community Church, Camas, Washington	Kengaraga Baptist Church, Riga	1998	Evangelism, Bible teaching

1996	First Baptist Church, Houston, Texas	Pavila Baptist Church, Liepaja	1997	Evangelism, pastoral support
1997	Christmas Valley Community Church, Christmas Valley, Oregon	Tilza Baptist Church and Conference Center, Tilza	Still active	Hope '99, construction, youth ministry, leadership development, summer camps, public school ministry, orphan care, agricultural development, mutual visits, financial assistance, home fellowships
1997	First Baptist Church, Richardson, Texas	Vilandes Baptist Church, Riga	Still active	Dallas-Riga 2000, Latvia 2002, evangelism, baby school, children's and youth ministry, orphan ministry, music ministry, leadership development, church and playground construction, economic development, women's ministry, financial support, education abroad, English language instruction, mutual visits, sports ministry
1998	Calvary Church, Los Gatos, California	Salvation Temple, Riga	Still active	Hope '99, evangelism, construction, technical assistance, children's and youth ministry, education abroad, Bible teaching, leadership development, financial assistance, music and drama ministry, mutual visits, secretarial training, sports ministry
1998	Calvin Presbyterian Church, Corvallis, Oregon	Tilza Baptist Church, Tilza	Still active	Hope '99, evangelism, construction, summer camps, English language instruction, agricultural development, music and drama ministry, mutual visits, financial assistance
1998	Christmas Valley Community Church, Christmas Valley, Oregon	Berzgale Baptist Church, Berzgale	Still active	Hope '99, evangelism, agricultural development, leadership development
1998	First Baptist Church, Bend, Oregon	Sigulda Baptist Church, Sigulda	Still active	Hope '99, evangelism, summer camps, financial assistance, Sunday school ministry, Bible teaching, children's and youth ministry, mutual visits, church planting
1998	Grace Community Church, Minden, Nevada	Madona Baptist Church, Madona	2003	Hope '99, Bible teaching, construction, financial support, mutual visits

1998	Sisters Community Church, Sisters, Oregon	Trinity Baptist Church, Ogre	Still active	Hope '99, leadership development, humanitarian aid, orphan care, mutual visits, publishing, youth outreach, children's ministry, summer camps, financial support, construction, military outreach
1999	First Baptist Church, Houston, Texas	Jelgava Baptist Church, Jelgava	Still active	Evangelism, children's ministry, construction, church planting, seniors' ministry, summer camps, music ministry, counseling, specialized conferences, mission exchange and mobilization, mutual visits, sports ministry
1999	Foothills Community Church, Santa Rosa, California	White Russian Baptist Church, Daugavpils	Still active	Hope '99, evangelism, leadership development, public school ministry, mime, children's and youth ministry, Christian education
1999	Grace Chapel, Wilsonville, Oregon	Vilaka Baptist Church Plant, Vilaka	2004	Hope '99, evangelism, public school ministry, summer camps, financial support, music ministry
2000	First Baptist Church, Richardson, Texas	Gipka Baptist Church, Gipka	Still active	Construction, financial support, children's ministry, preaching, evangelism
2000	Lake Tapps Community Church, Sumner, Washington	Mersraga Baptist Church, Mersrags	Still active	Evangelism, public school ministry, children's ministry, mutual visits
2000	Highland Community Church, Renton, Washington	Reformed Bible Church, Riga	Still active	Mutual visits, summer camps, church planting assistance
2000	Highland Community Church, Renton, Washington	Riga Reformed Church, Riga	Still active	Mutual visits, summer camps, church planting assistance
2001	Living Faith Community Church, Philomath, Oregon	Kandava Baptist Church, Kandava	Still active	Summer camps, youth ministry, preaching, evangelism, mutual visits
2001	Abundant Life Center, Jefferson, Oregon	Jelgava Pentecostal Church, Jelgava	Still active	Preaching, Bible teaching, children's and youth ministry, mutual visits
2002	First Baptist Church, Canton, Texas	New Evangelical Baptist Church, Riga	Still active	Campground construction, summer camp, preaching, evangelism, VBS, mutual visits

2003	First Baptist Church, Richardson, Texas	Vilaka Baptist Church Plant, Vilaka	Still active	Financial support through Vilandes Baptist Church
2003	Immanuel Baptist Church, Highland, California	Matthews Baptist Church, Riga	Still active	Senior ministry, specialized conferences, mutual visits, sports ministry, development consulting
2003	The HUB of Philomath Community Church, Philomath, Oregon	Matthews Baptist Church Youth Ministry, Riga	2004	Youth ministry, music and mime outreach, mutual visits, military outreach
2004	Bear Valley Baptist Church, Denver, Colorado	Talsi Baptist Church, Talsi	Still active	Children's ministry, music ministry, preaching, evangelism
2004	First Baptist Church, Longview, Texas	Pavila Baptist Church, Liepaja	Still active	Orphan care, children's ministry, preaching, economic development
	SPECIALIZED PARTNERSHIPS			
1991	Western Baptist Seminary, Portland, Oregon	Latvian Baptist Union Theological Seminary, Riga	1998	Latvian students studied at Western, eight Western profs guest-lectured at LBUTS, library assistance, mutual visits
1992	Santiam Christian School, Adair Village, Oregon	George Barbins Christian School	Still active	Initial concept consultation, student supplies, mutual visits, MissionFest '98 (music and outreach), guest teaching, student exchange
1996	KALS 97.1 Christian Radio Station, Kalispell, Montana	Latvian Christian Radio, Riga	2001	General and accounting system consultation, equipment supply
1997	Evangelical Development Ministry, Texas/California	Mission Pakapieni, Barbins School, Baptist Seminary, Tilza Training Center, Matthews Center, Salvation Temple, Latvian Christian Radio	2003	EDM specialists Holmes Bryan and Andy Read provided numerous group and individualized training sessions on the topics of leadership, management, and fund development.
1998	Venture Latvia Teams, Oregon and Texas	A variety of entrepreneurs who are operating small businesses	Still active	Small business loans and ongoing consultation have been provided to seven small businesses, including leather goods, clothing, construction, pig farming, diesel mechanics, computer repair, and videography.

1999	Hope for Farm Families Team, Oregon	Regional Farmers, Rezekne	Still active	Financial assistance, distance program management, veterinary consultation, local farmer seminars, feed production consultation
2000	Alliance of Saturation Church Planting, Budapest, Hungary	A variety of church planting specialists and missionaries	Still active	Church planting research, training, promotion, and publishing.
2000	The Latvian Evangelical Alliance Bashkortostan Outreach Team	Bashkortostan	Still active	Led by Peteris Eisans, the Bashkortostan outreach team is comprised of Latvians who are partially financially supported by Americans to spread the gospel in this predominantly Muslim Russian republic.
2001	CitiReach International, Colorado Springs, Colorado	Riga City Council, The Protein Youth Leadership Network, Partners and BBI	Still active	Eric Swanson and Sam Williams have provided teaching, consultation, and resources to help Latvian youth develop numerous practical service projects to local communities.
2001	Multnomah Publishers, Sisters, Oregon	Atklasme (Discovery) Christian Publishers, Riga	Still active	Financial assistance, initial establishment consultation, access to titles, ongoing consultation
2001	World Christian Publishers	Atklasme Christian Publishers, Riga	Still active	Ongoing publishing consultation – twice a year by Peter Cunliffe
2002	Buckner Orphan Care International, Dallas, Texas	A variety of governmental and social care agencies	Still active	Humanitarian aid, orphan care, orphanage renovation, summer ministry to orphanages, foster care program establishment, high level government consultation
2002	The Latvian Nehemiah Project Team, Texas and Oregon	Latvian Christian Radio	Still active	A joint project between Latvians and Americans to construct a Christian recording studio for Latvian Christian musicians to record music in their own language.
UNIQUE INDIVIDUAL MINISTRIES				
1999	Dr. Dan White & Sam Bradley Dental Care	Mission Pakapieni and Talsi Christian School	Still active	Every year a Texas dentist provides gratis care to more than 100 impoverished people, mostly children. He uses BBI's portable dental clinic.

2000	Dr. Gunars Iesalnieks, Portland, Oregon	Ventspils Evangelical Christian Pentecostal Church, Ventspils	Still active	Book translation, discipleship seminars, evangelism, financial assistance
2001	Ed and Kathi Beacham, Beacham Clock Company, Sisters, Oregon	The Latvian Museum and Monument Commission and the Dome Cathedral, Riga	2001	Ed and Kathi went to Latvia to repair and restore the historic wrought-iron "Birdcage" clock movement of the Dome Cathedral clock.
2002	Paula Hewitt, Calvin Presbyterian Church, Corvallis, Oregon	Tilza Baptist Church, Tilza	2002	Paula spent three months in Tilza for leadership development, fellowship, community relationship building, English language instruction, and project preparation.
2002	Paula Gamble	Tilza Baptist Church, Tilza	2002	As a part an internship to fulfill requirements for her master's degree at Western Seminary, Paula spent the summer in Latvia learning the language, leading worship, and fellowshipping with the people of Tilza.
Katie 1991 Dan 1998	Dan and Katie Roth, Christmas Valley, Oregon	Tilza Baptist Church, Tilza	Still active	Both Dan and Katie lead the youth group at Tilza Baptist Church. They also both help run the conference and training center located next to the church, Dan is a part of the Hope for Farm Families program, and Katie teaches English at Tilza High School.
2003	Brian Lindsay, Lebanon, Oregon	Nehemiah Project and Latvian Christian Radio	Still active	Brian consults with and helps construct the recording studio in Latvia.
2003	Dr. David New, Eugene, Oregon	Riga Bible Institute, Riga and Jelgava	Still active	Itinerant Bible teaching and preaching in numerous Russian-language churches, especially in Jelgava.
2003	David Baker, Christmas Valley, Oregon	Tilza Baptist Church, Tilza	Still active	Youth ministry, English language instruction at the local public high school, general assistance at the conference center.
2003	Thomas Kinkade, Morgan Hill, California	Bridge Builders International, Partners, and Barbins Christian School	2004	Thom, Nanette, and their two oldest daughters took part in a Christian art camp at Barbins School, and Thom ministered in numerous settings utilizing his paintings.

THE LAUSANNE COVENANT

APPENDIX E

Bridge Builders International is committed to the biblical principle of the whole church bringing the whole gospel to the whole world. It wholeheartedly identifies with the purpose, theology, principles, and passion of the international Lausanne Movement as expressed by the Lausanne Covenant. This document was therefore adopted as the doctrinal statement of Bridge Builders International at the time of its inception.

Introduction

We, members of the Church of Jesus Christ, from more than 150 nations, participants in the International Congress on World Evangelization at Lausanne, praise God for his great salvation and rejoice in the fellowship he has given us with himself and with each other. We are deeply stirred by what God is doing in our day, moved to penitence by our failures and challenged by the unfinished task of evangelization. We believe the gospel is God's good news for the whole world, and we are determined by his grace to obey Christ's commission to proclaim it to all mankind and to make disciples of every nation. We desire, therefore, to affirm our faith and our resolve, and to make public our covenant.

1. The Purpose Of God

We affirm our belief in the one-eternal God, Creator and Lord of the world, Father, Son and Holy Spirit, who governs all things according to the purpose of his will. He has been calling out from the world a people for himself, and sending his people back into the world to be his servants and his witnesses, for the extension of his kingdom, the building up of Christ's body, and the glory of his name. We confess with shame that we have often denied our calling and failed in our mission, by becoming conformed to the world or by withdrawing from it. Yet we rejoice that even when borne by earthen vessels the gospel is still a precious treasure. To the task of making that treasure known in the power of the Holy Spirit we desire to dedicate ourselves anew. (Isa. 40:28; Matt. 28:19; Eph. 1:11; Acts l5:l4; John 17:6,18; Eph. 4:12; 1 Cor. 5:10; Rom. 12:2; II Cor. 4:7)

2. The Authority And Power Of The Bible

We affirm the divine inspiration, truthfulness and authority of both Old and New Testament Scriptures in their entirety as the only written word of God, without error in all that it affirms, and the only infallible rule of faith and practice. We also affirm the power of God's word to accomplish his purpose of salvation. The message of the Bible is addressed to all mankind. For God's revelation in Christ and in Scripture is unchangeable. Through it the Holy Spirit still speaks today. He illumines the minds of God's people in every culture to perceive its truth freshly through their own eyes and thus discloses to the whole church ever more of the many-coloured wisdom of God.(II Tim. 3:16; II Pet. 1:21; John 10:35; Isa. 55:11; I Cor. 1:21; Rom. 1:16; Matt. 5:17,18; Jude 3; Eph. 1:17,18; 3:10,18)

3. The Uniqueness And Universality Of Christ

We affirm that there is only one Saviour and only one gospel, although there is a wide diversity of evangelistic approaches. We recognize that all men have some knowledge of God through his general revelation in nature. But we deny that this can save, for men suppress the truth by their unrighteousness. We also reject as derogatory to Christ and the gospel every kind of syncretism and dialogue which implies that Christ speaks equally through all religions and ideologies. Jesus Christ, being himself the only God-man, who gave himself as the only ransom for sinners, is the only mediator between God and man. There is no other name by which we must be saved. All men are perishing because of sin, but God loves all men, not wishing that any should perish but that all should repent. Yet those who reject Christ repudiate the joy of salvation and condemn themselves to eternal separation from God. To proclaim Jesus as "the Saviour of the world" is not to affirm that all men are either automatically or ultimately saved, still less to affirm that all religions offer salvation in Christ. Rather it is to proclaim God's love for a world of sinners and to invite all men to respond to him as Saviour and Lord in the wholehearted personal commitment of repentance and faith. Jesus Christ has been exalted above every other name; we long for the day when every knee shall bow to him and every tongue shall confess him Lord. (Gal. 1:6-9; Rom. 1:18-32; I Tim. 2:5,6; Acts 4:12; John 3:16-19; II Pet. 3:9; II Thess. 1:7-9; John 4:42; Matt. 11:28; Eph. 1:20,21; Phil. 2:9-11)

4. The Nature Of Evangelism

To evangelize is to spread the good news that Jesus Christ died for our sins and was raised from the dead according to the Scriptures, and that as the reigning Lord he now offers the forgiveness of sins and the liberating gift of the Spirit to all who repent and believe. Our Christian presence in the world is indispensable to evangelism, and so is that kind of dialogue whose purpose is to listen sensitively in order to understand. But evangelism itself is the proclamation of the historical, biblical Christ as Saviour and Lord, with a view to persuading people to come to him personally and so be reconciled to God. In issuing the gospel invitation we have no liberty to conceal the cost of discipleship. Jesus still calls all who would follow him to deny themselves, take up their cross, and identify themselves with his new community. The results of evangelism include obedience to Christ, incorporation into his church and responsible service in the world.(I Cor. 15:3,4; Acts 2:32-39; John 20:21; I Cor. 1:23; II Cor. 4:5; 5:11,20; Luke 14:25-33; Mark 8:34; Acts 2:40,47; Mark 10:43-45)

5. Christian Social Responsibility

We affirm that God is both the Creator and the Judge of all men. We therefore should share his concern for justice and reconciliation throughout human society and for the liberation of men from every kind of oppression. Because mankind is made in the image of God, every person, regardless of race, religion, colour, culture, class, sex or age, has an intrinsic dignity because of which he should be respected and served, not exploited. Here too we express penitence both for our neglect and for having sometimes regarded evangelism and social concern as mutually exclusive. Although reconciliation with man is not reconciliation with God, nor is social action evangelism, nor is political liberation salvation, nevertheless we affirm that evangelism and socio-political involvement are both part of our Christian duty. For both are necessary expressions of our doctrines of God and man, our love for our neighbour and our obedience to Jesus Christ. The message of salvation implies also a message of judgment upon every form of alienation, oppression and discrimination, and we should not be afraid to denounce evil and injustice wherever they exist. When people receive Christ they are born again into his kingdom and must seek not only to exhibit but also to spread its righteousness in the midst of an unrighteous world. The salvation we claim should be transforming us in the totality of our personal and social responsibilities. Faith without works is dead. (Acts 17:26,31; Gen. 18:25; Isa. 1:17; Psa. 45:7; Gen. 1:26,27; Jas. 3:9; Lev. 19:18; Luke 6:27,35; Jas. 2:14-26; John 3:3,5; Matt. 5:20; 6:33; II Cor. 3:18; Jas. 2:20)

6. The Church And Evangelism

We affirm that Christ sends his redeemed people into the world as the Father sent him, and that this calls for a similar deep and costly penetration of the world. We need to break out of our ecclesiastical ghettos and permeate non-Christian society. In the church's mission of sacrificial service evangelism is primary. World evangelization requires the whole church to take the whole gospel to the whole world. The church is at the very centre of God's cosmic purpose and is his appointed means of spreading the gospel. But a church which preaches the cross must itself be marked by the cross. It becomes a stumbling block to evangelism when it betrays the gospel or lacks a living faith in God, a genuine love for people, or scrupulous honesty in all things including promotion and finance. The church is the community of God's people rather than an institution, and must not be identified with any particular culture, social or political system or human ideology. (John 17:18; 20:21; Matt. 28:19,20; Acts 1:8; 20:27; Eph. 1:9,10; 3:9-11; Gal. 6:14,17; II Cor. 6:3,4; II Tim. 2:19-21; Phil. 1:27)

7. Cooperation In Evangelism

We affirm that the church's visible unity in truth is God's purpose. Evangelism also summons us to unity, because our oneness strengthens our witness, just as our disunity undermines our gospel of reconciliation. We recognize, however, that organizational unity may take many forms and does not necessarily forward evengelism. Yet we who share the same biblical faith should be closely united in fellowship, work and witness. We confess that our testimony has sometimes been marred by sinful individualism and needless duplication. We pledge ourselves to seek a deeper unity in truth, worship, holiness and mission. We urge the development of regional and functional cooperation for the furtherance of the church's mission, for strategic planning, for mutual encouragement, and for the sharing of resources and experience. (John 17:21,23; Eph. 4:3,4; John 13:35; Phil. 1:27; John 17:11-23)

8. Churches In Evangelistic Partnership

We rejoice that a new missionary era has dawned. The dominant role of western missions is fast disappearing. God is raising up from the younger churches a great new resource for world evangelization, and is thus demonstrating that the responsibility to evangelize belongs to the whole body of Christ. All churches should therefore be asking God and themselves what they should be doing both to reach their own area and to send missionaries to other parts of the world. A re-evaluation of our missionary responsibility and role should be continuous. Thus a growing partnership of churches will develop and the universal character of Christ's church will be more clearly exhibited. We also thank God for agencies which labour in Bible translation, theological education, the mass media, Christian literature, evangelism, missions, church renewal and other specialist fields. They too should engage in constant self-examination to evaluate their effectiveness as part of the Church's mission. (Rom. 1:8; Phil. 1:5, 4:15; Acts 13:1-3; I Thess. 1:6-8)

9. The Urgency Of The Evangelistic Task

More than 2,700 million people, which is more than two-thirds of mankind, have yet to be evangelized. We are ashamed that so many have been neglected; it is a standing rebuke to us and to the whole church. There is now, however, in many parts of the world an unprecedented receptivity to the Lord Jesus Christ. We are convinced that this is the time for churches and para-church agencies to pray earnestly for the salvation of the unreached and to launch new efforts to achieve world evangelization. A reduction of foreign missionaries and money in an evangelized country may sometimes be necessary to facilitate the national church's growth in self-reliance and to release resources for unevangelized areas. Missionaries should flow ever more freely from and to all six continents in a spirit of humble service. The goal should be, by all available means and at the earliest possible time, that every person will have the opportunity to hear, understand, and receive the good news. We cannot hope to attain this goal without sacrifice. All of us are shocked by the poverty of millions and disturbed by the injustices which cause it. Those of us who live in affluent circumstances accept our duty to develop a simple life-style in order to contribute more generously to both relief and evangelism. (John 9:4; Matt. 9:35-38; Rom. 9:1-3; I Cor. 9:19-23; Mark 16:15; Isa. 58:6,7; Jas. 1:27; 2:1-9; Matt. 25:31-46; Acts 2:44,45; 4:34,35)

10. Evangelism And Culture

The development of strategies for world evangelization calls for imaginative pioneering methods. Under God, the result will be the rise of churches deeply rooted in Christ and closely related to their culture. Culture must always be tested and judged by Scripture. Because man is God's creature, some of his culture is rich in beauty and goodness. Because he is fallen, all of it is tainted with sin and some of it is demonic. The gospel does not presuppose the superiority of any culture to another, but evaluates all cultures according to its own criteria of truth and righteousness, and insists on moral absolutes in every culture. Missions have all too frequently exported with the gospel an alien culture, and churches have sometimes been in bondage to culture rather than to the Scripture. Christ's evangelists must humbly seek to empty themselves of all but their personal authenticity in order to become the servants of others, and churches must seek to transform and enrich culture, all for the glory of God. (Mark 7:8,9,13; Gen. 4:21,22; I Cor. 9:19-23; Phil. 2:5-7; II Cor. 4:5)

11. Education And Leadership

We confess that we have sometimes pursued church growth at the expense of church depth, and divorced evangelism from Christian nurture. We also acknowledge that some of our missions have been too slow to equip and encourage national leaders to assume their rightful responsibilities. Yet we are committed to indigenous principles, and long that every church will have national leaders who manifest a Christian style of leadership in terms not of domination but of service. We recognize that there is a great need to improve theological education, especially for church leaders. In every nation and culture there should be an effective training programme for pastors and laymen in doctrine, discipleship, evangelism, nurture and service. Such training programmes should not rely on any stereotyped methodology but should be developed by creative local initiatives according to biblical standards.(Col. 1:27,28; Acts 14:23; Tit. 1:5,9; Mark 10:42-45; Eph. 4:11,12)

12. Spiritual Conflict

We believe that we are engaged in constant spiritual warfare with the principalities and powers of evil, who are seeking to overthrow the church and frustrate its task of world evangelization. We know our need to equip ourselves with God's armour and to fight this battle with the spiritual weapons of truth and prayer. For we detect the activity of our enemy, not only in false ideologies outside the church, but also inside it in false gospels which twist Scripture and put man in the place of God. We need both watchfulness and discernment to safeguard the biblical gospel. We acknowledge that we ourselves are not immune to worldliness of thought and action, that is, to a surrender to secularism. For example, although careful studies of church growth, both numerical and spiritual, are right and valuable, we have sometimes neglected them. At other times, desirous to ensure a response to the gospel, we have compromised our message, manipulated our hearers through pressure techniques, and become unduly preoccupied with statistics or even dishonest in our use of them. All this is worldly. The church must be in the world; the world must not be in the church. (Eph. 6:12; II Cor. 4:3,4; Eph. 6:11,13-18; II Cor. 10:3-5; I John 2:18-26; 4:1-3; Gal. 1:6-9; II Cor. 2:17; 4:2; John 17:15)

13. Freedom And Persecution

It is the God-appointed duty of every government to secure conditions of peace, justice and liberty in which the church may obey God, serve the Lord Christ, and preach the gospel without interference. We therefore pray for the leaders of the nations and call upon them to guarantee freedom of thought and conscience, and freedom to practise and propagate religion in accordance with the will of God and as set forth in The Universal Declaration of Human Rights. We also express our deep concern for all who have been unjustly imprisoned, and especially for our brethren who are suffering for their testimony to the Lord Jesus. We promise to pray and work for their freedom. At the same time we refuse to be intimidated by their fate. God helping us, we too will seek to stand against injustice and to remain faithful to the gospel, whatever the cost. We do not forget the warnings of Jesus that persecution is inevitable. (I Tim. 1:1-4; Acts 4:19; 5:29; Col. 3:24; Heb. 13:1-3; Luke 4:18; Gal. 5:11; 6:12; Matt. 5:10-12; John 15:18-21)

14. The Power Of The Holy Spirit

We believe in the power of the Holy Spirit. The Father sent his Spirit to bear witness to his Son; without his witness ours is futile. Conviction of sin, faith in Christ, new birth and Christian growth are all his work. Further, the Holy Spirit is a missionary spirit; thus evangelism should arise spontaneously from a Spirit-filled church. A church that is not a missionary church is contradicting itself and quenching the Spirit. Worldwide evangelization will become a realistic possibility only when the Spirit renews the church in truth and wisdom, faith, holiness, love and power. We therefore call upon all Christians to pray for such a visitation of the sovereign Spirit of God that all his fruit may appear in all his people and that all his gifts may enrich the body of Christ. Only then will the whole church become a fit instrument in his hands, that the whole earth may hear his voice. (I Cor. 2:4; John 15:26,27; 16:8-11; I Cor. 12:3; John 3:6-8; II Cor. 3:18; John 7:37-39; I Thess. 5:19; Acts 1:8; Psa. 85:4-7; 67:1-3; Gal. 5:22,23; I Cor. 12:4-31; Rom. 12:3-8)

15. The Return Of Christ

We believe that Jesus Christ will return personally and visibly, in power and glory, to consummate his salvation and his judgment. This promise of his coming is a further spur to our evangelism, for we remember his words that the gospel must first be preached to all nations. We believe that the interim period between Christ's ascension and return is to be filled with the mission of the people of God, who have no liberty to stop before the End. We also remember his warning that false Christs and false prophets will arise as precursors of the final Antichrist. We therefore reject as a proud, self-confident dream the notion that man can ever build a utopia on earth. Our Christian confidence is that God will perfect his kingdom, and we look forward with eager anticipation to that day, and to the new heaven and earth in which righteousness will dwell and God will reign for ever. Meanwhile, we rededicate ourselves to the service of Christ and of men in joyful submission to his authority over the whole of our lives. (Mark 14:62; Heb. 9:28; Mark 13:10; Acts 1:8-11; Matt. 28:20; Mark 13:21-23; John 2:18; 4:1-3; Luke 12:32; Rev. 21:1-5; II Pet. 3:13; Matt. 28:18)

Conclusion

Therefore, in the light of this our faith and our resolve, we enter into a solemn covenant with God and with each other, to pray, to plan and to work together for the evangelization of the whole world. We call upon others to join us. May God help us by his grace and for his glory to be faithful to this our covenant! Amen, Alleluia!

Drafted and adopted by the International Congress on World Evangelization, Lausanne, Switzerland, July 1974; adopted, by formal action of the Board of Directors, as the Doctrinal Statement of Bridge Builders International, December 9, 1994.